Dear Reader,

Welcome to the Galileo Press *Discover SAP* series. This new series has been developed as part of our official SAP PRESS imprint to help you discover what SAP is all about, and to explain how to use the wide array of applications and tools to make your organization much more efficient and cost effective.

Each book in the series is written in a friendly, easy-to-follow style that guides you through the intricacies of the software and its core components. Beginning with "Discover SAP," the first book in the series, you'll find a detailed overview of the core components of SAP, what they are, how they can benefit your company, and the technology requirements and costs of implementation. Once you have a foundational knowledge of SAP, you can explore the other books in the series covering NetWeaver, Financials, HCM, BI, and more. In these books you'll delve into the fundamental business concepts and principles behind the tool, discover why it's important for your business, and evaluate the technology and implementation costs for each.

Whether you are a decision maker who needs to determine if SAP is the right enterprise solution for your company, you are just starting to work in a firm that uses SAP, or you're already familiar with SAP but need to learn about a specific component, you are sure to find what you need in the *Discover SAP* series. Then when you're ready to implement SAP, you'll find what you need in the SAP PRESS series at *www.sap-press.com*.

Thank you for your interest in the series. We look forward to hearing how the series helps you get started with SAP.

Jenifer Niles
Vice President

Galileo Press, Inc.
100 Grossman Drive
Suite 205
Braintree, MA 02184

SAP PRESS

SAP PRESS is a joint initiative of SAP and Galileo Press. The know-how offered by SAP specialists combined with the expertise of the publishing house Galileo Press offers the reader expert books in the field. SAP PRESS features first-hand information and expert advice, and provides useful skills for professional decision-making.

SAP PRESS offers a variety of books on technical and business related topics for the SAP user. For further information, please visit our website: *www.sap-press.com*.

Planning Your SAP CRM Implementation
George Fratian
2008, ~320 pages, $69.95
ISBN 978-1-59229-196-0

Maximizing Your SAP CRM Interaction Center
John Burton
2008, ~450 pages, $69.95
ISBN 978-1-59229-197-7

Service with SAP CRM
Markus Kirchler, Dirk Manhart
2008, ~400 pages, $69.95
ISBN 978-1-59229-206-6

mySAP CRM
Rudiger Buck-Emden, Peter Zencke
2004, 462 pages, $59.95
ISBN 978-1-59229-029-1

Srini Katta

Discover SAP® CRM

Bonn • Boston

ISBN 978-1-59229-173-1

1st Edition 2008

Editor Jenifer Niles
Technical Development Editor John Burton, SAP
Copyeditor Julie McNamee
Cover Design Silke Braun
Production Editor Todd Brown
Design Vera Brauner
Typesetter Publishers' Design and Production Services, Inc.
Printed and bound in Canada

To my mom and my wife
The two most beautiful and lovable women in my life
I Love You!

Contents at a Glance

1	Customer Relationship Management	27
2	SAP CRM Detailed Overview	43
3	SAP CRM Marketing	61
4	SAP CRM Sales	79
5	SAP CRM Service	99
6	SAP CRM Interaction Center	123
7	Web Channel Enablement Solution	153
8	SAP CRM Mobile Applications	177
9	SAP CRM Partner Channel Management	199
10	The Technology and Tools Behind SAP CRM	229
11	Master Data	253
12	Working with SAP Industry Vertical Solutions	279
13	SAP CRM Analytics	305
14	SAP CRM User Access	343
15	Building an SAP CRM System	355
16	Varian Medical Systems Case Study	371
A	Glossary	375

Contents

Acknowledgments 19
Preface 21
    Whom This Book Is For? 21
    What You'll Discover 22
    Navigational Tools in This Book 22
    What's in This Book? 23

1 Customer Relationship Management 27

What Are Your Industry Verticals? 28
What Type of Business Are You In? 28
Who Are Your Customers? 29
What Are Your Products and Services? 29
    Which Channels Does Your Company Use? 31
    What Are Your CRM Business Needs? 31
    What Is Your Company Culture? 33
    How Big Is Your Company? 34
    Are You Global, Regional, or Local? 34
    Competitiveness of Your IT Infrastructure and
    Architecture 35
Core CRM Principles 36
    Customer First 36
    Designing a Customer- First CRM Initiative 37
    Customized Product and Service Offerings for
    Customers 39
    Increase Customer Lifetime Value 39
What Functionality Should Your CRM Application
Provide? 40
    What Drives CRM Technology? 41
Conclusion 41

2 SAP CRM Detailed Overview 43

What Is SAP CRM? 43
    SAP CRM Strengths 44

The Three Key Components of SAP CRM 45
    SAP CRM Solution Map 47
SAP CRM Marketing 48
SAP CRM Sales 49
    E-Commerce (Formerly Internet Sales) 50
SAP CRM Service 51
Analytics 53
    How Can SAP CRM Analytics Help Your Company? 55
SAP CRM Solutions for Small- and Medium-Size
Businesses 55
SAP CRM On-Demand Solutions 58
    Benefits of SAP CRM On-Demand for SMBs 58
Conclusion 58

3 SAP CRM Marketing **61**

SAP CRM Marketing Component 63
    Marketing Resource Management (MRM) 64
    Market Planning and Budgeting 65
    Segmentation 67
    List Management 68
    Campaign Management 70
    Trade Promotion Management (TPM) 71
    Lead Management 73
    Backend ERP Integration 75
    Marketing Analytics 75
Case Study 77
Conclusion 78

4 SAP CRM Sales **79**

Discover SAP CRM Sales 80
    Accounts and Contact Management 81
    Activity Management 84
    Planning and Forecasting 84
    Territory Management 85
    Opportunity Management 86

Product Configuration and Pricing 87

Quotation and Order Management 89

Billing and Contract Management 91

Incentives and Commissions Management 93

Time and Travel Management 93

Sales Analytics 94

Case Study 96

Conclusion 98

5 SAP CRM Service **99**

Discover SAP CRM Service 100

Installed Base Management 101

Warranty Management 103

Contract and Entitlement Management 105

Resource Planning 107

Knowledge Management 108

Case Management 110

Service Order and Service Ticket 111

Complaints and Returns 114

In-House Repair 115

Service Analytics 117

Business Drivers 118

Case Study 119

Conclusion 121

6 SAP CRM Interaction Center **123**

Interaction Center Strategy 125

Consolidating Standalone Telephone, Email,
and Chat Applications 127

Customer-Facing Tools and Interfaces 132

Telephone and Interactive Voice Response 133

SAP CRM Interaction Center Capabilities 139

Agent Desktop Productivity Tools 139

Multi-Channel Integration 140

SAP CRM Marketing Integration 141

SAP CRM Sales Integration 142

SAP CRM Service Integration 143

Blended Business Scenarios 145

Shared Service Centers 147

Running Your Interaction Center: Operations and
Administration 148

Case Study 148

Conclusion 150

7 Web Channel Enablement Solution 153

E-Marketing 156

Demand Generation 156

Catalog Management 157

Personalization 158

E-Commerce (Formerly E-Selling) 158

Interactive Selling 159

Pricing 162

Order to Cash 163

Web Auctions 170

E-Service 170

Knowledge Management 171

Service Management 172

Web Channel Analytics 173

Conclusion 174

8 SAP CRM Mobile Applications 177

Introduction to SAP CRM Mobile Technology 179

SAP CRM Mobile Sales 182

Mobile Sales Laptop 183

Mobile Sales Handheld 186

Mobile Sales Online 189

SAP CRM Mobile Service 191

Mobile Service Laptops 191

Mobile Service Handheld (for SAP CRM 4.0) 193

Case Study 194

Conclusion 196

9 SAP CRM Partner Channel Management 199

Why Use Channel Partners? 200
Channel Management and SAP 201
Partner Management 203
    Partner Recruitment 203
    Partner Profiling and Segmentation 205
    Partner Training and Certification 205
    Partner Networking 207
    Partner Compensation 208
    Partner Planning and Forecasting 208
Channel Marketing 208
    Partner Communication 209
    Catalog Management 209
    Campaign Management 209
    Lead Management 210
    Channel Marketing Funds 210
    Partner Locator 211
Channel Sales 212
    Account and Contact Management 213
    Activity Management 213
    Opportunity Management 214
    Channel Sales Analytics 214
Partner Order Management 215
    Quotation and Order Management 215
    Interactive Selling and Configuration 216
    POS and Channel Inventory 216
    Collaborative Showrooms 217
    Distributed Order Management 218
Channel Service 220
    Knowledge Management 221
    Live Support 222
    Service Order Management 222
    Complaints and Returns Management 223
Partner and Channel Analytics 223
Case Study 224
Conclusion 226

10 The Technology and Tools Behind SAP CRM 229

SAP NetWeaver Introduction 229
    Enterprise Service-Oriented Architecture
    (Enterprise SOA) 231
SAP NetWeaver Integration 232
    People Integration 233
    Information Integration 234
    Process Integration 234
    Application Platform 235
SAP NetWeaver for SAP CRM 236
    SAP NetWeaver Web Services for SAP CRM 236
    SAP NetWeaver Mobile for SAP CRM 238
    SAP NetWeaver Process Integration (PI)
    for SAP CRM 238
    SAP NetWeaver Java for SAP CRM 240
    SAP NetWeaver Enterprise Portal for SAP CRM 240
SAP CRM Technology 242
    SAP CRM Middleware 242
    Groupware Integration with SAP CRM 243
    SAP CRM Mobile 244
    People-Centric User Interface (PCUI) 245
    Business Server Pages (BSP) 246
    SAP CRM WebClient (New with SAP CRM
    2006s and SAP CRM 2007) 247
    SAP CRM Business Object Layer (BOL)/Generic
    Interaction Layer (genIL) 247
    ABAP 248
Case Study 249
Conclusion 250

11 Master Data 253

Business Partner (BP) Master Data 255
    Business Partner Design in SAP CRM 256
    Business Partner Categories 256
    Business Partner Roles 257

BP Classification 258
BP Relationships 260
Product Master Data 262
SAP CRM Product Master Data Design 262
Product Types 263
Product Attributes and Attribute-Set Types 264
Product Categories and Hierarchies 265
Product Relationships 266
Organizational Master Data 267
Organizational Objects 268
Organizational Attributes and Business Attributes 269
Pricing Master Data 272
SAP Internet Pricing and Configurator (IPC) 272
Condition Technique and Condition Records 274
Case Study 275
Conclusion 277

12   Working with SAP Industry Vertical Solutions 279

Automotive 280
Chemical Industry 281
Consumer Products (CP) 283
Engineering, Construction, and Operations 285
High Tech 286
Oil and Gas 287
Life Sciences (Pharmaceutical) 287
Financial Services (Banking and Insurance) 289
Leasing 291
Media 293
Professional Services 294
Public Sector 297
Retail 298
Telecommunications 299
Utilities 300
Case Study 303
Conclusion 303

13 SAP CRM Analytics 305

SAP CRM Analytics 306
Marketing Analytics 311
    Market Budget Planning 312
    Campaign Planning 312
    Target Group Optimization 313
    Market Plan Analysis 314
    Campaign Monitoring and Success 314
    Lead Analysis 315
    External List Analysis 316
    External List Cost and Revenue Analysis 318
Sales Analytics 320
    Territory Management Analysis 321
    Activity Management Analysis 321
    Opportunity Management Analysis 321
    Sales Quotation and Order Management Analysis 322
    Contract Management Analysis 323
    Sales Pipeline Analysis 324
    Sales Funnel Analysis 324
    Sales Performance Analysis 325
    Billing Analysis 326
Service Analytics 327
    Service Quality Analysis 328
Customer Analytics 334
    Customer Migration Analysis 334
    Churn Management 335
    Customer Lifetime Value (CLTV) 336
    Customer Satisfaction and Loyalty Analysis ... 337
Product Analytics 337
    Cross-Selling Proposals 338
    Product Profitability Analysis 338
Interaction Channel Analytics 339
    Web Channel Analytics 340
    Interaction Center Analytics 340
Conclusion 341

14 SAP CRM User Access 343

User Access Modes 344
    Desktop/Laptop 344
    Notebook Computers 345
    PDA Companion 345
    Tablet PC 346
    Handheld Devices 347
    Smartphone 348
SAP CRM Enhanced Usability 349
    Design Layer Customizing 351
Conclusion 352

15 Building an SAP CRM System 355

Discover Your Business Needs 356
    Set Up a Team and/or Hire an SAP CRM
    Business Application Consultant 356
    Conduct Discovery Sessions 356
Business Scenario Analysis 357
Design and Development 358
    Functional Design 358
    Technical Design 359
    Implementation/Configuration/Development 359
End-to-End Deployment 359
Project Methodologies 360
    ASAP Methodology 360
    Cycle Methodology 366
    Conference Room Pilot (CRP) Methodology 367
Conclusion 368

16 Varian Medical Systems Case Study 371

Business Challenge 371
Business Objectives 372
Technology Challenge 374
Solution Deployment 376

Value Achieved 377
Lessons Learned 378
    Have a Focused Approach and Implement SAP
    CRM in Small Pieces 378
    Get Key Users Involved Very Early, Preferably During
    Sandbox Testing 379
    Establish Direct Communication with SAP Product
    Developers — Especially in a Ramp-Up Scenario 379
    Pilot with a Smaller Group If Possible to
    Mitigate Risks 379
    Get the Right People on the Bus 380
Relieve the Core Team of Users from Their Daily
Jobs So They Can Dedicate Their Time to the Project 381
Have Dedicated Project Managers from the Business
and IT Teams 382
Use SAP Best Practices for SAP CRM 382
Looking Ahead 383

A   Glossary 385

Index 399

Acknowledgments

I would like to thank the following individuals for their invaluable contributions:

John Burton, Product Manager, SAP, a great friend for taking the time out of his busy work schedule to review the chapters and make necessary content updates.

Satish Subramanian, Manager (EAS), in particular, and Varian Medical Systems, Inc. for providing their SAP CRM implementation as a case study for the book.

Jenifer Niles, VP Galileo Press, Inc. for her constant encouragement when I was going through the blues and struggles of writing my first book. In the process, I learned that writing a successful book requires the support of an experienced hand from a quality publishing company.

Iris Warkus, Production Director, Galileo Press, Germany in making me comfortable with templates and Todd Brown, Production Manager at Galileo Press, Inc. for resolving the mystery behind why "clear type" setting in **Windows XP display • Appearance • Effects** is turned on automatically even when it is manually turned off.

Anil Shah, Global Business Solutions Manager, HP, for relieving me from our project to focus on completing the book.

Clients, client managers, and SAP for giving me various opportunities to sharpen and apply CRM skills in delivering successful CRM projects.

Michael Weiner, Dave Lawlor, and Brian Rikuda from iServiceGlobe, Inc. for permitting to use their names and pictures in the book

iServiceGlobe India Pvt. Ltd, for helping me with the system access and providing the necessary support when requested.

My wife for making endless cups of green tea to help me stay awake late while I was writing.

I thank my friends Paul Jones and Bob Rich from myiTgroup, and other friends and family members who have indirectly been supportive in making this book a possibility.

Thank you all for making my dream come true!

Preface

This is certainly not the first book on SAP CRM. Many books are available that address particular SAP CRM technologies and solutions, but *Discover SAP CRM* is the only book that explains the fundamentals of customer relationship management, the foundations of SAP CRM, and the business solutions SAP CRM makes possible.

This book explains customer relationship management in general and SAP CRM in an easy to understand way, including valuable examples and business case studies on how to leverage SAP CRM business solutions to optimize your company's customer relationships and revenue channels.

Whom This Book Is For?

In general, *Discover SAP CRM* is geared toward those involved in the customer relationship management process on many levels; however, the following groups of people will find this book especially helpful:

> C-level executives who need a quick reference guide on SAP CRM solutions to help them make decisions about the future course of their company's SAP CRM platform

> Managers who want to know about SAP CRM in detail before kicking off an SAP CRM project, but are often scared off by the thought of sifting through volumes of documentation and tons of PowerPoint presentations to learn SAP CRM

> Business analysts who know their company's business processes very well and are scratching their heads about how to map those processes with the SAP CRM system because they are new to SAP CRM solutions and technologies

> Senior consultants who worked with non-SAP CRM solutions and technologies in the past and are planning to make a career move to the SAP CRM platform

> Senior SAP CRM consultants who haven't had an opportunity to work with the full suite of SAP CRM solutions and want to know the full details of the 360-degree view offered by SAP CRM

> College graduates who want to make a career in SAP CRM and need a comprehensive guide to understand the solutions and technologies available

What You'll Discover

In this book, you'll learn about the entire suite of SAP CRM business applications that you'll use when creating CRM strategies and solutions that work for your customers and your company. You'll also find an overview of each of the major products with sample case studies so you can see how each product works in the real world.

Navigational Tools in This Book

Throughout the book, we've provided several elements that will help you access useful information:

> Tips call out useful information about related ideas and provide practical suggestions for how to use a particular function.

> Notes provide other resources to explore, or special tools or services from SAP that will help you with the topic under discussion.

> Examples provide real-world scenarios and illustrations of how the tools are used.

This is a marginal note

> Marginal text provides a useful way to scan the book to locate topics of interest for you. Each marginal note appears to the side of a paragraph or section with related information.

What's in This Book?

This book provides you with a detailed overview of SAP CRM. You'll learn about everything from the three core applications of Marketing, Sales, and Service, to the interaction center, channel management, master data, analytics, access modes, and more.

Read the book in sequence or go to specific chapters or sections as needed

Chapter 1

This chapter provides the definition and fundamentals of customer relationship management and discusses CRM business needs and CRM core principles.

Chapter 2

This chapter introduces SAP CRM, its components, and the 360-degree view of customer relationship management.

Chapter 3

This chapter focuses on the definitions and basics of the SAP CRM Marketing application and discusses the business uses of the various components.

Chapter 4

This chapter provides elaborate details concerning the SAP CRM Sales application, including account and contact management, order management, sales planning, incentive and commission management (ICM), and various sales analytics.

Chapter 5

This chapter discusses SAP CRM Service, which is the strongest application in the CRM marketplace. The Service application supports both enterprise and small- to mid-size businesses (SMB).

Chapter 6

This chapter covers the SAP CRM interaction center, which is more than just a call center. The interaction center provides multi-channel communication interfaces to prospects/customers, and interfaces with the Marketing, Sales, and Service applications.

Chapter 7

This chapter explores how the SAP CRM Web channel (formerly known as E-Commerce) can easily open the Web as a prominent sales and service channel wherein customers, dealers, and distributors can interact with your business 24/7.

Chapter 8

This chapter describes the business mobility solutions provided by SAP CRM to keep your employees connected with your core business systems so they can make informed decisions.

Chapter 9

This chapter explains the SAP CRM partner channel management solution that addresses the business network of dealers, distributors, and retailers that are involved in business today. You'll learn the practical details of channel management and how to implement channels to optimize your channel relationships.

Chapter 10

This chapter delves into the SAP CRM technology landscape, including the original SAP-developed proprietary programming language, ABAP, which has been the workhorse of SAP engines for more than 30 years. You'll also learn about SAP's innovative NetWeaver technology that supports your challenging and ever growing business needs.

Chapter 11

This chapter helps you understand and apply master data as the core fundamental building block of any SAP CRM business process.

Chapter 12

This chapter, along with the previous 11 chapters, will put you in the cockpit and get you ready to take off on your journey into SAP CRM by describing the business solutions SAP CRM offers your industry.

Chapter 13

This chapter uncovers the analytical techniques for identifying your most profitable customers with easy to understand examples.

Chapter 14

This chapter explores the new SAP CRM 2007 user interface (UI) that is easy to configure and use to create a robust and flexible CRM business system.

Chapter 15

This chapter covers the various ASAP project methodology variants used in successful SAP CRM implementations to meet particular business and industry verticals.

Chapter 16

This chapter provides an in-depth, real-world example of SAP CRM in action. Learn why Varian Medical Systems (VMS) chose SAP CRM to meet its business needs.

Appendix

The appendix is a glossary of the SAP and enterprise computing terminology used in this book.

In addition, the book includes an index that you can use to go directly to certain points of interest.

I hope this book's straightforward and practical approach will give you the the information you need to assess your individual business needs and to determine your own SAP CRM road map for making your implementation a great success.

1

Customer Relationship Management

Customer Relationship Management, commonly referred to as CRM, is about all of the interactions a company has with existing and prospective customers. CRM includes business processes, such as Marketing, Sales, Service, and Analytics, as well as the software used to automate these business processes. In addition, CRM is a strategy for studying, analyzing, and learning about your customers' needs, wants, and expectations. You can use CRM to ensure that your company's products and services meet those needs, wants, and expectations satisfactorily. In essence, there is no one single CRM strategy that every company can follow. Your strategy will be unique to your company, but all CRM strategies have the same goals: to acquire and retain customers to ensure that you conduct business profitably.

Many factors will greatly influence your company's CRM model and strategy, including the following:

> Industry verticals
> Type of business
> Customers served

> Products or services offered

> Distribution channels

> Strategic business needs

> Company culture

> Size of your business

> Whether your company is local or global

> Quality of your IT architecture

Let's briefly discuss each of these factors.

What Are Your Industry Verticals?

An *industry vertical* is a particular industry or group of companies in which similar products and services are developed, marketed, and sold. The industry vertical to which your company belongs and the industry verticals to which your company markets, sells, and provides service are important influencers in determining your company's CRM strategy.

 Example

Different types of industry verticals include High Tech, Manufacturing, Pharmaceutical, the Public Sector, and so on.

What Type of Business Are You In?

As you know, there are many types of businesses. Some businesses produce and sell products, whereas others provide services. Some are owned independently, and others have shareholders. But whatever your business is, it will greatly influence the CRM model and design that you adopt. For example, a consulting company in the defense sector has to comply with government rules, regulations, and procedures, so, its CRM application should support all necessary regulatory compliance requirements. Likewise, the CRM application for a consulting company in the defense sector must be sure that its organization meets the defense industry compliance issues, including having staff with all necessary security clearances.

Who Are Your Customers?

The type of customers your organization deals with also affects your CRM strategy. Types of customers include Business to Business (B2B), Business to Consumer (B2C), or a mix of both. Companies that operate in the B2B model sell their products and services directly to other companies. For example, specialty chemical and plastics companies, such as Dow Chemical, Dow Corning, or BASF, typically sell their products to other manufacturing companies rather than to end consumers.

Whereas a food-packaging company that manufactures plastic milk cartons might routinely order truckloads of ethylene oxide, clearly an end consumer would never drive his new Toyota Camry over to the chemical plant and toss a tank of toxic, highly flammable, explosive gas into the back seat. Another difference between B2B and B2C business models is that B2B companies typically have full-time purchasing departments with professional buyers and purchasing agents whose sole job is to buy things — every week, every day, all day long. This is quite different from a B2C business model in which a customer might only buy a new computer, mobile phone, or MP3 player once every couple of years or so.

When planning your CRM strategy, you clearly need to consider who your customers are.

 Tip

> Did you know that law enforcement agencies use a CRM system to classify criminals as customers? Some of their criminal customer types include single offenders, prolific offenders, low-level offenders, and migrating offenders. Every type of business, public or private, has some form of customer.

What Are Your Products and Services?

Only a few companies today still sell a single product or service. Most companies sell a variety of products and services to a variety of different customer segments. The types of products and service you sell and the types of customers you sell them to have a big influence on your CRM strategy. Let's take the example of a high-tech computer company that sells servers, PCs, storage media, printers, hand-held devices, and software, along with providing consulting and IT services. The three different types of customer segments that the company offers products for are listed here:

Customer segments

> Large enterprise businesses (i.e., government, health, and education, etc.)
> Small and medium businesses (SMB)
> Home and home office businesses (HHO)

The company will need a different strategy for each type of customer.

Let's consider what the SAP CRM strategy should be for the HHO product and service offerings. Because most HHO customers don't have a full-fledged purchasing department, the company owners make most of the purchase decisions. Therefore, the high-tech computer company's CRM Strategy for HHO customers should probably leverage e-commerce, including Internet sales and Internet customer self-service, to allow home business owners to make purchases and receive service online. So, the CRM strategy would give HHO customers the flexibility to purchase products by visiting the company's 24/7 e-commerce web shop.

This would also allow customers to search the website for FAQs and solutions to common problems and issues. If the customer is unable to find a solution for the issue on the Web, the customer can log a trouble ticket online, which will automatically create a service ticket in the underlying CRM application on behalf of the customer.

Now let's consider what the high-tech computer company's CRM strategy should be for its large enterprise customers. The sales cycle and purchasing decisions of enterprise customers are more lengthy and complex and include numerous sales visits, telephone calls, quotation proposals, contract negotiations, and so on. This involves frequent communication between the company via telephone, email, fax, and certified postal letter. Therefore, the CRM strategy for large enterprise customers needs to be broader than the strategy for HHO customers to support all of these business processes and communication channels.

Which Channels Does Your Company Use?

Companies use a variety of business models to reach customers. For example, some companies sell directly to customers. Other companies use wholesalers, distributors, or value-added resellers, and still other companies sell to consumers through retailers. These different business models require different business channels to reach the end customers. For example, a PC company such as Dell that mainly sells directly to consumers would use the Web channel to set up an e-commerce Web shop, perhaps supplemented by an interaction center for handling customer complaints, returns, and trouble ticketing.

Business channels

On the other hand, an original equipment manufacturer (OEM) such as AMD or Intel that sells microprocessors to systems integrators or PC manufacturers might leverage channel and partner management for making sales tools and collaterals available to those channel partners. Finally, a consumer products company such as Colgate-Palmolive or Proctor and Gamble that sells through retailers might set up an interaction center for business to business (B2B) sales, as well as a separate interaction center for consumer complaints. So, your business model will ultimately influence your channel requirements as well as your overall CRM strategy.

What Are Your CRM Business Needs?

It's critical for your business to first identify and prioritize your CRM needs so that you can properly define and implement a suitable CRM solution. For example, let's assume you have a very pressing need that is driving your search for a CRM solution. Perhaps your sales force is consistently causing headaches for the company by not reporting their sales leads or tracking their sales opportunities in your current homegrown, Excel-based system until the end of each quarter. As a result, your manufacturing department is caught by surprise each quarter and not able to produce the required amount of products, causing orders to be delayed and cancelled.

Define your CRM business needs

31

Perhaps your sales force is also losing productivity by spending several hours a week doing shadow accounting to calculate their own commissions because they don't have access to a real-time incentive and compensation management system. This would show their projected commissions and allow them to conduct "what if" scenarios to see how their commission would go up or down if they won or lost a particular sales deal.

Choose a full-featured CRM application to address short- and long-term needs

Based on these pain points, you might be tempted to rush out and buy a standalone sales force automation package rather than a full-blown CRM product or enterprise business suite. But, you probably have several other pain points just about to spring up. What happens when the next emergency arises? If you address each point as it arises with separate non-integrated standalone point solutions, you'll eventually end up with a very fragmented IT landscape without the possibility for easy process integration or consolidated reporting. Additionally, such systems are very costly to maintain and require a large assortment of IT staff and expertise, each trained on the different products and technologies.

One major advantage of a full-featured CRM application — or an enterprise business suite that includes CRM as well as Enterprise Resource Planning (ERP) and other products — is that you can start small by immediately addressing your most pressing current pain points and then add on other features and capabilities as needed. Because you're using a single product suite from a single vendor with one consistent underlying technology platform, you can integrate end-to-end business processes and leverage consolidated reporting. And, of course, total cost of ownership (TCO) is naturally lower due to the simplified IT landscape and reduced need to support disparate technologies and tools.

Start small but think big

Before designing or implementing a CRM solution, however, be sure to carefully consider what your needs are — not just your current needs but your short-term and long-term needs as well. Start small, but think big. Today you might need a sales force automation solution, but maybe tomorrow you'll need a customer-service center, an employee help desk, or an IT help desk. Make sure you consider how the tactical topics you're working on today fit into the larger, more strategic long-term project or program. Even the best individual solutions are of little value if they don't play well with your complete IT infrastructure.

What Is Your Company Culture?

Company culture defines the degree of readiness and adaptability to business process and IT changes. Most companies understand and acknowledge that customer-facing business initiatives such as CRM should be driven by the business rather than the IT organization. However, in reality, many CRM initiatives are still driven and controlled by the IT organization. This can lead to difficult situations in which the business feels that its needs are not being considered or addressed.

Know your
company's culture

Take the following fictitious — but realistic — example based on a fast-growing widget company named Widgets-R-Us that recently acquired several smaller widget companies. The CIO of Widgets-R-Us decides that he wants to consolidate his fragmented CRM and IT infrastructure to reduce TCO and to allow all of the company's locations to share customer data. The CFO loves the idea because it will save millions of dollars by allowing the company to retire its various home-grown IT systems that have become very costly to maintain. Senior management doesn't understand all of the little details but doesn't want to appear unknowledgeable by asking dumb questions, so they give it the thumbs up as well.

However, no one ever bothers to consult the Line of Business (LoB) owners or the end users. The system is rolled out smoothly ahead of time and under budget. The project teams throw a big party to celebrate. However, a month later, management notices that sales revenues are down, service costs are up, and customer satisfaction is worse than ever. It turns out, the end users were never trained on the new system and are still doing things the way they used to with the old system.

We can learn a lot from the mistakes of Widgets-R-Us. For example, to succeed, every project needs top-level management support — not just top-level management sign-off. Also, CRM projects need to be driven by the business and supported by IT, not the other way around. Finally, CRM projects are not just about IT, they are about changing the way people work and re-engineering business processes. If the culture of the company isn't open to change and has not been primed for business process re-engineering, any CRM efforts are likely to fail.

How Big Is Your Company?

If you're a small or medium business (SMB), you may have limited business and IT resources available for a new CRM project because day-to-day activities tie up all of your resources. Unfortunately, SMB companies often allocate minimal resource time to developing a CRM strategy. However, implementing a CRM strategy could actually free up some of the resources by automating certain business processes, such as customer support, service agreement fulfillment, and so on. In contrast, large enterprises are often able to allocate substantial resources and funds to new processes and strategies that will improve efficiency. But, large companies sometimes try to do too much, running the risk of creating a CRM strategy so broad that it tries to involve every division without having a clear business purpose.

 Tip

> Know your business goals, business drivers, and business objectives for your CRM requirements, and stay focused while building your CRM strategy. Diligently fight scope creep, and resist the urge to add "just one more" cool feature or functionality. New features are like potato chips: you can't have just one.

Are You Global, Regional, or Local?

The legal and cultural aspects of different countries, regions, and states greatly influence your CRM strategy. Many companies start local and then go global as they grow and expand. So it's very important that you develop a strategy from the beginning with flexibility to go global and accommodate different legal and cultural requirements. Taking a "we're a local company" approach today may impact your ability to go global later.

In addition, many global companies that already have operations around the world decide to roll out new CRM programs or new CRM features on a regional basis. For example, when rolling out an upgraded CRM solution, a large global company decided to start with only a handful of users in Portugal. Then, over the next year, the company slowly rolled the solution out to more than 13,000 users across Europe, Asia, and North and South America. The key to going global is to first master the basics in one particular region or location and then to re-duplicate the success from one location to the next. Very few companies attempt a global "big bang" CRM implementation all at once.

 Tip

Build a single CRM strategy that meets your global business needs, but also supports your local culture and legal requirements. Start local, but always be thinking global.

Competitiveness of Your IT Infrastructure and Architecture

Many people assume that if the IT department stays competitive, the company will too. In reality, your IT architecture only supports your business needs — not your customers' business needs. Your IT architect is only asked to provide an IT architecture that supports what your company needs for its own business operations.

Know your IT strengths and weaknesses

It's possible that your company's IT architect and your business leaders did not see CRM as a necessary tool when originally developing your IT infrastructure. However, having a solid IT system as part of your CRM strategy can help increase the efficiency with which your customers interact with you and, in turn, increase your brand value, develop profitable customer relationships, facilitate communication with your customers, and much more.

If your IT structure has not been updated periodically, it may not be able to support a CRM implementation or development of new dimensions of CRM initiatives. So as part of your CRM strategy planning, you need to perform a SWOT (Strengths, Weaknesses, Opportunities, and Threats) analysis of your current IT infrastructure and IT resources. For example, if your IT team is still using magnetic tape, punch cards, 8-inch floppy diskettes, and Commodore 64 computers, it might be time to buy them some new equipment and send them to a training class or two.

 Tip

Business goals and objectives should lead your CRM strategy, and technology should support it.

Now that we've reviewed the major factors to consider when developing your CRM strategy, let's move on to discuss a few core CRM principles.

Core CRM Principles

Just as human cultures are focused on people, CRM is also focused on people — customers to be exact. Customers are the key to success for your company. A CRM approach is based on core principles and a strong foundation. Let's take a look at these principles.

Customer First

CRM is focused on people

"Customer First" is a common mission statement for many companies. Clearly, it should be the strategy of every company, but only a few companies achieve this mission and establish profitable and sustainable relationships with their customers. Your CRM initiative should be customer-centric. If all your employees, products, and services are positioned to meet the needs and expectations of your customers, then you have a solid start in developing a customer-centric CRM strategy.

 Note

> Amazon is a good example of a customer-first company. Everything the company does ties into providing for its customer's needs by offering a plethora of products and then customizing the customer experience so that it seems as if the Amazon site and products were designed for that customer alone.

Designing a Customer-First CRM Initiative

Regardless of the size of your organization, you should have a Chief Customer Officer (CCO) who is charged with envisioning, designing, executing, and deploying a CRM Business and IT solution that provides profitable, optimum customer satisfaction.

 Examples

> ❯ Amazon envisioned, designed, executed, and deployed a click-and-sell bookstore where customers with access to the Internet can browse, review, and order books from the comfort of their homes.
>
> ❯ eBay envisioned, designed, implemented, and deployed a digital auction hall successfully.
>
> ❯ Netflix changed the movie rental business landscape by creating an online video rentals business model in which movies are delivered to the customer's mailbox, and customers can return movies without late fees.
>
> All of these companies developed products with the customer in mind. They made the customer experience easy, customizable, and hassle-free.

The "Customer-First" strategy must be designed to ensure that you understand your customers (and prospective customers) thoroughly. Conducting regular customer satisfaction surveys about your products and services will give you valuable insights into their experiences, preferences, and suggestions. Knowing the customer is an ongoing

Build your CRM strategy as "Customer –First"

process that must evolve as customer needs and wants change over time.

 Example

> The Hilton, Holiday Inn, Hyatt, and Marriott hotel chains usually request that customers complete a survey via email after a stay at one of their hotels or resorts. The surveys typically ask about the customer's experience and how the customer would rate the ambience of the hotel, comfort level of the suite, arrival and departure experiences, quality of the breakfast if provided, and what other services the customer would like or recommend. They also ask about the likelihood of the customer staying at the hotel again. This type of information is invaluable for planning future renovations, expansions, and service changes. And as part of their CRM strategy, it is integrated into the hotel's systems and made available in a variety of usable forms.

Customer Market Segments

Use CRM to automate customer market segmentation

Another important factor about the customer-first approach is to remember that every customer fits into a particular market segment. So, your company's products and services must be tailored to meet the specific needs and wants of a particular market segment. SAP CRM offers marketing and campaigning applications to automate market segmentation so that you know the needs and wants of customers in a particular market segment.

For example, a large number of Apple®'s iPod® consumers are part of what some researchers call the millennial generation. These customers were born between 1977 and 1998, are technologically perceptive, and usually have significant disposable income. Knowing this about their largest market segment makes it possible for Apple to tailor advertising, promotions, and pricing specifically to meet the millennial generation's needs.

Customers Change

Customer needs and wants change over time, so monitoring their profile changes allows companies to better match products and services with customer needs and wants. Your CRM application should provide the ability to collect and analyze customer profile updates at every possible touch point, such as phone calls, email updates, Web notices, customer visits, and so on.

 Example

> Blockbuster initially refused to change its brick and mortar movie rentals to an online order and delivery model. They also insisted on continuing with their late fee policies, which allowed rival Netflix to gain significant market share. Blockbuster has recently changed its policies though, and they are now "changing with the times and customer preferences."

Customized Product and Service Offerings for Customers

In addition to changing with the times, your product and service offerings should be as customizable as possible to meet specific customer needs. Many high-tech companies provide customers with an option to configure products based on their needs. Dell, Fujitsu, HP, Lenovo, Sony, and Toshiba all provide product configuration tools on their e-commerce websites that allow customers to build personalized desktops and notebooks. If your products can be customized, it's important to let your customers know it.

Provide timely customer service with your CRM system

Increase Customer Lifetime Value

Finally, it's increasingly important to maintain long-term customer relationships. Customer Lifetime Value (CLTV) is a new concept featured in customer-centric aspects of CRM software. It's based on the present value of future cash flows that will come from a customer relationship. CLTV places greater emphasis on customer satisfaction rather than short-term sales, and CRM programs designed to increase CLTV help increase customer loyalty, brand loyalty, and product loyalty (iPod, Skype, Windows, Google, etc.). A company with loyal and committed customers earns repeated revenues from the same customers.

Create lifetime value

Note, however, at most companies, 20% of the customers generate about 80% or more of the revenue and profits, which is known as the 80/20 business rule. In addition, because recent studies show that on-

80/20 rule

line shopping has decreased brand and product loyalty due to the low, or no cost of switching brands, it's increasingly important to maintain your core customers. Statistics say that Web shoppers go to their favorite search engine (Google, Yahoo!, etc.) to search for products and services. They don't search for a particular product brand anymore! This is true even in the B2B scenario.

Clearly, everything we have discussed so far is important when developing your CRM strategy, but it's safe to say that putting your customers first in your strategy is essential.

Now let's take a quick look at the technology requirements for a CRM strategy to be implemented.

What Functionality Should Your CRM Application Provide?

Now that we have a clear definition of CRM and its core principles, let's look at the basic functionalities a CRM application should be able to do:

> Collect the most relevant information about your customers and prospects, their preferences, needs, and necessities, so that you can meet their expectations well. Today's customers search before every purchase they make, so you not only have to satisfy them but also make them want to come back.

> Match the products and services offered with the customer's needs and then make an offer to the customer.

> Assist your business in improving the quality of products and services by providing comprehensive reports about product issues or suggested improvements reported by customers.

> Be easy to use for customers and employees.

> Improve and increase lifetime value (CLTV).

As mentioned, this is just a quick overview of what the CRM system should provide. We'll discuss this in more detail throughout the book. For now, let's take a quick look at the technology requirements.

What Drives CRM Technology?

Innovative business ideas and cost effective business process changes can drive CRM developments. Technology savvy companies drive developers of CRM applications to deliver additional out-of-the-box solutions to support new business needs. On average, out-of-the-box CRM functionality lags a year behind what businesses need, so your company's CRM strategy is limited by the features and solutions available from CRM application vendors. You do have the option of custom development, but that requires skilled IT resources. The recommendation is to stay with the out-of-box tools and expand your CRM model with the new or enhanced functionalities that your CRM vendor delivers with each release. This way, you let the vendor take care of your IT needs, while you work on growing your business. In Chapter 10 we'll talk about the SAP-specific technology in depth.

CRM is business driven and technology supported

Conclusion

As we discovered throughout this chapter, CRM provides a win-win environment for customers and companies who implement the right CRM strategy. You need to ask many questions when developing your CRM strategy to ascertain the following:

> Industry verticals
> Type of business
> Customers served
> Products or services offered
> Distribution channels
> Strategic business needs
> Company culture
> Size of your business
> Whether your company is local or global
> Quality of your IT architecture

We also briefly discussed how technology is a key component of your CRM strategy, and that CRM is business driven and IT supported. In the next chapter, you'll learn what SAP CRM provides for achieving your CRM strategy.

2

SAP CRM Detailed Overview

In Chapter 1, you learned about CRM in general terms, so now let's look at SAP's approach to customer relationship management and see how the technology has developed around the principles of CRM. Throughout the chapter, we'll introduce the core components of SAP CRM and briefly review their functionality.

What Is SAP CRM?

SAP CRM is a software tool based on a customer-centric business philosophy. SAP CRM manages all aspects of the customer relationship throughout the marketing, sales, and service operations within a business. It helps companies gain operational efficiency for winning and retaining customers, and it can help your company improve overall market value, share, and profitability by improving your customers' experiences with your products and services. SAP CRM is truly a powerful, well-rounded tool that you can use for various aspects of your customer relationship management strategy. Let's look at the major strengths of SAP CRM.

SAP CRM Strengths

SAP CRM has many strengths, and in the newest release, SAP CRM 2007, it continues to improve in both functionality and usability. The key strengths include:

> Provides a 360-degree view of customers, including all interactions with them. You can determine who your most profitable customers are and build lasting, loyal, and profitable relationships (Figure 2.1).

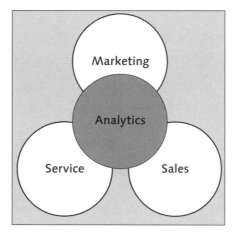

Figure 2.1 360-Degree View of SAP CRM

> Supports Web Services by providing enterprise service-oriented architecture (enterprise SOA), which we'll define later in the book.

> Provides a browser-based, zero footprint SAP CRM WebClient user interface (UI).

> Comes in *SAP CRM on-demand* and *SAP CRM on-premise* versions.

> Provides seamless integration to SAP ERP applications using out-of-the-box SAP CRM middleware.

> Allows Single Sign-On to all connected SAP systems.

> Includes standard business content for providing analytics by connecting to the SAP NetWeaver BI system. (We'll talk about standard business content in detail in later chapters.)

The Key Components of SAP CRM

The key components of SAP CRM are Marketing, Sales, Service, and Analytics. These key components of SAP CRM provide the necessary tools and automated processes to engage the customer, process and fulfill sales orders, and provide customer service and support.

The components of SAP CRM are also known as cycles within SAP CRM, so SAP CRM is sometimes referred to as a full-cycle solution

The components of SAP CRM: Marketing, Sales, Service, and Analytics

1. **Marketing**
   Informs the customer about new products and services via marketing and campaigning programs.

2. **Sales**
   Creates opportunities, quotations, and sales orders, logistics management, such as order delivery, tracking, and billing.

3. **Service**
   Responds to the customer service requests, collects feedback from the customers about the products and services, and runs analytics.

4. **Analytics**
   Provides feedback that can be used to fine-tune future marketing programs and campaigns as the SAP CRM process continues (see Figure 2.2).

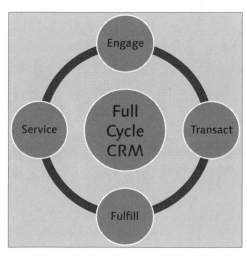

Figure 2.2 Full Cycle CRM

45

SAP CRM is made up of many applications, which we'll discuss throughout this chapter. SAP CRM begins with marketing and the generation of qualifying leads. Leads are then converted into opportunities — either manually or by an automated process — and handed over to the sales department for further engagement with the customer (Figure 2.3).

During the sales cycle, product and price quotations may be provided to the customer. If the customer accepts the quote, the quotation is converted into a sales order, sales contract, or business agreement. After the sale, customers can take advantage of SAP CRM Service to request service or repairs, log trouble tickets for malfunctioning equipment, file complaints for problems with sales orders or invoices, or return damaged or defective items. Customer data and business transaction data are then exported to BI and used for planning further marketing efforts. So, the closed-loop SAP CRM process continues.

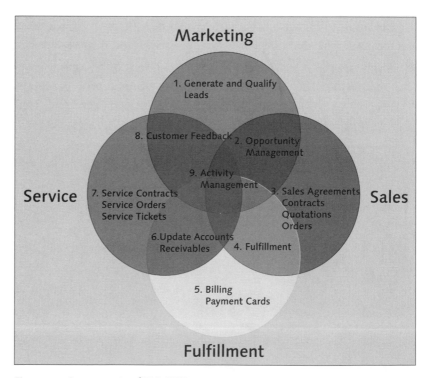

Figure 2.3 Components of SAP CRM

Now let's review the SAP CRM Solution Map for Marketing, Sales, Service, and Analytics.

SAP CRM Solution Map

The solution map helps you understand the SAP CRM applications provided by SAP CRM. The solution map in Figure 2.4 gives a complete view of the SAP CRM applications, including processes (marketing resource management, sales planning, forecasting, etc.) as well as business channels (Web channel, interaction center, and channel partner management).

SAP CRM solution map

Figure 2.4 SAP CRM Solution Map

 TIP

> The SAP CRM Marketing, Sales, and Service functionality can be accessed differently by different types of SAP CRM users. For example, a sales manager, a mobile sales person, and an interaction center agent might all access the same underlying customer data record from different applications. The sales manager will pull up the customer details via the standard SAP CRM screen, and the field reps will be using the mobile sales application on a laptop or handheld device. And, the interaction center agent will access the customer record from the interaction center using the interaction center specific view of the customer data.

Let's take a brief look at the key components of Marketing, Sales, Service, and Analytics.

SAP CRM Marketing

Every organization, whether it be for profit or not, needs to market its products, services, and concepts to its customers. The SAP CRM Marketing component provides a central marketing platform that helps businesses analyze, plan, develop, and execute all marketing activities through all customer touch (interaction) points. An integrated solution like this gives the marketing team detailed business insights to help them make smart business decisions and drive end-to-end marketing processes. The Marketing component supports important marketing processes, including marketing resource management, segment and list management, campaign management, trade promotion management, telemarketing, e-marketing, lead management, and marketing analytics.

> **Marketing resource management**
  Assists the marketing manager in designing a marketing plan with budget and resources.

> **Segment and list management**
  Enables delivery of complete marketing campaigns, including planning, content development, audience definition, market segmentation, and communication.

> **Campaign management**
  Enables delivery of complete marketing campaigns, including planning, content development, audience definition, market segmentation, and communication.

> **Trade promotion management**
  Enables brand managers to optimize trade funds to maximize sales volume and optimize brand awareness.

> **Lead management**
  Allows development of new leads through lead qualification, routing, tracking, and eventually the delivery of sales leads to opportunity management.

> **Marketing analytics**
  Helps managers understand the effectiveness of their marketing activities to improve marketing efforts that didn't work. (We'll talk about SAP CRM Analytics in detail in Chapter 13.)

SAP CRM Sales

Today's sales paradigm requires you to win the confidence of your customers by demonstrating and showcasing your company's products and services and by solving customer problems quickly and efficiently. By doing so, you help build trusted and long-term relationships with your customers.

Become a trusted and dependable partner for your customers

The SAP CRM Sales component helps sales professionals achieve this by providing the functionality they need to turn insight into action and acquire, grow, and retain profitable relationships. Using the Sales application, companies can plan and analyze the entire sales lifecycle, find new ways to speed the sales cycle, uncover new areas of revenue potential, and determine new methods for improving sales productivity. The Sales solution supports a number of business processes, including the following:

> Sales planning and forecasting

> Territory management

> Accounts and contacts management

> Activity management

> Opportunity management

> Quotation and order management

> Product configuration and pricing

> Billing and contract management

> Incentive and commission management

> Time and travel management

> Sales analytics

We'll look at each of these in depth in Chapter 4.

In addition to these capabilities, the Sales component supports customer touch points (phone, email, chat, Web, customer visit, etc.) with specific applications, such as E-Commerce (formerly Internet Sales), interaction center, channel partner management, and field sales.

E-Commerce (Formerly Internet Sales)

Use SAP CRM Web Channel to keep your business open 24/7

E-Commerce (formerly called Internet Sales) is part of the SAP Web channel (formerly called E-Commerce), which gives customers and prospects access to dedicated information, such as product catalog, content, pricing, solutions, and self-service functions (order entry and tracking orders) via the Internet. E-Commerce is a cutting-edge solution for companies that want to develop the Internet as a strategic sales channel. The fact that E-Commerce is integrated with other SAP applications plays a major role in providing an end-to-end business process.

 Example

An order created in an SAP CRM system via a Web shop is fulfilled by the integrated backend ERP application.

Interaction Center

Using telesales in the interaction center allows agents to qualify leads (either manually or automatically via built-in marketing survey integration), leverage cross-selling and up-selling opportunities, and process and update sales orders on behalf of customers.

Partner Channel Management

The high-end reselling models use Web-based channel management, in which distributors log on to the E-Commerce application and create orders for end customers.

Field Sales

Your sales force consists of many road warriors who need access to customers, products, and price list data, as well as the ability to create quotations and orders whether connected to the SAP CRM system or not. SAP CRM provides an offline SAP CRM Sales solution that is installed on a laptop or PDA with its own database — consisting of all necessary data around the customer and products that the sale rep sells — and is a subset of the main SAP CRM database. The sales person will be able to create new accounts using the offline application and upload the account info to the main SAP CRM server when connected. Likewise, the sales person receives updates to the products and customers and the other relevant data from the SAP CRM main server to the laptop application during the data synchronization.

You may choose to use a laptop to run the mobile sales application if your sales person needs a full strength Sales application. However, you also have handheld sales on PDA if only a light sales application is needed. Let's look into those details.

Mobile Sales on a Laptop

Mobile Sales is a complete suite of sales components made available on a laptop to the sales person to work offline from the SAP CRM server. The accounts, contacts, products, and pricelist are made available on the laptop for the sales person to create a quote or order during a customer visit. The laptop is connected to the central SAP CRM server at the next available connectivity to get and send data updates.

Handheld Sales

Handheld devices, such as GPRS-enabled (Global Pocket Radio Services) Wireless Application Protocol (WAP) access phones and Personal Digital Assistants (PDAs), have been integrated into SAP CRM Sales to enable sales people to access accounts and contact information, and process light duty activities and opportunities remotely from the SAP CRM server. Handheld Sales comes in On-Mode when a wireless connectivity is available and Off-Mode when no connectivity is available.

SAP CRM Service

SAP CRM Service allows you to provide onsite, telephone, or self-service options to your customers. Customer service includes all of the activities designed to enhance customer satisfaction by meeting the customer expectations of a product or service. Customer service can be provided onsite by a field service technician; over the telephone, email, or chat by an interaction center agent; or via customer self-service.

Customer self-service is becoming more and more widely used by companies because it gives customers the ability to handle things themselves. For example, if you've ever visited a company website to register your products or check the status of your order, you've experienced customer self-service.

Although customer self-service can provide a low-cost option for delivering basic customer service, many companies prefer to use the interaction center (especially for high-value customers, products, or industries) because it allows the company to differentiate itself and reinforce its brand image via excellent service. The interaction center also provides superior opportunities for cross-selling and up-selling via trained sales people, rather than a static hyperlink on a self-service website that says "click here to buy accessories."

The SAP CRM Service application maximizes service profitability by helping keep profitable customers loyal, decreasing service costs through efficiency, and increasing service revenue. In the past, customer service departments were often seen as cost centers, or operations that don't make a profit and just add to the cost of running a company. Customer service was viewed as an obligatory requirement of doing business.

Today, customer service is expected to be profitable and to contribute to the bottom line of a company's income statement. Service operations need to keep costs down by automating and re-engineering redundant and inefficient business processes and by resolving customer issues on the first attempt. But keeping costs down is only half of the equation. Service departments are also expected to sell extended service contracts and high-uptime service level agreements. Service contracts are, in fact, often much more profitable than the actual product itself, due to the high profit margin on services and the relatively lower profit margin on manufactured products.

The following are the individual components of SAP CRM Service.

> Service order management
> Service contract management
> Complaints and returns management
> In-house and depot repair
> Case management
> Installed-base management
> Warranty management
> Resource planning
> E-service
> Service analytics

As you can see, the SAP CRM Service application is a feature-packed tool that can help you meet all of your SAP CRM strategy goals. We'll cover SAP CRM Service in much greater depth in Chapter 5.

Analytics

SAP CRM Analytics provide actionable intelligence that helps managers and customer-facing employees make better business decisions. Organizations can view vital information from all business functions across the company, including marketing, sales, service, the interaction center, Web channel, and partner channel management. In the next sections, we'll highlight the various analytics that are delivered standard out of box with integration into SAP NetWeaver BI. Take it easy for now if you don't understand some of the analytics because there is a dedicated discussion about the analytics in Chapter 13.

Analytics — actionable intelligence about your customers

> **Marketing analytics**
Managers can leverage SAP CRM marketing analytics to make profitable business decisions by keeping an eye on metrics such as Customer Lifetime Value (CLTV), churn propensity, or customer satisfaction. Marketing analytics provide insight into why certain marketing activities were successful and why other marketing ac-

tivities didn't work as intended. Marketing analytics can also help predict customer behavior and anticipate customer needs, allowing marketers to create targeted marketing messages and campaigns.

> **Sales analytics**

Sales departments need more than historical reports showing sales volumes for the previous quarter. SAP CRM sales analytics allow companies to monitor their sales pipeline and respond in real time as necessary. Organizations can forecast sales volumes, monitor their sales pipeline, and make on-the-fly adjustments to achieve forecasted revenue goals. Sales managers can also analyze competitive win and loss data to determine what is working and what needs to be further improved.

> **Interaction center analytics**

Companies can measure and improve their interaction center operations by viewing analytical reports relating to customer service issues, inbound email and telephone volumes, and performance metrics. Out-of-the-box reports are available showing service ticket volume, history, and average lead time (sometimes also referred to as average turnaround time). Standard reports are available for email showing email volume, average handling, average response time, and service level compliance. It's also possible to import CTI data from communication management software products to view more traditional call-center telephone statistics, such as service level, connection volume, average handling time, average speed of answer, and call abandonment rate.

> **Service analytics**

Service departments can leverage SAP CRM Service analytics to reduce service costs, increase service profitability, and keep customers loyal and profitable. Service analytics allow companies to identify undesirable trends or other issues and to take corrective action before the trends become a problem. Managers can also compare the effectiveness of existing service territories and check planned values against actual values.

How Can SAP CRM Analytics Help Your Company?

SAP provides standard business content to be used with SAP NetWeaver BI for SAP CRM Analytics. SAP CRM customer analytics provide metrics around customer behavior, CLTV, and so on. These analytics provide an in-depth analysis of your customer's behavior and lifetime value by analyzing the customer touch points, performance of products purchased by the customer, and service requests around the products owned by the customer.

The customer experience with your company at each touch point is measured and monitored by conducting customer satisfaction (C-SAT) surveys and analyzing the same. The resulting corporate metrics could raise alerts if any decline in customer satisfaction from the preset levels is found. You'll learn a lot more about this later, but for now, just know that you can get tremendous insight into your customers with the Analytics tool.

> C-SAT means customer satisfaction

For the rest of this chapter, let's take a quick look at the SAP solution offerings for small- and mid-size companies. These products are new tools that expand the reach of SAP products and bring the power of a SAP CRM solution to all size businesses.

SAP CRM Solutions for Small- and Medium-Size Businesses

In 2002, SAP launched the Smart Business solutions program for the small and medium business (SME or SMB) market. Since then, SAP has been adding new functionality continuously.

Advances in enterprise computing now make addressing the needs of this market easier than ever. SAP's 35 years of gathering knowledge of back-office and front-office best practices is integral to their success with smaller businesses. SAP products offer several technical features:

> Preconfigured templates (so-called *Best Practices*)
> Tools to accelerate the implementation of industry-specific solutions

> SAP NetWeaver platform to support integration

> Easy-to-use interfaces

> Enterprise service-oriented architecture (eSOA) approach that hides the underlying programming complexity

Robust enterprise computing is now becoming much more affordable and predictable, even for small businesses. In 2007, SAP committed their resources, and even launched a new business model that includes a retooling of their own internal processes, to deliver solutions to a larger customer base. In future years, SAP will use innovative methods of delivering their products and services, including a try-run-adapt model that allows customers to try out products via Internet-hosted services before they buy.

The SAP SME portfolio
Beyond the financial opportunities of the small- to midsize market, SAP recognizes that the market is unique in its needs. SMBs vary a lot in their structure, systems, and needs. Far from being simpler than larger companies, their needs are often just as complex; however, they are much less risk-tolerant because of their often tight profit margins and niche markets.

Consequently, SAP offers the SMB market a portfolio of three products: SAP Business One, SAP Business All-in-One, and the newest offering, SAP Business ByDesign.

SAP Business One
> **SAP Business One**
This affordable solution is targeted directly at small businesses. This product helps companies manage their entire business across several key functions, including financials, sales, customers, and operations, with a single system. With SAP Business One, small businesses can streamline their end-to-end operations and get quick access to information that helps them respond faster to market pressures. SAP Business One can typically be implemented in about a month.

SAP Business All-in-One
> **SAP Business All-in-One**
SAP All-in-One solutions are designed for midsize companies that have more sophisticated business processes and specific industry functionality. These companies may have global operations and

several channels of distribution and typically have an IT staff that can customize business solutions. SAP All-in-One solutions are very configurable and can often be implemented in about two to four months.

> **SAP Business ByDesign**
> SAP Business ByDesign is for nontraditional, integrated suite customers. This on-demand solution provides a hosted solution with a great deal of choice and flexibility for its adoption and configuration. All three of these offerings also provide SAP CRM functionality including the following:

SAP Business
ByDesign

> **Business partner management**
> Provides master data management of partners and resellers to track sales leads, opportunities, and customer touch point summaries (customer visit, phone call, etc.), account balances, and sales pipeline analysis.

> **Sales and opportunity management**
> Manages the sales process during different phases, tracks sales opportunities, forecasts revenue potential, and provides sales and opportunity analyses dashboard reports.

> **Customer service and support**
> Provides an integrated management of warranties, service calls, service contracts, and customer interactions.

> **Web access to SAP CRM**
> Provides sales people a secure access to customer information via the Web, and customers can log in to the system to check an order status and log inquiries.

> **Microsoft Outlook integration**
> Synchronizes contacts, tasks, and activities created in SAP Business One with MS Outlook.

So if you own or work for an SMB, SAP also offers you the right SAP CRM solution. Let's take a look at one more solution: SAP CRM On-Demand.

SAP CRM On-Demand Solutions

SAP CRM
On-Demand
solutions

SAP has extended SAP CRM solutions to provide on-demand solutions (subscription-based Web solutions) using the SaaS (Software as a Service) model for the Marketing, Sales, and Service applications. SAP created the first hybrid SAP CRM solution that transcends on-demand and on-premise. You can start with an on-demand SAP CRM solution to provide an effective sales tool to sales persons quickly.

Then, you can transcend later to the on-premise solution when the complexity and needs of your sales processes warrant it. The switch from on-demand to on-premise will be smooth and won't shock the sales person because the same intuitive on-demand UI is also available in the on-premise solution with the new unified UI approach. In the on-premise model, the customer owns the systems and software, and systems are typically installed on the customer premise. In the on-demand model, SAP offers the SAP CRM solution in SaaS with a monthly subscription fee that starts around $75 per user.

Benefits of SAP CRM On-Demand for SMBs

Subscription-based
model

One of the most appealing features of this solution is that there are no upfront costs for establishing the system landscape and purchase of software because this is a subscription-based model. The hosted Web-based application can be rapidly deployed with faster user adoption and minimal training. Productivity is also enhanced because the solution can be synchronized with desktop office applications, such as MS Outlook, Lotus Notes, and so on. On-demand can be integrated with ERP and Supply Chain Management (SCM) systems as well.

Conclusion

We covered a lot of material in this chapter, but don't worry about remembering every detail at this point because each topic is covered in a detailed chapter later in the book. Some key points to remember as you move on include the following:

> SAP CRM provides a 360-degree view of customer relationship management with a full-cycle solution.

> The SAP CRM Solution covers all components of Marketing, Sales, Service, and Analytics.

> The new SAP CRM Web UI offers enhanced functionality and an improved UI.

> The Analytics capabilities of SAP CRM provide detailed information on your customers that can improve your relationships and establish new ones.

> SAP also provides SAP CRM solutions for SMB customers, including SAP Business One, SAP Business All-in-One, and SAP Business ByDesign.

> SAP CRM comes in on-premise and on-demand versions.

In the next chapter, we'll explore the SAP CRM Marketing component in detail.

3

SAP CRM Marketing

If you want to sell your products (including service products), you need to let customers know what you have to offer. In today's competitive marketplace, getting your products known is essential to your growth. To put it simply, marketing is everything you do to make sure your customers and prospects know about your products.

One of the key goals of marketing, therefore, is to generate customer awareness and demand for your products. Like all successful activities, marketing begins with a strategy and a plan. A marketing strategy defines conceptually at a high level how you want to use your limited marketing resources to best optimize brand awareness and sales revenue to create a competitive advantage. For example, perhaps you're a consumer packaged goods company and decide that you want to rely on in-store trade promotions — essentially paying grocery store retailers to prominently display and advertise your products in the store. Or, perhaps you're an enterprise software company that decides to launch a television and print media campaign to make a push into the lucrative small- and medium-business (SMB) market.

Whereas a marketing strategy defines the goals you want to accomplish, a marketing plan describes the details of how you plan to achieve those goals. With your marketing plans, you decide what your customers should know about your products or services, allowing them to distinguish your products from the many other choices available. A marketing plan is composed of marketing plan elements, namely campaigns and trade promotions:

> A *campaign* contains information such as the campaign objectives, tactics, priority, channel (email, telephone, mail, print media, etc.), and target market.

> A *trade promotion* contains information such as the trade funds (or budget), trade activities, maximum price discount, maximum duration, whether there is allowed overlap with other promotions, and so on.

But whether you're targeting customers directly through campaigns or indirectly through retail trade promotions, the goal is the same: to acquire new customers, to increase your market share of existing customers, and to protect and retain your most valuable customers from competitors.

When people think of marketing, they often focus on outward activities such as advertising and telemarketing designed primarily to capture new customers. However, an important but sometimes overlooked role of marketing is to identify and *retain* a company's most valuable and profitable customers. Much has been written in the past few years about how it's 5 to 10 times more expensive to acquire new customers than to sell to existing customers.

However, a disproportionate amount of marketing budgets are still focused on efforts to acquire new customers rather than efforts to retain profitable existing customers. But this can be a real mistake! Many experts recommended that companies focus most of their marketing efforts on activities designed to increase customer loyalty and to prevent customer churn and defections.

For example, SAP Real-Time Offer Management (which will be discussed later in this chapter) can identify and propose the optimal marketing retention offer for at-risk customers during a real-time customer interaction. On one hand, it's important to prevent customer defections by offering an appealing retention offer. On the other hand, with shrinking profit margins and increased competition, companies can't afford to give away more discounts and incentives than is absolutely necessary to retain a customer. It's important to pick just the right retention offer that provides enough of an incentive to keep the customer but doesn't needlessly waste money and resources by providing far more than is necessary.

SAP Real-Time Offer Management

It's important for companies to be able to justify marketing budgets by accurately estimating returns on the marketing dollars spent. Companies also need to be able to align and coordinate the marketing activities to ensure effective timing with product releases and such. And to make campaigns really effective, you need to be able to break down your activities by customer segment. This is where SAP CRM Marketing shines. SAP CRM Marketing helps you identify which customers you should target with which of your products. It also maintains information about those customers so you can close your deals more efficiently. So let's take a look at everything you'll find in the Marketing component.

SAP CRM Marketing Component

SAP CRM Marketing assists your company in planning, budgeting, executing, analyzing, and optimizing all aspects of marketing and campaign execution. In the next sections, we'll take a detailed look at each of the eight major components as shown in Figure 3.1.

Figure 3.1 SAP CRM Marketing Solution Map

Marketing Resource Management (MRM)

A successful marketing campaign requires tools and resources that are flexible enough to meet your company's marketing needs. SAP CRM Marketing Resource Management (MRM) provides the tools to increase efficiency and visibility of your marketing resources. Marketers have limited resources, and those resources need to be maximized. For example, almost all managers will tell you that they never seem to have enough people, time, or budget. Marketing managers, in addition, also need flexibility to respond to changing dynamics. Most marketers would agree that marketing is probably more of a skill — or even an art — than an exact science.

MRM manages
resources for
running successful
marketing
campaigns

MRM manages all of the resources that businesses need to run successful marketing campaigns. You can plan and forecast, manage costs and budgets, control digital assets (brands, logos, collaterals, and so on), and publish calendars of marketing events. For example, marketing teams need to know what events are happening when and where — whether it's a trade show, analyst briefing, Web cast, or television or print media campaign. The marketing calendar tool is used as the central entry point for marketing professionals. The tool can be used to view, edit, and interlink campaigns and promotions (Figure 3.2).

Sales people also need access to the most up-to-date marketing collaterals and assets relevant for their job, while preventing expired or inappropriate collaterals from being accidentally circulated.

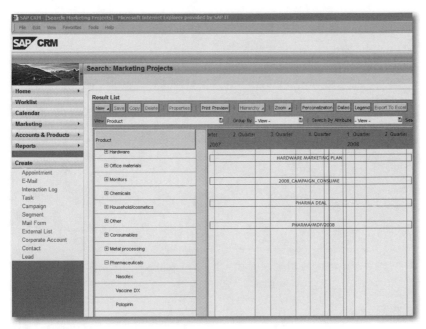

Figure 3.2 Marketing Calendar Functionality in SAP CRM

Market Planning and Budgeting

Any organization's marketing plans depend on the allocated budgets. Marketing budgets drive your planning options. SAP CRM integration with SAP NetWeaver BI helps analyze past market budgets and create a budget forecast based on historical data. You can run budget scenarios with each of the marketing planning scenarios you have on the table. Your marketing planning decisions are based on business needs and marketing budgets. SAP CRM Marketing comes integrated to SAP Project Systems (PS), part of the controlling components of SAP ERP. The marketing planning can be managed either in Microsoft Project (MSP) or in the SAP ERP Project Systems component (Figure 3.3).

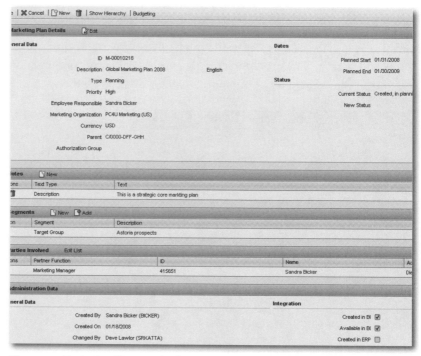

Figure 3.3 Marketing Planning Application in SAP CRM

MRM versus marketing automation

 Tip

Marketing Resource Management (MRM) is sometimes confused with another marketing concept called marketing automation. However, the two are quite distinct. *Marketing automation* is, as its name suggests, primarily concerned with automating processes such as customer segmentation and customer list creation. Often marketing automation is associated with direct marketing and telemarketing. MRM on the other hand is a much more broad and comprehensive approach that gives marketing managers all of the tools they need to run a successful marketing campaign, including budgeting, forecasting, managing digital assets, and managing marketing calendars.

Segmentation

Every customer has specific needs and wants. However, groups of customers who exhibit similar attributes and needs fall into what are known as *customer segments*. Customer segmentation — the process of grouping customers with similar attributes into segments that can be used as the basis of marketing campaigns — can be performed using various criteria or attributes.

Customer segments

 Example

> A video game company is getting ready to roll out two new games in time for the Christmas buying season, and it wants to target customers from its existing customer database with an email or a short message service (SMS) message. One video game is entitled *Axe Maniac on Parole* and is targeted at young males between the ages of 12 and 26 who enjoy violent first-person shooter games. The second video game is entitled *Marathon Shopper: New York City* and is targeted at anyone who bought the "Marathon Shopper: San Francisco" game, as well as female video game players who live in New York or New Jersey. Creating targeted customer segments allows the company to reduce marketing costs (because not every customer will receive the email or SMS) and also helps the company avoid annoying or offending existing customers by offering a game that they are likely not interested in.

The SAP CRM Marketing functionality includes a tool called the Segment Builder that can be used to build target groups for marketing campaigns based on marketing attributes such as age, income, geographical location, hobbies, buying behavior, RFM (recency, frequency, monetary) values, and so on.

The Segment Builder can access customer data from a variety of sources, including SAP NetWeaver BI, SAP ERP, or even rented or purchased customer lists. To speed up the process of searching for and retrieving customer data, the Segment Builder takes advantage of a high-speed business partner search using the SAP NetWeaver TREX search engine. Additionally, the Segment Builder offers a number of other advanced features such as predictive modeling, dynamic filtering, segment duplication, target group optimization, clustering, data mining, decision trees, and ABC analysis based on profitability and retention scores. Spend a couple of minutes on Figure 3.4, so that you can understand the Segment Builder application.

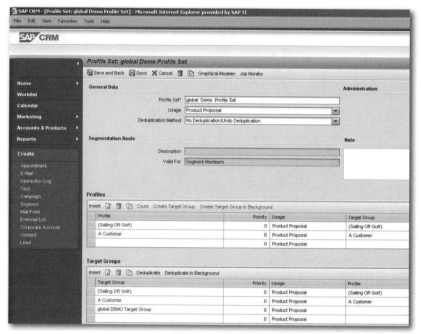

Figure 3.4 Marketing Segment Builder in SAP CRM

List Management

List management

Often, companies buy or rent lead lists from list-management companies (e.g., Hoovers, Dun & Bradstreet, etc.) or use leads generated by trade shows conducted by channel partners. SAP CRM External List Management (ELM) provides data mapping between source data fields and SAP CRM data fields, duplicate check (between owned and acquired leads), data cleansing, address validation, measurement of list quality (number of duplicate records, address errors, etc.), and list analysis. ELM helps companies manage customer master records, including cleansing, de-duping, and flagging expired or already used records for deletion (e.g., for rented lists). And, of course, list data can be exported to SAP NetWeaver BI and merged with other business data (such as sales data) to track the success of each list.

Ex Example

One SAP customer, an American news agency, had been purchasing expensive third-party lead lists for a number of years. The company had no way of tracking how many of the customer names on the list actually resulted in a sale, but the company was beginning to suspect that the lead lists were not generating significant sales. After implementing SAP CRM, including ELM and SAP NetWeaver BI integration, the company confirmed that the lists were not resulting in nearly any sales. Rather, almost all of the company's sales were coming from customers who had contacted the company via the Web on the company's website. So, of course, they stopped purchasing the expensive lead list and put more efforts into making their website even easier to use.

Figure 3.5 shows the steps and settings required to import list data from an external file, map the data, process the data, and save the data in SAP CRM using ELM.

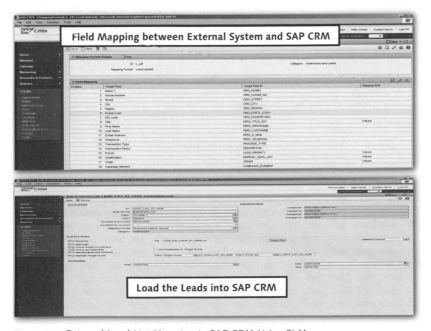

Figure 3.5 External Lead List Mapping in SAP CRM Using ELM

Campaign Management

Campaign
management —
tools for running a
campaign from start
to finish

SAP CRM campaign management provides tools for setting up and running a campaign from start to finish, beginning with market analysis, continuing with the execution of the campaign, and ending with analytics. The results of the campaign then, of course, can be used for planning future campaigns to enable closed-loop SAP CRM. Using SAP campaign automation tools, you can graphically model a campaign and conduct campaign simulation. An easy-to-use graphical interface provides a clear overview of the campaign process flow, including support for multi-channel and multi-wave campaigns.

For example, you might choose to execute your campaign as an email campaign, a telephone campaign, both, or via other channels such as fax, SMS, and so on. If you're conducting an email campaign, you can use the Marketing Mail Form tool to create email templates to support the campaign. You can also attach surveys to the emails. If you're conducting a telephone campaign via the interaction center, you can use the Interactive Script Editor tool to create call scripts to guide the interaction center agents through telephone conversations with prospects and customers. The campaign management application supports both B2B and B2C scenarios, as well as mixed B2B/B2C scenarios. The most typical campaign scenarios are multi-wave campaigns, recurring campaigns, and event-triggered campaigns (Figure 3.6).

Ex Example

A retail catalog sporting goods company wants to target customers who have signed up for the company's newsletter on the website but have not yet made any purchases with the company. To entice these new customers to give the company a try, the company might generate an email campaign offering free shipping on orders over $50 for the next two days. The email could also contain a promotion code in case the customer would prefer to call the interaction center and have an agent assist them with placing the order rather than using the Internet. When the customer provides the campaign promotion code to the interaction center agent, the agent could automatically pull up the correct interactive call script containing details about the promotion. Even though the outbound portion of the campaign was communicated via email and not via the outbound call list in the interaction center, the company still had the option to allow the interaction center to support the campaign.

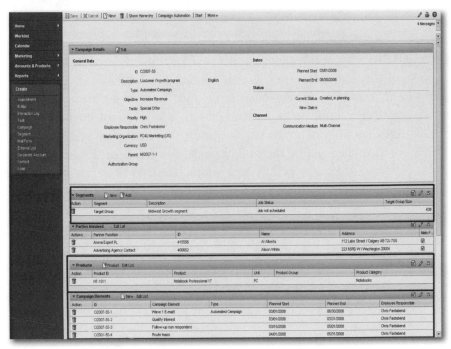

Figure 3.6 The Campaign Management Application in SAP CRM

The campaign management application also provides real-time monitoring of ongoing campaigns and allows managers to adjust campaigns for optimum results. The system provides campaign-specific pricing and supports tracking of sales triggered from a campaign.

Trade Promotion Management (TPM)

TPM helps organizations increase the effectiveness of their in-store retail promotions. Many manufacturers spend a significant percentage of their sales revenue on trade promotions — refunds or discounts given by manufacturers to retailers in hopes that the retailer will in exchange lower the price of the product and pass the savings on to consumers, generating more demand for the manufacturer's product.

Trade Promotion Management (TPM) increases retail promotion effectiveness

Trade promotion (also sometimes referred to as *trade spend*) is most commonly associated with the consumer packaged goods (CPG) industry but is also quite common in other retail-based industries, such as footwear and apparel as well as consumer electronics. Many recent studies are raising questions about the effectiveness of trade promotions, suggesting that manufacturers aren't able to accurately track how much revenue results from any particular trade promotion.

Additionally, studies suggest that up to a third of most trade promotion funds may go directly to the retailer's bottom line, rather than being passed on the customer in the form of reduced prices. Retailers have been found to use techniques such as forward-buying to buy large quantities of product at a discounted promotional price and then — rather than selling the product right away at a discounted price — holding on to the product and selling it after prices return to their normal levels. National retailers also take advantage of regional trade promotions to buy large quantities at the discounted price in a certain region and then ship the product across the country to their stores in other locations where the product can be sold at full price. Nonetheless, despite all of these issues, trade promotions have steadily increased over the past 10 years and still seem to be increasing.

SAP TPM addresses these concerns by giving manufacturers the tools to make sure retailers can demonstrate that they sold the required quantity of product in the appropriate retail location. For example, retailers receive compensation only for the units that they can prove were sold from a valid retail location within a valid time period specified by the promotion. This concept is sometimes referred to as *pay-for-promotion*.

TPM begins with deciding how to use allocated funds — based on sales targets and budgets — across various possible promotions to optimize sales revenue and brand awareness. After the trade promotions are created, you can use forecasting tools to pre-analyze planned trade promotion spending. If things look good, you can release the promotions, which will trigger accruals and fund use. SAP TPM is fully integrated with SAP CRM, SAP ERP, SAP Supply Chain Management (SCM), and Business Process Simulation (BPS) – Strategic Enterprise Management (SEM). The integrated TPM system handles creating, executing, monitoring, and optimizing TPM programs at the key account level (e.g., a national grocery chain) as well as in-store promotions (e.g., for a local promotion in your neighborhood grocery store). SAP CRM TPM provides trade funds management, trade spend budgeting, account/product allocation, deductions management, and payment processing (Figure 3.7).

Ⓔ Example

An international beverage bottler is spending over 50% of its annual advertising budget (which equates to around 30% of its annual sales revenue) on trade promotions with large retailers such as Sam's Club, Costco, and Wal-Mart. The retailer has historically invested heavily in trade promotions providing various price discounts, rebates, refunds, free and subsidized in store displays, and so on. However, the company feels that perhaps only a quarter of the money it's spending is actually providing measurable results. The company wants more transparency and control over the management of its trade promotions with retailers, as well as stronger optimization, simulation, and analytical capabilities.

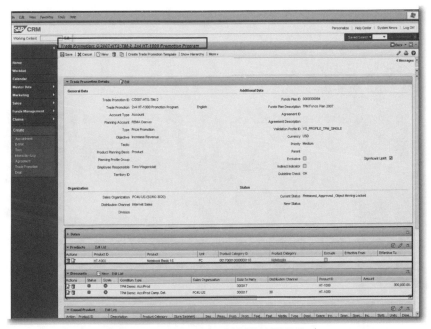

Figure 3.7 Setup Trade Promotions Using the SAP CRM TPM Tool

Lead Management

So far, we've discussed marketing planning, budgeting, customer segmentation, list management, campaign management, and trade pro-

Manage leads across all marketing channels

motion management. Let's assume that your marketing efforts are a mega success, and customers and prospects are responding positively to your campaign. Customers are contacting you via email, phone, and the Web asking for more information. Now you need a tool to capture the leads and customer information. SAP CRM lead management functionalities allow you to manage leads across all marketing channels, including telemarketing, email marketing, Web-based promotions, and so on.

Lead management provides capabilities to generate leads on the Web as well as to automatically qualify leads or to dispatch leads for qualification using workflow or business rules. You can also automatically generate follow-up activities with reference to leads. As shown in Figure 3.8, leads created in SAP CRM will have the following main fields:

> Main Partners

> Qualification Level

> Lead Group

> Lead Priority

> Lead Origin

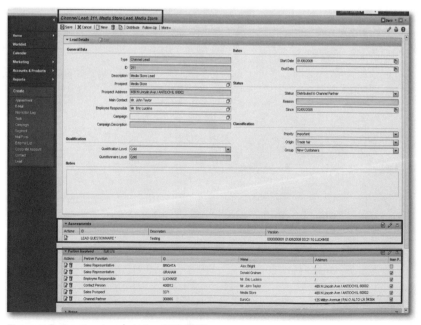

Figure 3.8 Creating Leads Using SAP CRM

Example

> A large international software company uses the SAP CRM Interaction Center to qualify leads generated from trade shows, conferences, and customer events. Inside sales people telephone the customer to assess the level of interest in the company's products. The interaction center agents use a survey tool, which is integrated into the interaction center lead screen, to automatically qualify the lead based on the customer's responses to questions about the level of interest, desired quantity of product, product type, and expected time frame of purchase. If the customer indicates an interest but doesn't plan to buy for at least six months, the system might automatically qualify the lead as warm, rather than hot. However, if the agent also knows that a competitor is speaking with this customer, the agent might manually qualify the lead as hot. The manual qualification is recorded separately and does not override the automatic survey-based qualification. After the agent saves the lead, the SAP CRM system automatically routes the lead to the responsible sales person using business routing rules that the customer maintained via a tool called the SAP CRM Rule Modeler.

Backend ERP Integration

SAP CRM comes with standard out-of-the-box integration with the SAP ERP backend system. You may want to transfer a marketing project and marketing budget to SAP ERP Project Systems (PS), which checks and monitors the marketing costs and sends alerts if you go over the planned budgets or if the planned costs are not compatible with the available funds. You can also set up integration with SAP ERP Controlling Profitability Analysis (CO-PA) if you want to enter marketing costs and sales revenue and settle them to CO-PA.

Marketing Analytics

SAP CRM is integrated with both SAP ERP and SAP NetWeaver BI, providing closed-loop marketing analytics that measure, predict, plan, and optimize marketing plans. Analytics help you to understand the effectiveness of your marketing activities, allowing you to convert data into actionable intelligence. For example, you can gain insights into why certain marketing activities didn't work and avoid duplicating them down the road. You can also discover which activities worked well and leverage them again for future marketing efforts.

Various types of marketing analytics are available, including campaign analytics, lead analytics, and trade promotion analytics. For example, you can view reports about customer marketing attributes, CLTV, churn propensity, and customer satisfaction level. Based on this data, you can more accurately predict customer behavior, anticipate customer needs, and generate appropriate marketing messages. See Figure 3.9 for full details regarding the analytical capabilities of SAP CRM Marketing.

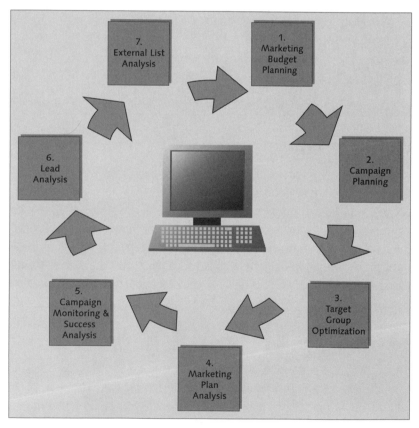

Figure 3.9 Closed-Loop SAP CRM Marketing Analysis Components

Case Study

The company in this case study is a world leader in digital media creation tools for film, video, audio, animation, games, and broadcast professionals. In fact, this company's technology may be behind a great movie you've watched recently. The company had sales revenues of $1 billion in 2007.

The business challenges facing this company include a standalone marketing system currently running on Onyx and an apparent disconnect between the marketing and sales departments. Because of this, the success of a marketing campaign was hard to estimate.

To face these challenges, the company has the following business objectives:

> Monitor campaign effectiveness in real time by measuring the sales revenue generated by a campaign.
> Create integrated marketing analytics that help analyze and adjust the marketing programs.
> Improve overall customer and dealer satisfaction.

On the technology side, the company is faced with two challenges: integrating the marketing and sales system, and creating a CRM system that integrates seamlessly with the backend SAP R/3 system.

The solution deployed to meet these challenges initially included an SAP CRM 3.0 system, an SAP R/3 4.6C system, and an SAP BW 3.1 system. The SAP CRM system was later upgraded to SAP CRM 4.0.

The value achieved by deploying this solution included an integrated marketing and sales system where in a prospect is created and upgraded to customer when an order is placed. As a result, the customer data redundancy when a standalone marketing system was used was eliminated.

Another benefit is that all of the interactions with the prospect/customer are visible in the customer interaction history.

Finally, the marketing programs are being managed, monitored, and adjusted in real time using marketing analytics.

Conclusion

In this chapter, we covered the major components of SAP CRM Marketing. The key things you should remember about this component include the following:

> SAP CRM Marketing is a comprehensive tool that supports marketing as well as campaign planning and execution using a variety of communication channels, such as telephone marketing, email marketing, Web-based marketing, and postal mail marketing.

> SAP CRM Marketing provides all of the tools necessary for marketing managers to successfully execute marketing campaigns.

> SAP CRM Marketing is fully integrated with SAP ERP and SAP NetWeaver BI.

This chapter has provided you with the details you need to understand what a great tool CRM Marketing is and how you can benefit from using it.

In the next chapter, we'll move on to cover SAP CRM Sales.

SAP CRM Sales

Now that you have a good understanding of the SAP CRM Marketing application, let's move on to SAP CRM Sales. If you have a sales force, and one of your customer relationship management strategies is to implement a sales application, the SAP CRM Sales application has much of what you need and allows you to customize the application for your own unique requirements.

Many sales tools have complex interfaces because they have to work with other applications, such as credit, logistics fulfillment, legal, and finance. They also have to interface with functions, such as pricing-to-market, credit ratings, and product offer engines. This can make them complicated to use and slow to perform. However, in today's competitive market, sales people aren't only responsible for selling, they are expected to perform everything in real time, including providing good customer service with timely pricing quotes, product order placements, and closing deals. If their application doesn't provide this support, they could lose a sale.

So for a sales person, the ideal sales system is designed to recognize customer priorities and customer product interests, and to provide competitive prices based on the past buying patterns of that cus-tomer. This system should also be capable of notifying the sales per-son with alerts and messages during the negotiations with a customer to provide support and the information needed to close the deal. The sales order entry should also auto-complete most of the informa-tion needed, requiring minimal manual input or navigation between screens for the sales person.

The dream sales system may sound difficult to find, but it's not im-possible. SAP CRM offers many of the tools you need to build an effi-cient and user-friendly sales system. So let's look at the available sales applications that come with SAP CRM.

Discover SAP CRM Sales

Key components of
SAP CRM Sales

The SAP CRM Sales application helps sales people become more ef-ficient and effective in turning their knowledge into action to help them acquire, grow, and retain profitable relationships. Using the Sales application, companies can plan and analyze the entire sales execution cycle, find new ways to speed the sales cycle, uncover new areas of revenue potential, and determine new methods for improving sales productivity. To get the most out of the Sales ap-plication, it's helpful to look at each of the following components in detail:

> Sales planning and forecasting

> Territory management

> Accounts and contacts management

> Activity management

> Opportunity management

> Quotation and order management

> Product configuration and pricing

> Billing and contract management

> Incentives and commissions management

> Time and travel management

> Sales analytics

Figure 4.1 The SAP CRM Sales Solution Map

Accounts and Contact Management

This component let's you capture, monitor, store, and track all critical information about customers, prospects, and partners, as well as perform contact management, account planning, segmentation, relationship management, and interaction tracking.

Using SAP CRM Sales, the sales manager or sales person can break sales planning down to the account level. The sales person simply searches for the customer in the customer contacts and updates the information, if changed. The sales person can also create, edit, update, and delete the customer contacts.

All of the interactions with the customer, such as phone calls and visits can be recorded in the system as activities and follow-ups. And, the activities and follow-ups are visible to all sales people and sales managers who have access to the customer information. Easy-to-use accounts and contact management functionality is a key for the success of the sales force.

Ex Example

Kim is a sales person at Smart Inc, where she manages the ABC Corporation account. During a meeting with ABC, she learns that current purchase manager, Joe, is being transferred to another division, and John Doe is assuming the role of purchase Manager from January 1, 2008. Kim carries a Smartphone to meetings all the time that has key accounts and contacts data downloaded from the central SAP CRM server. She pulled the ABC Corp account and set the end date of Joe's relationship as purchase manager of ABC Corp. to December 31, 2007. At the same time, she created John Doe as a contact person for ABC Corp., set up his relationship at ABC Corp. as a purchase manager, assigned a start date of January 1, 2008, and kept the end date as open. These changes are updated to the main SAP CRM server when Kim synchronizes the Smartphone with the main SAP CRM system. Any communications with regard to products and services offered to ABC Corp. would go to John Doe automatically from January 1, 2008. This is a good example of how SAP CRM Sales can help companies have up to-date-information from the field go directly to the central sales system seamlessly (Figures 4.2 and 4.3).

Figure 4.2 Account Management in SAP CRM

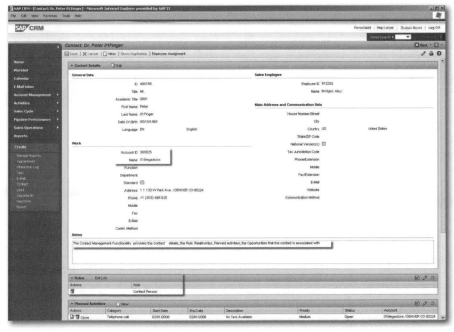

Figure 4.3 Business Partner Relationships Feature in SAP CRM

Activity Management

This component helps you develop loyal and profitable customer relationships. You can achieve complete visibility into all sales activities, collaboration, and team efficiency, with support for visit planning, account profiling, and bidirectional synchronization with leading groupware solutions (Figure 4.4).

Figure 4.4 Activity Management Functionality in SAP CRM 2007

Planning and Forecasting

Accurate planning
and forecasting are
essential

This component helps you plan and forecast accurately across all sales channels, manage budgets and opportunities, and allocate resources efficiently. It also lets you proactively handle trends, shortfalls, and opportunities; optimize supply chain planning and execution; perform strategic planning and account planning; and monitor the planning cycle.

SAP CRM is integrated with SAP NetWeaver BI and SAP ERP to provide sales planning and forecasting functionality. Strategic planning and operational planning are the two components of Sales Planning. SAP CRM Sales strategic planning is about what, where, and to whom to sell. It's also about market share, profit, revenue, market leadership, and penetration. Operational planning provides demand forecasting based on historic and real-time data coming from pipeline analysis and sales bookings. SAP CRM with SAP NetWeaver BI and SEM-BPS (Business Planning and Simulation) generate sales planning and forecasting. You'll learn more in Chapter 13 on analytics.

Territory Management

With this tool, you can optimize your account coverage with clear territory definition, assignment, and scheduling, as well as have complete visibility into team distribution. You can recognize and rapidly respond to shifting market demands by placing the right resources in the right locations to optimize team performance.

Territory management also lets you manage the assignment of sales people to accounts. Using territory management, your company can define sales territories and territory hierarchies and assign sales people and managers to the territories, update the sales territories in sync with changing sales markets, and generate sales performance reports by territory (Figure 4.5).

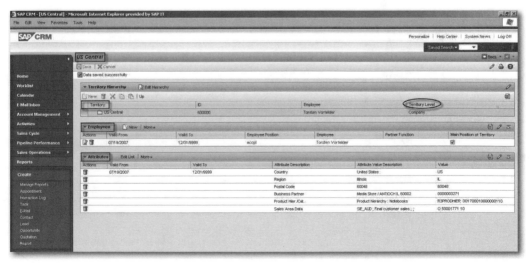

Figure 4.5 Territory Assignment in SAP CRM 2007

Ex **Example**

MyBev is a food and beverage company with a large global sales force. Their sales force structure is very complex, so it was very difficult to make any changes to the structure before implementing SAP CRM territory management. They now use SAP territory management to define geographic territories as well as to assign customers, products, and responsible sales people to the territories. This functionality allows MyBev to easily make changes to territory assignments. Territory management made the top-down and bottom-up sales planning easy. Sales managers can now view territory sales reports with the click of a button.

Opportunity Management

Manage your sales opportunities effectively

With this tool, you can manage your sales cycle more effectively, predictably, and at a lower cost. Obtain full visibility into the opportunity pipeline, improve team communication, and route leads to the right sales people. You'll also improve opportunity planning, team selling, influence modeling, opportunity hierarchies, and sales processes and selling methodologies (Figure 4.6).

Figure 4.6 Opportunity Management in SAP CRM

Using this component, sales people create documents — called *opportunities* — in the SAP CRM system to capture sales-relevant data such as expected sales volume and sales value, probability of success, and estimated closing date. The sales people also record the names of the members of the sales team working on the opportunity as well as the members of the customer's buying center — the group of employees from the customer's organization who are the decision makers for the current opportunity, including so-called gatekeepers and influencers.

Opportunities typically have phases such as discovery, development, decision making, and so on. Each phase results in certain activities, which are captured in the system. SAP CRM provides an SAP-proprietary sales methodology — based on guided selling — that helps maintain high-quality sales processes throughout the sales engagement.

Opportunity management, as part of SAP CRM Sales, is linked directly with the SAP CRM Marketing functionality, allowing marketing leads to be converted into sales opportunities. Opportunity management provides functionality to create an opportunity with reference to a lead when the status of the lead was, for example, set to "hot." The sales person responsible for the account will be automatically notified about the opportunity. Additionally opportunities can be dispatched to the appropriate sales person using routing rules configured in the SAP CRM Rule Modeler tool.

Convert your marketing leads into sales opportunities

Opportunity management is also integrated with real-time monitoring, reporting, and analytical tools. For example, opportunity management provides real-time updates to the pipeline analysis by transferring the data to SAP NetWeaver BI after the opportunity is saved. Also, data about opportunities and their results can be exported to SAP NetWeaver BI for detailed analysis.

Product Configuration and Pricing

This component helps you guide your sales people through the product configuration process, enforcing business rules to ensure that correct product combinations are recommended to customers and that pricing is tailored to each sales channel or customer. You also get up-to-date information based on centrally maintained pricing rules and conditions, and you can perform contractual pricing, discounting, promotional pricing, and customer-specific pricing.

SAP CRM leverages the SAP Internet Pricing and Configurator (IPC) tool for pricing in SAP CRM. The IPC was designed to support product configuration and pricing on the Internet, for example, for Internet sales. However, IPC can also be used by SAP CRM Enterprise Sales. The IPC consists of the Sales Pricing Engine (SPE), Configuration Engine (SCE), and product-modeling environment (PME). The SPE manages pricing, including variant pricing; the SCE supports configurable products and variant configuration; and the PME is used for master data maintenance of product configuration data.

The IPC is a Java 2 Enterprise Edition (J2EE) based engine. Customers can upload pricing records and conditions to the IPC from a backend ERP application. In such cases, all pricing logic will then be maintained and provided using the IPC. Alternatively, customers can also integrate SAP ERP pricing and variant configuration with certain SAP CRM scenarios — such as telesales in the interaction center — leveraging the ABAP-based (Advanced Business Application Programming) pricing condition tables of the connected backend ERP application. Customers can even integrate third-party, non-SAP pricing engines into SAP CRM.

A topic very closely related to pricing is — you guessed it — taxes. For calculating taxes such as sales tax, VAT (value added tax), or GST (goods and service tax), SAP CRM leverages the Transaction Tax Engine (TTE) to manage county, state, and federal taxes effectively. The TTE is a J2EE-based engine, delivered as part of the IPC that integrates with SAP CRM pricing, providing comprehensive and flexible pricing functionality.

Contract management is another topic that, although not technically considered part of pricing, is very closely related. Using the SAP CRM contract management functionality, you can, for example, create long-term purchasing agreements and sales contracts with customers that allow customers to buy products and services at special prices and with favorable delivery terms over a predetermined period. A contract typically specifies the exact terms and conditions, pricing agreements, specific releasable products, authorized customer companies, and completion rules. Contract management assists your company in the following:

> Creating long-term agreements with price and product agreements for a customer

> Guiding the sales person through the follow-ups with the customer and recording the follow-ups in the system

> Capturing the touch points with the customers during contract negotiation

> Monitoring the sales process from inquiry through the contract completion

> Preventing sales people from giving discounts or price reductions beyond a specified threshold price

> Tracking whether the customer has been buying products as agreed in the contract

> Tracking the competitors' pricing for the same products and their sales strategies

> Analyzing customer satisfaction during the contract period

> Keeping clearly defined communications between your company and your customers

Quotation and Order Management

You can generate accurate quotes and configurations, place orders, confirm product availability in real time, and track order status with this tool. You can also provide order information to the supply chain for planning and fulfillment and help synchronize billing and fulfillment.

The orders that you create with SAP CRM Sales orders are documents that can be used as an inquiry, quotation, or firm order by setting the line-item status (inquiry, quotation, firm order) as a differentiator at the item level. Your sales force may love handling the entire sales process with one document rather than working with several documents and struggling to keep them linked. However, you also have the option to create separate inquiry, quotation, and sales order documents if desired (Figure 4.7).

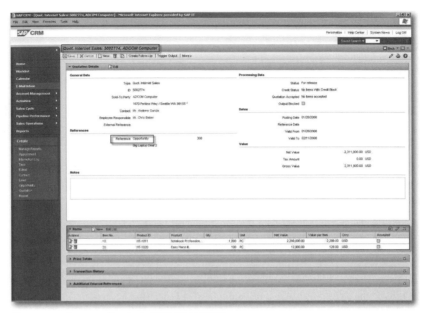

Figure 4.7 Create a Quote in SAP CRM 2007

 Tip

> Inquiries are more commonly used in SAP ERP than in SAP CRM. Many SAP CRM customers prefer to work with leads and opportunities, rather than inquiries. There are a number of advantages to working with leads and opportunities. For example, leads can be automatically qualified with built-in survey integration. Both leads and opportunities can be routed to the appropriate sales person using routing rules defined in the SAP CRM Rule Modeler, and opportunities can be easily tracked and analyzed with SAP NetWeaver BI.

Sales order management via real-time interfacing with SAP ERP

After a quotation is converted into a sales order, various channels can be used for sales order management. For example, sales managers can access sales orders directly or view sales order data as part of pipeline performance management. Interaction center agents can access sales orders on behalf of customers, whether via telephone, email, chat, or other communication channels.

Regardless of the channel, SAP CRM sales order management provides real-time interfaces with SAP ERP for things such as product availability check (also known as Available-to-Promise [ATP] check) and credit check. Optionally, an interface with the Advanced Planner and Optimizer (APO) is available for product availability check if APO is used instead of SAP ERP to manage the supply chain processes (Figure 4.8).

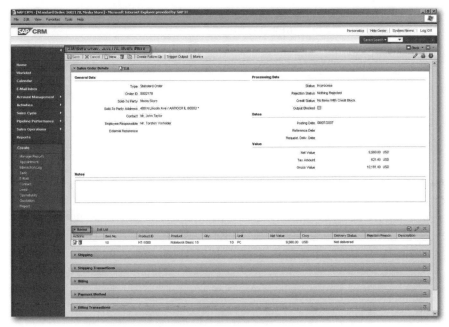

Figure 4.8 Sales Order Management in SAP CRM 2007

Billing and Contract Management

These components allow you to develop and manage long-term customer contracts, incorporate customer agreements into ongoing processes, monitor the sales process from inquiry to completion, and seamlessly integrate these activities with backend financial and accounts receivable (AR) processes.

You'll also be able to manage value-based and quantity-based contracts, sales agreements, collaborative contract negotiation, release-order handling, cancellation processing, credit management, invoicing, and payment processing.

Of course, billing is an essential part of most sales and service processes, especially for companies that like to remain profitable and solvent (e.g., with liquid assets). Your company can close big sales deals and celebrate, but if you can't handle your billing and invoicing, you won't be in business very long.

SAP CRM billing can be done either in SAP CRM or in SAP ERP (or another integrated third-party billing system). For example, many companies in the telecommunications industry may have legacy Telco billing systems that they can't or don't want to replace.

SAP CRM supports two main billing scenarios: transaction-related billing and delivery-related billing. However, external billing and non-billing (for non-billing-related transactions) are also supported. *Transaction-related* billing includes billing options such as usage-based billing and transaction-related billing after completion. For example, a utility customer might be billed based on the amount of electricity or gas the customer consumed, whereas a hospital would be billed, per transaction, for each diagnostic imaging machine that was repaired.

Delivery-related billing, on the other hand, generates a billing document in SAP CRM only after a delivery is created in SAP ERP based on a goods issue. With this billing option, the billing documents are always created in reference to specific deliveries, keeping things simple and easy to track (Figure 4.9).

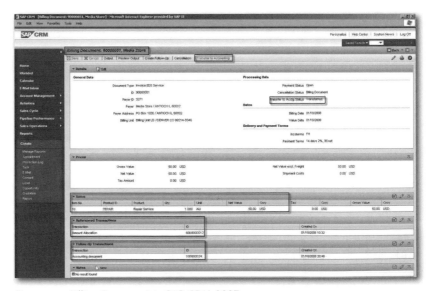

Figure 4.9 Billing Document in SAP CRM 2007

Incentives and Commissions Management

If your company wants to increase sales revenues, you need either to make better products, provide better service, or hire better sales people. Talented sales people are one of a company's most valuable assets, second perhaps only to loyal customers. Good sales managers and sales people can cultivate long-term profitable relationships with your most valuable customers, increase your wallet share among existing customers, and increase your market penetration and your market share against competitors. However, great sales people are a lot like great athletes, great musicians, or great entertainers — they feel that their time is more valuable than anyone else's (probably because it actually is), and they sometimes don't like to follow rules or be told what to do.

Sales force automation

One of the challenges, therefore, is to get sales people to trust your SAP CRM sales force automation (SFA) system and to use it regularly and correctly. Sales people are very busy and don't want to waste time using a system that they perceive as difficult to use — or worse yet, unreliable. For example, if a sales person has had problems in the past, even just once, where the SFA system did not correctly calculate the sales person's commission, the sales person won't trust the system again and will spend hours every week doing shadow-accounting, that is, maintaining a separate Excel spreadsheet to track commissions.

SAP CRM incentive and commissions management provides your company's sales force with easy and accurate visibility into possible commissions if a sales deal is closed. Sales people can perform "what-if" analysis to see how much their commission would increase if they closed a particular deal. With the expected incentives and commissions information, the sales force is in position to spend all of its time driving sales toward closure — rather than playing with custom Excel macros!

Time and Travel Management

Time and travel management is a very important business function of companies that have a field sales force, a field service department, or a professional services organization. As more and more businesses

Measure and manage time and travel costs effectively

93

continue to become international or global, travel budgets and costs increase. On one hand, companies need a system to accurately measure, manage time, and travel costs. On the other hand, employees normally disdain filling out expense reports and time logs, feeling that they eat up productive time that could be spent performing their job.

SAP applications provide an integrated solution that can help you keep your travel costs — and your employees — under control. The integrated solution includes SAP CRM, SAP ERP, and SAP xApps Mobile Time and Travel Solutions for time and travel. The time and travel solutions provide offline access to the time and travel component to record working times and expenses. The application is installed on a mobile device and is very convenient for employees such as outside sales people, consultants, or any other traveling employees that need to book their time and expenses offline and synchronize up with the enterprise system at any available moment.

This tool enables the sales force to focus more on pursuing opportunities and less on tracking expenses using paper-based processes. It will also help you enforce corporate travel policies, and monitor and control the costs associated with the activities of the sales force. And, you'll improve time tracking, expense reporting, and assignment of costs to sales activities.

Sales Analytics

Standard out-of-the-box business content with SAP Sales analytics

This critical component helps you monitor and respond to needs in real time, forecast accurately, remain below budget, optimize resource alignment, and position the team to achieve revenue goals.

SAP CRM Sales analytics provide standard out-of-the-box business content to enable reporting on the complete sales process, from territory management to billing. The SAP CRM Sales analytics provide sets of analytical data geared for both sales managers and sales people. Easy slice-and-dice functionality allows sales managers and sales people to view sales statistics by region, area, territory, and key account level. The delivered sales analytics also provide comparison of planned and actual sales using SAP NetWeaver BI and SEM-BPS.

Supported sales performance analytics include pipeline analysis, sales volume analysis, Top N opportunities, order and contract analysis, sales funnel analysis, win/loss analysis, and customer profitability, and Customer Lifetime Value (CLTV) analysis. SAP CRM provides business content for sales analytics in the Sales Manager and the Sales Representative business roles, accessible via the SAP CRM WebClient in SAP CRM 2006s and beyond. In previous releases, such as SAP CRM 5.0, this functionality was available via the People-Centric User Interface (PCUI) as part of the enterprise portal (Figure 4.10).

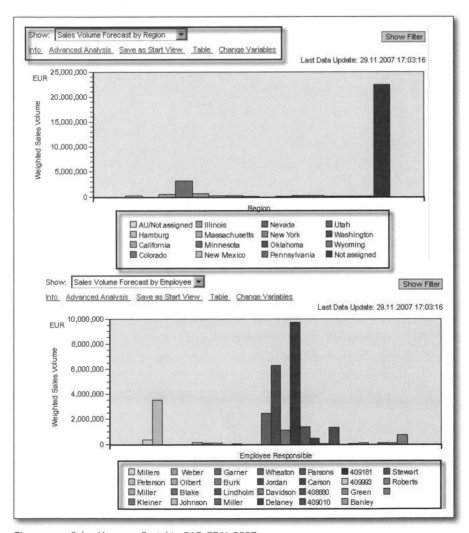

Figure 4.10 Sales Manager Portal in SAP CRM 2007

Case Study

A U.S.-based supplier of global communications equipment, systems, and services — including radio towers, microwave antennas, and power amplifiers — with more than 11,000 worldwide employees and over $2 billion in annual sales revenue was having trouble managing its enormous global sales pipeline. The company had been doing business for more than 60 years and had recently acquired eight other smaller companies, each with its own incompatible software systems. The company was now struggling to keep track of its customers and prospects in more than 100 countries, including both original equipment manufacturers (OEMs) such as Motorola and Ericsson, as well as telecommunications carriers such as Verizon and Cingular.

Each of the company's product lines seemed to have its own sales force automation (SFA) tools, making it difficult to provide accurate, aggregated sales forecasts. Additionally, there were few — if any — tools for collaboration across the company's 260-person sales force. A sales person who called on a local division of a multinational account would often have no visibility into the global operations and installed product base of the global account. And, to add insult to injury, when sales people left the company, they would take their knowledge of the account with them — leaving the company in the dark.

The company, already an existing long-time user of SAP ERP, decided to implement SAP CRM to manage its sales processes. The short-term goal was to automate the entire order-to-cash process. One of the key focus areas of the SAP CRM Sales project was Mobile Sales, because the company operates in many parts of the world where wireless Internet access isn't always available — making an offline, disconnected mode absolutely necessary. In the first phase of the project, the company rolled out SAP CRM Mobile Sales to handle basic sales processes such as activity management, contact management, and opportunity management/forecasting.

As with any project, there were challenges and obstacles that had to be overcome. The company learned that although implementing and supporting SAP CRM Mobile Sales isn't difficult, it does require certain skill sets that the average IT person (or SAP developer) does not necessarily possess, such as familiarity with Sun Java Virtual Machine (JVM), Microsoft .NET Framework, and Microsoft SQL Server. Additionally, the company discovered that when dealing with a large user base, support can't be delegated to just one person — even if that person is currently the only one in the organization with the necessary skills and experience. To ensure that the project was a success, the company developed its own custom installation scripts and troubleshooting tools that allowed even less skilled employees to help with support and troubleshooting.

Based on the challenges and obstacles that the company faced, it came up with the following list of recommendations to help other customers who implement Mobile Sales:

> Installing Mobile Sales requires experts familiar with a variety of technologies, including SAP CRM Mobile Sales, Sun JVM, Microsoft SQL Server, Microsoft .NET Framework, and Microsoft Windows Dynamic Link Library (DLL). Make sure you have experts on your team familiar with each of these technologies.

> Relying on just one Mobile Sales "guru" in your team can cause bottlenecks — especially if you need to support a large user base. Make sure that you have adequate resources commensurate to the size of your organization.

> Installing and troubleshooting Mobile Sales can be long and painful or short and easy — depending on whether you choose to do things manually by hand or whether you choose to use automated tools. Hint: use automated tools!

> When providing end users with training environments, it's far better to take the extra time to install the application on the end user's actual machine than to give the user access to a separate training system. Users need to see that an application will actually work in their environment and not just in a controlled laboratory setting.

Using these practices, the company successfully replaced its collection of disjointed customer tracking systems and standardized sales forecasting methodologies across all business units with a single SAP CRM Mobile Sales system. Senior management now has an accurate and dependable view into the global sales pipeline, allowing for accurate and confident sales forecasts and planning. Additionally, local sales people now have a complete overview of global accounts and no longer go into sales opportunities with only a partial view of the client. And finally, when a sales person leaves the company, a new person is able to seamlessly take over and keep the sales process moving, because all information about the customer and the opportunity is now stored centrally in the SAP CRM system — not in a sales person's head or notebook.

Now that the company has its sales processes under control and running smoothly, the company plans to extend its SAP CRM footprint to include SAP CRM Marketing and the interaction center for lead management.

As in the case study, the design of the SAP CRM system is driven by the business objectives and drivers that are the outcome of the business discovery sessions.

Conclusion

In this chapter, we've provided a brief look into all of the functions of the Sales component of SAP CRM. You may be amazed at the depth and breadth of this solution, which supports light sales processes such as lead generation as well as highly complex processes such as multiple opportunities tied into a master opportunity with several managers and sales persons generating several hundred activities and touch points. SAP CRM presents vital sales statistics about an account at a click of a button, and it helps sales people close deals faster. The key things to remember about SAP CRM Sales include the following:

> SAP CRM supports sales across all possible touch points.

> The Sales application supports anytime-anywhere-sales processes to transact with the customers.

> Using Enterprise Sales, organizations can plan and forecast sales accurately and analyze the sales pipeline in a timely manner.

> The Sales analytics enable organizations to review and adjust sales plans and performance analysis.

In the next chapter, we move on to explore the SAP CRM Service component.

5

SAP CRM Service

Service is, without a doubt, a critical area for all businesses, whether they're selling products or services. Customers want good service. And, in today's marketplace, customer service is being outsourced or offered as a self-service application, so ensuring that your business offers the best quality service available, regardless of your delivery method, is paramount.

In the previous two chapters, you learned about the Marketing and Sales applications of SAP CRM. In this chapter, we'll discuss SAP CRM Service. Customer service involves providing service before, during, and after the sale to a customer. For example, prospects may call an interaction center with questions about a product they are considering purchasing, or, during the sales process, customers may need to schedule an appointment for a product installation. Then after the sale, customers often need technical assistance or may have questions about their delivery or invoice. There are many variables to customer service these days, so you need to offer a service option that can be highly customized depending on the needs of the customer. This includes everything from high-touch service involving a live agent in the interaction center to low-touch service where customers use an E-Service (formerly Internet Customer Self Service) to fulfill their own service needs.

Provide service before, during, and after the sale

99

Providing the best quality service, pre- or post-sale can drive repeat purchases from satisfied customers. So when choosing your SAP CRM application, you should consider the level of customer service you need to offer your customers.

Discover SAP CRM Service

In this section, we'll talk about how SAP CRM supports service in all phases of the customer engagement cycle, and we'll review each of the components of SAP CRM Service.

Service is probably the most robust, versatile, and flexible application of the SAP CRM product. SAP CRM Service enables your company to provide proactive support to customers and to respond to customer service requests in a timely manner. It can help maximize profitability by keeping valuable customers loyal, decrease service-related costs through automation and efficiency, and help you increase service revenue through intelligent, real-time, cross-sell, and up-sell proposals. You can see the various SAP CRM Service components in Figure 5.1.

SAP CRM supports the following business processes, which we'll discuss throughout the rest of the chapter:

> Installed base management

> Warranty management

> Contract and entitlement management

> Resource planning

> Knowledge management

> Case management

> Service order and service ticket

> Complaints and returns

> In-house repair

> Service analytics

Figure 5.1 SAP CRM Service Solution Map

Installed Base Management

In SAP terminology, *installed base* *(IBase)* refers to all of the different pieces of equipment installed at a company site. Individual pieces of equipment, when not part of an installed base, are referred to as *individual objects, IObjects,* or just *objects*. However, when an individual piece of equipment belongs to a larger group of installed equipment, the object is referred to as a *component* of the installed base. Let's look at an example using heating ventilation and air conditioning (HVAC) equipment.

Installed base
management

Assuming that a company has multiple buildings on its campus with multiple floors per building and multiple pieces of HVAC equipment per floor, the HVAC installed base can get complicated. Luckily, SAP installed base management provides an easy way to visualize such multi-level installation hierarchies. Starting with the top level of the hierarchy — in this case, the company's campus — users can drill down in the hierarchy by expanding the folder structure to see the lower level buildings, floors, and individual air-conditioning units. Similarly, installed base management can be used to represent other types of installed equipment hierarchies, such as elevators, printers, hospital diagnostic and imaging equipment, software, and so on — as well as equipment hierarchies that aren't technically "installed," such as vehicle fleets or credit card products.

Installed-base information is very important in service-related situations where, for example, a service technician needs to locate a specific piece of equipment that requires service or repair. The installed base can also be useful internally to customers to keep track of their equipment and to determine when any particular installed-base component was last updated or serviced. Installed-base information also makes it very easy to manage customer service requests (see Figure 5.2).

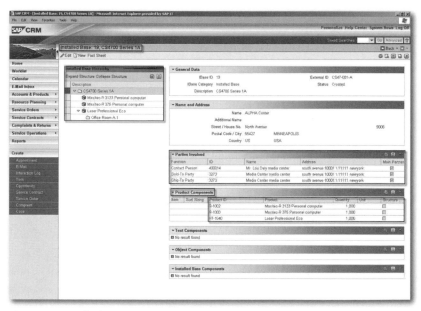

Figure 5.2 Installed Base Management in SAP CRM

The installed base can be viewed from most service-related SAP CRM applications, including E-Service, the Mobile Client for Field Service, the interaction center, and the SAP CRM WebClient user interface in SAP CRM 2006s and SAP CRM 2007. In SAP CRM releases 2005 and 4.0, the installed base is also visible from the People-Centric User Interface (PCUI).

Warranty Management

A warranty is a guarantee from a manufacturer or supplier that a product is free from defects and will remain operational for a specified period of time. Warranties define the terms and conditions of how repairs, replacement, and exchanges of defective products are handled. For example, a warranty will specify the length of time during which the product will be repaired or serviced by the manufacturer, vendor, or supplier at no cost to the customer. Essentially, warranties instill confidence in customers (Figure 5.3).

Customer and vendor warranty management

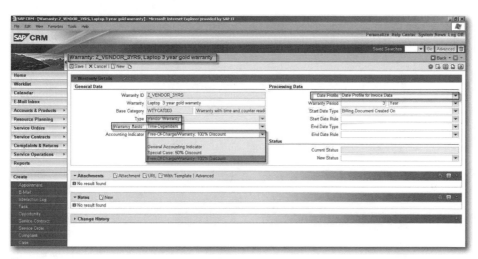

Figure 5.3 Warranty Management Using SAP CRM

SAP CRM Service supports two types of warranties: customer warranties and vendor warranties. A customer warranty is given by the *manufacturer* to the *customer* guaranteeing the finished product. A vendor warranty is given by a *supplier* (e.g., vendor) to the *manufacturer* guaranteeing a particular piece of equipment used by the manufacturer in the finished product. Both types of warranties can be tailored to meet the requirements of the customer. For example, an automobile manufacturer might offer a customer warranty for new automobiles covering the complete vehicle from bumper to bumper for 36,000 miles or 3 years — whichever comes first — but excluding normal wear-and-tear items such as tires, windshield wipers, and so forth. An automotive parts supplier might offer a vendor warranty to the vehicle manufacturer guaranteeing, for example, that the battery will last for 10 years or 100,000 miles.

SAP CRM Service also supports the warranty claims process, including the generation of return materials authorization (RMA) as well as receipt and inspection. A warranty claim is a request from the warranty holder for service, replacement, or exchange of a defective product as specified in the terms and conditions of the warranty. Figure 5.4 shows the warranty claims process with SAP CRM. An RMA is a unique code given to the customer that indicates the customer is authorized to return a defective product. The RMA might consist of the product ID followed by the complaint number field by the customer. For example, for product HT-1010 and complaint number 000576, the RMA number might be HT1010000576.

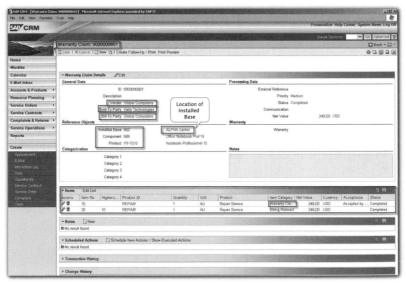

Figure 5.4 Warranty Claim

The following are the features of SAP warranty management:

> Create and maintain warranties representing warranty entitlements applicable to certain products.
> Register warranty assignment to customer products.
> Manage manufacturer warranties and vendor warranties.
> Recognize and validate warranty entitlement during service-related business processes.
> Manage warranty claims using case management.
> Track entitlement services provided to a customer through product warranty cost assignment.
> View warranty analytics.

The next business process supported by SAP CRM is Contract and Entitlement Management.

Contract and Entitlement Management

Service contracts are long-term agreements between companies and their customers in which the company, such as a retailer or manufacturer, offers to provide a certain level of service in exchange for a fixed fee. Service contracts are extremely profitable with profit margins as high as 50% to 60% or more depending on the industry. Considering that margins for products are sometimes as low as 5% to 10% in certain industries, you can see the importance for companies of being able to sell and manage service contracts and entitlement.

Contract management between you and your customers

Service contracts typically include a Service Level Agreement (SLA) in which the company specifies the response time and an availability time to which the customer is entitled.

Ex **Example**

A service contract may specify that a customer is entitled to 5 x 10 service with a three-hour response time, meaning that the customer is entitled to service Monday through Friday from 8 a.m. to 6 p.m., and that the company must resolve the issue (or start processing the issue) within 3 hours after the customer first reports the issue. To avoid giving service away for free, companies need to be able to perform entitlement checks to make sure the customer has a valid service contract and is indeed entitled to service.

SAP CRM Service contract management provides tools for managing service agreements, service contract quotations, and service contracts (Figure 5.5).

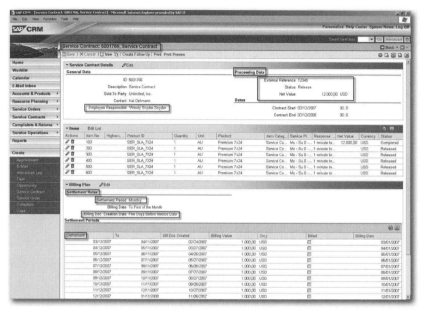

Figure 5.5 Service Contracts in SAP CRM 2007

Service agreements can be created for certain customer groups, specifying general parameters of service contracts such as pricing and discounts. SLAs and automatic entitlement both are supported, which allows service employees to know whether a customer is entitled to service and, if so, what type of service.

Keep your customers happy with good entitlement management

Entitlement management includes system-wide tracking of service entitlements as well as re-entitlement checks when data, such as damage codes, are changed in a service order. Escalation is also supported based on SLAs, which can be used to automatically warn a customer if a required spare part is out of stock or if a service technician is running late for an appointment. This type of proactive service not only increases customer goodwill but also lowers the cost of service by intercepting customers before they call the interaction center to file a complaint. It's far more costly to pay a live agent to spend 10 minutes trying to pacify an angry customer than it is to send a polite automated message ahead of time warning the customer of any expected delays or hiccups. This can be achieved with effective resource planning.

Resource Planning

The SAP CRM *resource planning application* (RPA) is used for scheduling and dispatching field service technicians to service-related customer appointments. When a customer contacts a company's interaction center to request installation of a new product, or maintenance or repair of an existing product, the interaction center agent will schedule an appointment for the customer based on the response and availability time specified in the customer's service contract or SLA. However, at this point, no actual service technician is yet assigned to the job. Rather, the customer is only told that someone will arrive during a certain time slot, say, between 8 a.m. and 12 p.m. on Friday. The actual assignment of a service technician is done later by a dispatcher using the RPA tool (Figure 5.6)

Resource Planning
Application tool
(RPA)

Figure 5.6 Resource Planning Overview

Of course, resource planning isn't just relevant for installations and repairs of equipment. Resource planning can also be used for any type of industry or business that needs to schedule onsite customer

Mobile scheduling
and resource
planning

visits, including insurance companies that do damage inspections, health-care professionals who conduct onsite evaluations, physical therapists, architects, real estate agents, and so on.

Resource planning can look for available internal or external service technicians based on factors such as geographical location, service type, skill set, and required skill level. As of SAP CRM 2007, the concept of "van stock" is also supported — allowing field service technicians to use their mobile devices to confirm whether they have the necessary parts and tools in their vehicle to perform the job, or to see whether a colleague or nearby central office has the required part or tool. *Route optimization* can also be incorporated into the solution via software from other vendors such as ServicePower or ClickSoftware. After a service task has been assigned to a service technician and the technician has accepted the initial assignment, the service order is transferred down to the mobile device of the technician. The technician then has access to all of the information he needs to properly service the customer.

 Tip

> In SAP CRM 2005, both a Web-based RPA and SAP GUI-based Resource Planning Tool (RPT) are provided. However, neither solution is available with SAP CRM 2006s. Only RPA is supported and available going forward with release SAP CRM 2007 and above.

Knowledge Management

Text Retrieval and Extraction (TREX) engine helps update your knowledge base

SAP CRM knowledge management provides users — such as interaction center agents, second-level engineers, and E-Service customers — with access to solutions, business transactions, and other knowledge gained from previous interactions with other customers. For example, when a new, previously undetected issue is reported by a customer, the company's engineers will come up with a solution or fix, and then make the solution available in the company's knowledge base.

The knowledge base is continually updated, so the next time a customer has the same issue, the customer can find the solution via a search. SAP provides a search engine tool known as the Text Retrieval and Extraction (TREX) engine, which works in conjunction with another layer of software known as the Software Agent Framework (SAF) that is responsible for continually updating, indexing, and compiling the knowledge base.

The knowledge management search can be used to access a variety of documents and business transactions across multiple knowledge bases. By default, knowledge management searches against the SAP-provided Solution Database (SDB). However, it's also possible to use TREX to index other data repositories and knowledge bases. For example, one SAP customer in the public sector who works in military procurement decided to index all of their SAP CRM service tickets to allow their interaction center agents to quickly locate and pull up an existing service ticket via a keyword search (Figure 5.7).

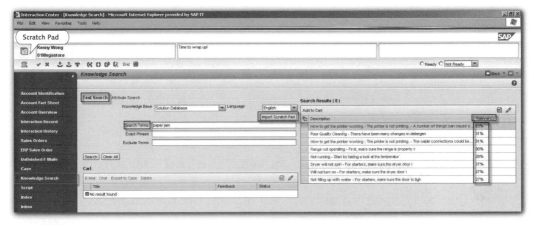

Figure 5.7 Knowledge Search

 Tip

Although TREX is part of SAP NetWeaver and is used for various high-speed searches across SAP CRM, including high-speed business partner searches in the interaction center and Marketing Segment Builder, a separate TREX installation is necessary for using TREX in conjunction with the SAF and knowledge management search.

Case Management

SAP CRM case management provides a central repository — essentially a virtual folder — for consolidating and keeping track of all of the different documents and information related to a single issue or case. For example, if a Telco provider experienced a service outage, it might create a case to keep track of all of the customers who called in to complain. An interaction center agent would create a unique service ticket for each customer, but the tickets would all be stored together as part of the same case.

Secure your
customer case
information
When the company's engineers had again successfully restored service, an automated email, SMS, or telephone call could be placed to all of the customers informing them that their issues had been resolved. Similarly, an insurance company might create a case in the event of a severe storm, flood, hurricane, tornado, mudslide, or fire to keep track of all of the policyholders who filed claims. A manufacturer or retailer might use a case to handle a product recall. In the public sector and higher education industries, cases can be used for keeping track of all of the documents related to a criminal investigation or a college entrance application, respectively.

Case management gives everyone involved in the case access to the most up-to-date information. For example, by entering notes electronically and storing them as part of the case notes log, there is no danger that the note will get misplaced in a file left on someone's desk or file cabinet. Case management also provides increased security because only those people involved in the case are allowed to access the information. Finally, case management helps reduce costs by reducing paper storage and manual processing; everything is automated and electronic workflow driven. See Figure 5.8 for an overview of case management.

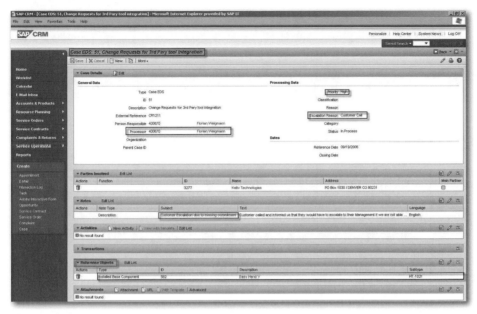

Figure 5.8 Case Management

Service Order and Service Ticket

SAP CRM service order management supports two types of service requests — the service order and the service ticket — both of which use the same underlying business transaction; the main difference is the UI layout of the screens. The service order view was originally designed for repair, maintenance, or installation situations where a service technician needed to perform some action, usually involving some piece of equipment, spare parts, or other so-called "service object." The service ticket was introduced in the interaction center with the SAP CRM 4.0 add-on. This was done for service industries in response to customers who were overwhelmed and confused by all of the functionality available in the service order and wanted a leaner, easier-to-use screen that better supported the interaction center service desk scenario.

It was also important for these customers that the service ticket contain SLA information, time-recording capabilities for engineers and technicians, and multi-level categorization for problem diagnosis. Although multi-level categorization and SLA information were originally only introduced with the service ticket, both of these features are also now

111

available with the service order. The main differences between the service order and the service ticket today are that the service ticket also contains time-recording capabilities, and that the service ticket does not contain any visible "service product" line items; rather the service ticket contains a hidden "dummy" line item (Figure 5.9).

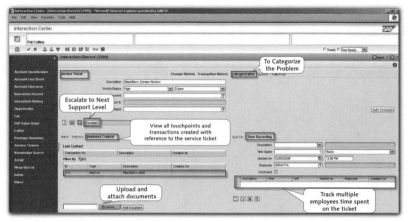

Figure 5.9 Service Ticket

➕ **Tip**

While the service *order* is available across all SAP CRM Service interaction channels, including E-Service, Field Service, and the interaction center, the service *ticket* is only available in the interaction center.

Support your service orders and tickets and create new quotes

In addition to supporting both the service order and the service ticket service request "flavors," SAP CRM Service order management also supports the creation of service quotations. Before creating an actual service order for the customer, you can first issue the customer a service order quotation that outlines the pricing and delivery conditions. If the customer accepts the quotation, an order can be created (see Figure 5.10).

The service order then performs all of the standard checks, including warranty and entitlement check, and service plan check based on the reference object (product, installed base, or IObject). The actual assignment of a service technician, in the event field service is required, it is done using the RPA tool (or optionally the RPT tool in SAP CRM 2005). The service order is closed upon customer confirmation of satisfactory service (see Figure 5.11).

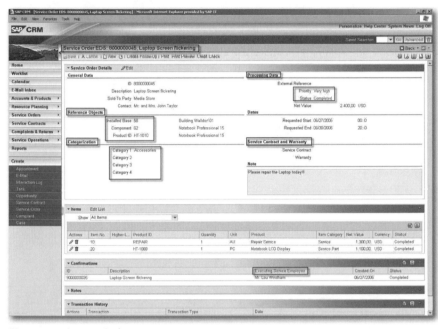

Figure 5.10 Service Order

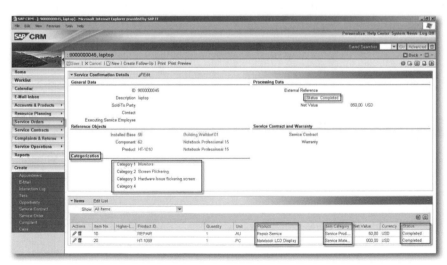

Figure 5.11 Service Confirmation

Complaints and Returns

Use complaints to
manage product
issues

SAP CRM Service provides complaints and returns functionality for managing the entire customer complaint process. In SAP terminology, a *complaint* is filed by the customer when the customer is dissatisfied or has an issue with a product (or service), shipment, or invoice. Complaints are typically not used for emotional issues — for example, where the customer felt offended by something an employee said or did — but rather complaints are filed if the customer received a damaged product, wrong product, or an incorrect quantity, or if the customer was over billed.

A complaint is typically created in reference to an existing business transaction such as a sales order or an invoice. After the reference transaction is selected, one or more line items (e.g., products) from the reference transaction can be transferred to the complaint. At that point, it's then possible to leverage complaint-specific functionality such as credit and debit memos, free-of-charge replacement shipments (Figure 5.12), RMAs, and QM notifications (also known as Quality Notifications outside SAP).

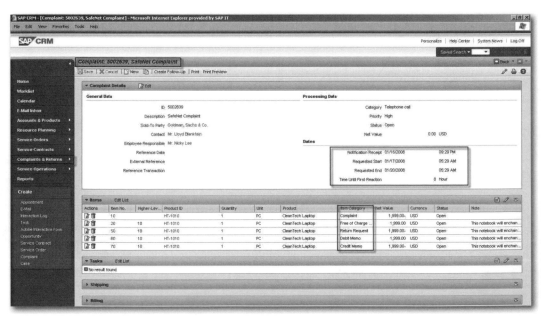

Figure 5.12 Complaints Management

114

Ex Example

If a grocery store ordered 100 units of Super-Fake-Cheese, but only 98 units arrived intact, the customer might request a credit for the two missing or damaged units; in this case, no items are actually returned. Or, if a consumer placed an order on the website of an online shoe company for one pair of black leather loafers but received three pair of blue alligator wingtips, the consumer would request an RMA to return the items. After the items are returned, they would undergo a quality inspection and then can be returned to stock, if they are undamaged.

The entire complaint and return process is fully automated and integrated with backend SAP ERP functionality for all of the financial and quality management processes, such as generating the credit/debit request, billing docs, QM notification, and so on. For example, if several customers start returning products that suffer from a common defect, such as a blotchy paint job, QM notifications can be automatically generated from the complaint in SAP CRM, which will trigger backend processes in the SAP ERP Quality Management component to inform engineering and production about the problem so that they can correct it. If this can be done in-house, the company can use the In-House Repair functionality.

In-House Repair

SAP CRM in-house repair assists your organization in managing your entire in-house repair process from the moment the customer requests an RMA to return a broken product, to the shipment of the repaired product back to the customer (see Figure 5.13).

The entire process is fully automated and includes tight integration with backend SAP ERP logistics and financials (see Figure 5.14). The company has complete visibility into which products are currently being serviced in the repair depot. If necessary, customers will be issued temporary loaners. For example, when a Porsche owner brings his new 911 Turbo into the dealer for an unexpected repair, the dealer will likely offer the customer a loaner car to drive while the car is being repaired.

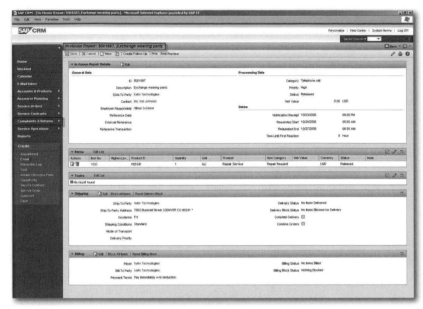

Figure 5.13 In-House Repair process in SAP CRM

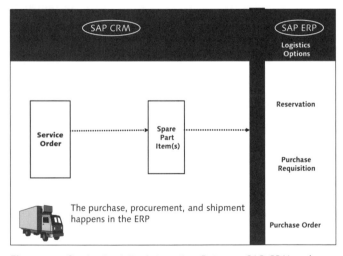

Figure 5.14 Service Logistics Integration Between SAP CRM and
SAP ERP Applications

Efficient repair processes with In-house repair

The in-house repair component of SAP CRM Service provides automatic warranty and service contract check and assignment to verify customer entitlement and ensure accurate billing. Repair quotations include cost estimates and allow customers to approve the quote before a repair is performed. A repair knowledge base is also provided — complete with repair steps, diagnostics, and damage and cause codes — so that repair technicians can leverage existing solutions rather than re-inventing the wheel for each repair. Templates are also available — including industry-specific templates — to handle even the most complex repair orders quickly and efficiently. Once the repair is performed and service complete, you can analyze the process with Service Analytics.

Service Analytics

Service analytics monitor the vital statistics of your service business, helping you react to emergencies and keep the business healthy. Analytics are provided for each of the Service components, including installed base management, warranty management, service contract and entitlement management, resource planning, case management, service order management, complaints and returns, and in-house repairs (Figure 5.15).

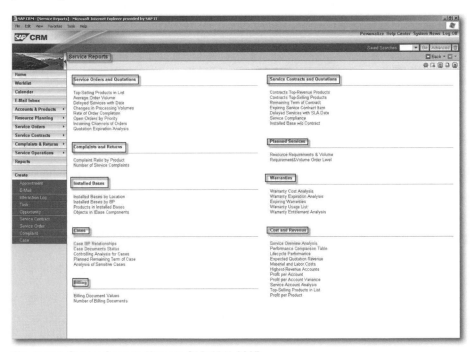

Figure 5.15 Service Reports Menu in SAP CRM 2007

For example, installed base analytics show the amount of money generated by orders for a particular product installation, enabling an analysis of cost, revenue, and profit by product installation. Similarly, service contract analysis allows you to look at billing information and planned versus actual contract usage to determine which service contracts are most profitable and which are unprofitable. Or, in-house repair analytics could be used to gather more information about the most common product defects and damage codes to drive closed-loop feedback back to engineering.

We'll discuss analytics in more detail in Chapter 13. Now we turn our attention to the business drivers and key performance indicators (KPIs) that guide your company's service model.

Business Drivers

Manage service business statistics with analytics

Typically, most SAP CRM Service projects are driven by concerns associated with costs, customers, and risks. Usually, a combination of these drivers will influence your service objectives. Cost-related drivers include the desire to reduce Total Cost of Ownership (TCO) by lowering operational and maintenance cost, and minimizing warranty claims costs.

Customer-related business drivers include goals such as increasing customer satisfaction, reducing customer churn, and generating greater cross-sell revenue during service interactions. These goals can be accomplished in part by decreasing turn-around time for service issues and increasing first call resolution. The risk-related drivers involve trying to meet legal and regulatory compliance requirements. For example, companies need to be able to identify potential product hazards and quickly track and recall the affected product. Companies also need to comply with regulatory guidelines such as the U.S. Consumer Product Safety Commission (Figure 5.16).

Now you should have a good understanding of the Service component of CRM, so let's look at the following case study to see Service in action.

NEWS from CPSC

U.S. Consumer Product Safety Commission

Office of Information and Public Affairs   Washington, DC 20207

FOR IMMEDIATE RELEASE
May 16, 2007
Release #07-190

Firm's Recall Hotline: (877) 607-6395
CPSC Recall Hotline: (800) 638-2772
CPSC Media Contact: (301) 504-7908
General Electric Media Contact: Kim Freeman, (502) 452-7819

General Electric Recalls Dishwashers Due to Fire Hazard

WASHINGTON, D.C. - The U.S. Consumer Product Safety Commission, in cooperation with the firm named below, today announced a voluntary recall of the following consumer product. Consumers should stop using recalled products immediately unless otherwise instructed.

Name of product: GE Dishwashers

Units: About 2.5 million

Manufacturer: GE Consumer & Industrial, of Louisville, Ky.

Hazard: Liquid rinse-aid can leak from its dispenser onto the dishwasher's internal wiring which can cause an electrical short and overheating, posing a fire hazard to consumers.

Incidents/Injuries: GE has received 191 reports of overheated wiring including 56 reports of property damage. There were 12 reports of fires that escaped the dishwasher. Fire damage was limited to the dishwasher or the adjacent area. No injuries have been reported.

Description: The recall includes GE built-in dishwashers sold under the following brand names: Eterna, GE, GE Profile™, GE Monogram®, Hotpoint®, and Sears-Kenmore. The dishwashers were sold in white, black, almond, bisque and stainless steel. The brand name is printed on the dishwasher's front control panel. The following model and serial numbers can be found inside the dishwasher tub on the front left side of the dishwasher.

Brand	Model Numbers Must Begin With	Serial Numbers Must Begin With

Figure 5.16 GE Dishwasher Recall

Case Study

In this case study, we'll look at a leading provider of enterprise communication solutions and unified messaging systems for enterprise customers. This company also provides contact center solutions. The company serves more than 6,000 customers, including nine of the world's largest financial institutions. The company's annual revenue is approximately $120 million, and it has about 600 employees.

The company's products include communication servers, gateways, digital phones, IP phones, mobile computers, and so on. The solutions include contact centers, unified communications, communication-enabled business processes, converged data, voice solutions, managed network solutions, and so on. The company, which started as a manufacturing company, has grown as a solutions company.

Their business challenge was to move the company from product-centric to customer-centric operations. They already had a thriving ecosystem of system integrators, channel partners, and distributors who faced the end customers day to day. The challenge was to provide a single system that supported this customer-facing ecosystem. So the company needed a single system that would support the customer-facing operations and revenue management system and calculate the

119

myriad service taxes and other applicable taxes on products and services. The solution would also need to provide a profitability analysis of value-based service contracts.

The high-level service business objectives were to do the following:

> Use AMC (Annual Maintenance Contract) pricing based on product group

> Create a value-added services contract

> Capture deviations from standard offerings

> Integrate with sales, service delivery, and installed base applications

> Calculate AMC as a percentage of PO value or based on reference price

> Attach contract information to every business process/system/product model/component

> Create a user-friendly interface for creating service contracts

> Cause AMC invoices to be based on payment terms

> Capture service tax and other applicable tax

> Use AMC debtors statements

> Provide end-to-end customer support

> Track expense/profitability of the contract

The company's technological challenge to provide an integrated system that would provide operational and analytic solutions was solved by implementing and integrating the SAP ERP, SAP CRM, and SAP NetWeaver BI system landscape supported by the Single Sign-On capabilities of SAP Enterprise Portal (EP).

The company deployed a 360-degree SAP CRM solution using the Marketing, Sales, and Service components with an emphasis on Service that used a Windows-based customer interaction center (CIC) application.

The company now uses SAP CRM to manage the service call, warranty, contract, and billing processes. The SAP CRM interaction center enables service agents to log calls, assign calls to an appropriate service engineer, and escalate calls as necessary. Finally, the SAP CRM E-Selling functionality supports channel partners for placing orders, tracking open orders, and viewing outstanding items in the Web shop.

Evidence of the value created by this deployment is provided by the company's report that it has generated more than 120% of the internal rate of return at the end of two years of deployment.

For the future, the company is looking to upgrade the SAP CRM 4.0 system to SAP CRM 6.0 (SAP CRM 2007) and further implement and enhance the following business processes:

> Lead management
> Opportunity management
> Quotations management
> Installed Base management
> Warranty management
> Channel management

Conclusion

In this chapter, we covered the major components of SAP CRM Service. The key things you should remember about what this component offers include the following:

> SAP CRM Service helps you decrease your service-related costs through increased efficiency, automated processes, and tight integration with SAP ERP backend processes.

> Service contract management can help you increase your service revenues and profits because selling service contracts is often more profitable than selling products.

> In-house repair depots allow you profit from fixing equipment that customers have returned or brought in for service, whereas the resource planning application (RPA) allows you to optimize your field engineers and technicians to minimize field service-related costs.

Chapters 3, 4, and 5 focused on the three core components of SAP CRM: Marketing, Sales, and Service. In the next four chapters, we'll shift our focus to the interaction channels by which customers interact with the core SAP CRM functionality. We'll begin in the next chapter with the Interaction Center. Then in Chapters 7, 8, and 9, we'll look at other interaction channels, including the Web channel (formerly E-Commerce), Mobile SAP CRM, and Partner Channel Management.

So let's turn our attention to the Interaction Center, which is one of the most commonly, used components within SAP CRM and often referred to as the *front door* of SAP CRM.

6

SAP CRM Interaction Center

At the heart of every company is an interaction center, where agents are standing by ready to take care of customers. You can think of the interaction center as the front door of any company — inviting customers to come in and do business.

Interaction centers let customers communicate and interact with companies through whichever communication channels the customer prefers, including telephone, email, Web chat, fax, postal letter, and other channels. The interaction center also allows companies to communicate with customers via telephone, email, Web chat, fax, and letter as well (Figure 6.1). Companies typically use the interaction center to provide product support and answer questions from customers, whereas some companies also use the interaction center for outbound marketing and sales.

The terms *call center* and *contact center* are sometimes used when discussing interaction centers, with call center referring to interaction centers that only support telephone communication, and contact center referring to interaction centers that support additional communication channels such as email or chat. Although the telephone is still the preferred communication channel for most customers, usage of

Call center versus contact center

Internet-enabled communication channels such as email, Web chat, and Web callback are widespread and continue to grow.

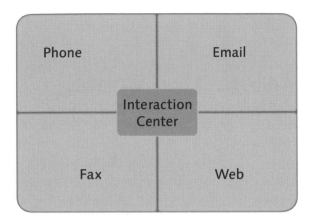

Figure 6.1 Multi-Channel Interaction Center

Traditionally, agents sat together in a large room, each person equipped with a computer and telephone headset. However, the industry is also shifting toward *virtual* interaction centers where there is no central office, and the interaction center agents work from home using their own computers. Regardless of how your interaction center is organized, the functions and purpose are the same: to increase customer loyalty and profitability.

Interaction centers facilitate two-way communication

Interaction centers facilitate two-way communication between customers and companies. For example, *customers* use the interaction center to contact companies to ask questions, request product information, place orders, check status of existing orders, file complaints or returns, or request service. *Companies* use the interaction center to contact customers and prospects to inform people about new products or promotions, follow up on sales leads and opportunities, schedule deliveries, and make service appointments.

Customers enjoy the freedom of being able to contact the company any time they want, via the communication channel they prefer. And companies benefit from actually being able to speak with their customers — who can otherwise be hard to contact due to increased privacy laws and do-not-call lists. This interaction with customers gives companies a chance to reinforce its brand image and marketing messages, to increase customer satisfaction and loyalty via excellent service, and to drive revenue and profitability via post-service cross-selling efforts.

Interaction Center Strategy

The interaction center is usually included as part of a broader SAP CRM program at a company, designed to help the company better understand and manage its customer relationships. However, the interaction center is also quite commonly implemented on its own, or as the first foray into a more comprehensive, longer-term SAP CRM initiative. For example, existing SAP ERP customers who want to start leveraging customer relationship management will often begin their SAP CRM project with the interaction center. These SAP ERP customers typically start with a help desk for providing customer-facing service and support. As the company becomes more and more committed to SAP CRM, it will expand its interaction center footprint to include telemarketing and telesales. And, many companies eventually even extend their SAP CRM efforts internally to employees, setting up IT help desks and employee interaction centers to provide internal IT and HR support.

Implement the interaction center independently or as part of CRM

The SAP CRM interaction center provides access to the complete SAP CRM Marketing, Sales, and Service functionality. Companies can use the interaction center to run their entire customer-facing marketing, sales, and service operations using any number of communication channels. However, as with any SAP CRM project, it's often best to start small with a specific business focus in a particular geographic region to address an immediate need or pain point. Later, you can gradually expand the scope of the interaction center project to include other lines of business, additional organizations, and more geographic regions.

Although the majority of interaction centers are set up as help desks with a primary focus on customer service and only peripheral support for sales and marketing processes, there are companies who use their interaction centers solely for telemarketing or telesales. For example, a manufacturing or bottling company might have a more pressing need to set up a business-to-business (B2B) sales support center to process sales orders from retailers or distributors than to implement a consumer help desk. Similarly, an OEM that sells computer processors to systems integrators and value-added resellers might already have a customer-facing trouble-ticketing system in place, but might want to roll out an internal employee-facing IT help desk to improve product quality.

Top 10 questions to ask before you start an IC project

The following is a list of 10 questions that companies should ask before starting an interaction center project. The answers to these questions will help determine on which features and capabilities of the SAP CRM interaction center a company should focus its initial efforts.

1. Are you currently running — or planning to run — one or more call centers to support your customers? Do you have the same technology and architecture in place across all systems, or are you struggling to hold together a fragmented landscape composed of disparate call center technologies?

2. Do you currently provide — or plan to provide — email support to customers? Is the email application integrated with the call center, or is the email application a standalone system?

3. Do you currently provide — or plan to provide — support for Web chat? Is Web chat integrated with your other communication channels such as telephone and email, or is chat handled separately.

4. Do you currently offer — or plan to offer — Web-based customer self-service? If yes, is it integrated with your call center or standalone?

5. What is the size of your organization? How many customers do you have? In how many countries do you operate? How many languages do you support?

6. How many products and services are currently supported by each communication channel (telephone, email, Web chat, Web self-service)?

7. How many customers are supported on average by each channel

on a daily, weekly, monthly, and yearly basis?

8. Does your call center also conduct sales at the point of service? Meaning, are your customer service representatives enabled to recommend accessories and cross-sell items and offer service contracts or extended warranties?

9. Does your call center also support your employees? For example, do you have an employee-facing internal HR help desk or IT help desk?

10. Are your call center applications integrated with your backend SAP ERP infrastructure?

The answers to the preceding questions will help you prioritize your business needs and provide guidance regarding how to approach and structure your interaction center implementation. For example, your most pressing business need might be to consolidate all of your existing, disparate call-center and email point solutions with an integrated multi-channel interaction center. Or, if you already have an interaction center deployed for customer service, your biggest need might be to roll out an employee-facing IT help desk or employee interaction center to handle your internal IT and HR issues.

Of course, if you don't yet have an interaction center, your challenges will be to determine what type of customer processes you want to support and then to roll out an interaction center from scratch. Among SAP customers and prospects — who are usually well-run established companies with a large customer base — the first scenario is probably the most likely (i.e., the need to consolidate a fragmented landscape of disparate call-center technologies). Let's look in detail at the issues facing a company as it migrates from a piecemeal legacy call center to a consolidated interaction center using SAP CRM.

Consolidating Standalone Telephone, Email, and Chat Applications

A call center, by definition, can of course only accept telephone calls. However, customers today demand to be able to contact a company any time they want, via whichever communication channel they prefer. In today's Internet economy, a customer might buy a product

Moving from call center to interaction center

online at the company's Web shop, call the company's interaction center for service or support, and then exchange the product in one of the company's brick-and-mortar retail locations. Companies who cling to outdated pre-Internet era business models — only providing customer service via telephone and only from Monday to Friday during normal business hours — are finding it increasingly difficult to hold on to customers. Today's customer demands the convenience of being able to reach your company any time of the day (or night), via telephone, email, SMS, or Web chat.

Provide consistent service from every channel

Unfortunately, it's not enough to simply support each communication channel with separate standalone solutions. Rather, customers expect to receive the same level of service and the same customer experience regardless of whether they contact you via telephone, email, or chat. Customers also naturally expect that if they send you an email and then later contact you via telephone, the person on the telephone should not only be aware of the email but already have it open right in front of them. Customers don't want to hear excuses or apologies about how emails are handled by a different system or another group of employees.

The challenge for companies that have deployed individual standalone point solutions — or have acquired an eclectic assortment of technologies via mergers and acquisitions — is to convert their legacy call center, email, and chat point solutions into a consolidated multichannel interaction center. The first step — after admitting you have a problem — is to undertake a technical migration. The following points should be considered before planning or initiating the technical migration from legacy point solutions to an integrated SAP CRM interaction center.

Telephone System Hardware

In the past, most telephone switching systems (i.e., PBXs) were hardware based. Although the majority of installed products in the field are still hardware based, over half of new telephone switching systems being sold are software enabled, or so called IP-PBXs. If you are using older — especially hardware-based — equipment, you might need to consider upgrading your equipment or verifying that your old equipment will be compatible with any new contact-center software you acquire to enable multi-channel integration in the SAP CRM interaction center.

 Tip

SAP does not directly certify any hardware, including telephones and telephone switches such as PBXs or IP-PBXs. To find out if your hardware is compatible with your contact center software, you will need to contact the vendor of your contact center software.

Contact Center Software

The SAP CRM interaction center doesn't come out-of-the-box with so-called "contact center software," which is the software that handles queuing, routing, and treatment of media such as telephone calls, emails, chats, and other communication channels. SAP does offer a contact center software product known as SAP Business Communications Management (BCM), but it's a separate product from SAP CRM and licensed and installed separately. However, like similar products from SAP partners such as Genesys, Avaya, Cisco, and others that can integrate via SAP-certified adapters, SAP BCM is also certified by SAP and can be integrated to the interaction center to allow integration of telephone, email, SMS, faxes, and other communication channels.

Add on the BCM contact center software

 Note

The contact center software is sometimes also referred to as Computer Telephony Integration (CTI), although technically CTI is an older term that only refers to telephone integration and does not include other newer channels such as email and chat.

A list of contact center software products supported by SAP-certified adapters is available from the SAP Partner directory. The technical migration will be easier if your current contact center software is SAP certified. Otherwise, you may have to migrate to SAP-certified software, or develop your own custom interface for SAP, which can be difficult and risky — although not impossible.

Tip

Certified adapters are available for contact-center software products from many vendors, including: Genesys, Avaya, Cisco, SAP BCM, Siemens, Ericsson, Cycos, Alcatel, Altitude, Aspect, Interactive Intelligence, Nortel, Philips-NEC, and so on. A full, up-to-date list of certified adapters per communication channel is available from the SAP Partner directory:

http://www.sap.com/partners/directories/SearchSolution.epx

> For ICI Telephony certified products and connectors choose CA-ICI-CTI 6.2 - Integrated Communication Interface - CTI 6.20.

> For SAPphone Telephony certified products and connectors choose BC-CTI 4.5 - Computer Telephony Integration (SAPphone) 4.5.

> For ICI email certified products and connectors choose CA-ICI-MAIL 6.2 - Integrated Communication Interface - Mail Add-On 6.20.

> For ICI chat certified products and connectors choose CA-ICI-CHAT 6.2 - Integrated Communication Interface - Chat Add-On 6.20.

Standalone Email and Chat Applications

Standalone email and chat applications

Most companies started adding standalone applications — first for email and then later for chat — as these Internet-based customer service and support tools became more popular with customers. However, rather than re-evaluating the current and long-term IT infrastructure requirements and designing an integrated solution, these standalone applications were just tucked into the overall IT infrastructure in little niches. This is a classic example of the downside of letting each line of business make its own IT decisions, rather than having a centralized IT strategy that supports the long-term business strategy.

Because email, chat, and telephone are managed as separate applications, there is often no centralized customer database. Each application has its own separate database, and companies end up maintaining multiple products. Whereas the SAP CRM interaction center is a channel-agnostic application; regardless of whether the customer uses the telephone, email, chat, or another application, the customer data and the details of the customer interaction are all stored in the SAP CRM system. All channels access and write data to a single database.

All communication channels have access to the same customer records, and all customer interactions are logged using the same format, regardless of the channel (Figure 6.2).

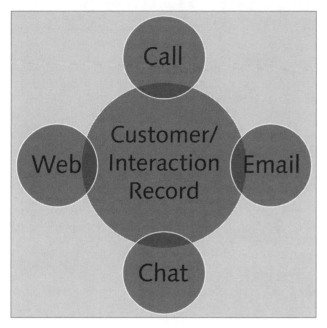

Figure 6.2 One View of the Customer Record Regardless of Communication Channel

 Tip

If you are using SAP ERP as your backend application, it's important to understand the differences in the data models between SAP CRM and SAP ERP. For example, SAP ERP has a "customer" master record, whereas SAP CRM uses a more generic object called a "business partner." Carefully consolidate, format, map, and prepare data migration to SAP CRM.

We already touched on one of the inherent risks of letting individual business units make their own IT decisions: you end up with a collection of best-of-breed solutions, none of which work with each other. This best-of-breed approach, due to its shortcomings, lays the foundation for a more integrated approach. The integrated approach takes advantage of the SAP CRM interaction center, which has complete access to the full customer-facing marketing, sales, and service functionality within SAP CRM, as well as integration to enterprise-wide functions, such as variant configuration and pricing, Availability-To-Promise (ATP), logistics, billing, and so on (Figure 6.3).

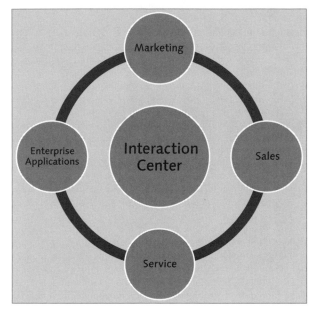

Figure 6.3 Integrated Interaction Center

Customer-Facing Tools and Interfaces

Before we look at the tools provided by the SAP CRM interaction center for agents and managers, let's spend some time talking about the generic tools that your customers may use to contact your interaction center. These tools are, of course, not part of the SAP CRM interaction center solution, but they are important nonetheless because you'll need to support them, and they define your customer's experience with your interaction center. Later we'll discuss the actual features and capabilities that the SAP CRM interaction center provides to agents and managers.

Telephone and Interactive Voice Response

The telephone itself becomes a user interface for customers when combined with an interactive voice response (IVR) system. As you may know, IVR is a telephony technology in which the user presses buttons on a touchtone telephone to interact with the computer system to retrieve or enter data from a database. IVR menus and responses are pre-recorded and don't involve an actual human operator. The IVR menus are designed to reduce the number of callers who need to speak with a human operator by automating the most common types of customer telephone interactions, such as retrieving account balances or updating customer information.

Telephone and IVR

IVR systems can often eliminate the need for a human agent, especially for simple or straightforward tasks such as retrieving account balances, activating new credit cards, making a payment, and so on. However, IVR systems usually also have an option to allow customers to transfer to a live agent, but they aren't well-suited for transactions that require human judgment, such as resolving customer billing disputes or making retention offers.

 Example

> To activate a credit card, banks and credit card companies advise customers to call an 800 number by using their home phone. The caller's telephone number is first verified by the computer system. If the telephone number matches the number in the customer database, the IVR instructs the customer to enter his unique 16-digit credit card number. If the customer is calling from a different telephone than their home phone, the caller will be connected to a live agent to verify the customer's identity.
>
> The IVR provides other services as well, such as verifying account balances. Some Telco companies also allow you to pay your monthly mobile phone bill via credit card by dialing 611 from your mobile phone and following a set of recorded instructions.

Web-Based "Push to Talk" and "Call Me Back" Options

Companies are increasingly using live voice chat or Web callback features such as "Push-to-talk" and "Call-me-back" in their online stores and websites to allow customers to contact interaction center agents

"Push to Talk" and "Call Me Back" options

with questions when shopping or browsing a company's website. For example, imagine that a customer is interested in ordering a particular product but can't find any information on the company's website about whether overnight shipping is available. The customer doesn't want to order the product if express shipping isn't possible.

In the past, this could have resulted in a lost sale because the customer might leave and look for another website that explicitly mentions overnight shipping. However, because the online store has a "Push to talk" feature, the customer clicks the button and is able to do a live voice chat with an interaction center agent using a USB headset or the speakers and microphone built into the laptop. Alternatively, if the customer does not have a USB headset or built-in microphone, the customer might click the "Call me back" button and then key in the preferred telephone number. A few seconds (or minutes) later, a live agent calls the customer.

Hybrid solutions using live voice chat and Web callbacks are gaining popularity among both customers and companies because they are more effective than IVR systems for addressing complex buying decisions where products and services have to be compared — resulting in more successful online shopping trips.

Web Forms

Web forms   A Web form is an area on a Web page typically composed of text boxes, drop-down values, and radio buttons or check boxes. This area allows customers to submit data to a company. The Web form often can mimic a real paper-based form and can be used for anything that a paper form would be used for, including sending requests for detailed product information, placing a sales order, or requesting service. The actual form is typically either submitted via a Web post to a CGI program for automated processing, or it's simply converted to an email and routed to an interaction center like a normal email. The agent would respond to the Web form request within an agreed time period just like a regular email (Figures 6.4 and 6.5).

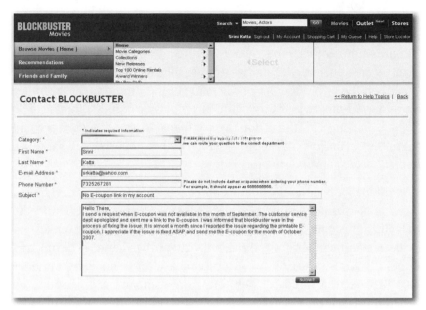

Figure 6.4 Blockbuster Customer Service Request Web Form (© Blockbuster)

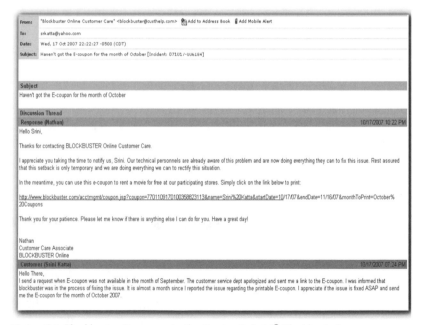

Figure 6.5 Blockbuster Response to the Service Ticket (© Blockbuster)

Many companies prefer Web forms over free-text email because they give the company control over how customers organize and submit information. For example, when writing a free-form email to a company's customer-service email address, the customer might forget to mention the order number or the name of the product. The customer might even mix two or three different topics or requests into a single email, making it difficult for the company to use automated email response management tools to automatically categorize and route the email to the appropriate processor.

Additionally, if different interaction center agents or engineers need to work separately on each of the different topics mentioned in the email, it becomes difficult to keep track of the various email exchanges and conversation threads. On the other hand, if a company doesn't publish a customer-service email address but only provides a URL link to a standard Web form, the company can control how customers structure their messages. For example, the Web form could have a mandatory field where the customer has to enter the affected product or the customer's sales order number. And, of course, the customer would need to log a separate Web form submission for each problem rather than lumping three different issues together in the same email.

Internet Customer Self-Service Portals

Self-service customer support
Customer self-service portals, such as SAP CRM Internet Customer Self-Service, provide customers with tools to resolve their own customer-service needs without assistance from a live interaction center agent. A self-service portal normally contains a list of Frequently Asked Questions (FAQs) as well as a knowledge search to help the customer locate solutions, knowledge base articles, or other relevant documents. A self-service portal might also offer software downloads for device drivers, bug fixes, or recent product updates.

SAP's CRM Internet Customer Self-Service (ICSS) application isn't actually part of the SAP CRM interaction center, although the two applications are somewhat aligned in that they leverage the same underlying data model and database. For example, if a customer is unable to find a resolution to an issue on the self-service portal, the customer might create a service ticket from the portal. The customer would naturally be able to check the status of the ticket by logging into the portal. However, the customer might also choose to call the interaction center to check on the status of the issue. Even though the ticket was logged on the self-service portal, the interaction center agent should be able to locate the ticket and provide the customer with the current processing status. If the customer needs assistance, they can use Web chat.

Web Chat

In today's Internet economy, customers research product information online, order products from a company's Web shop, and try to resolve service issues on their own by visiting the company's Web self-service portal. However, even today's self-reliant, Web-savvy customers still occasionally need a little help from a real person. Web chat allows a Web user to have an immediate, real-time typed online conversation with an interaction center agent without picking up the phone and without leaving the website. Chat can be used for any issue or topic for which other channels such as email or telephone are used.

However, one of the most common uses of chat is for customers to report technical issues and request customer support. Some companies also provide chat as a service to assist customers who are shopping for big-ticket or high-value items on a website. For example, a company might have an automated process that sends a chat request to a customer who has been on the same Web page for more than two minutes and might be experiencing a problem finding a product or need help making a decision.

Different companies use different technologies to enable chat on their websites. Often chat works out of the box with no special settings or actions necessary on the part of the user. Occasionally, however, a small chat application (typically a browser plug-in or ActiveX control) needs to be installed on the user's browser to enable the chat application. Most sites allow anonymous chat where anyone can chat with an interaction center agent. However, other sites require customers to be authenticated or to register by providing a name, email address, product ID, or serial number prior to initiating a chat session (see Figure 6.6 and 6.7).

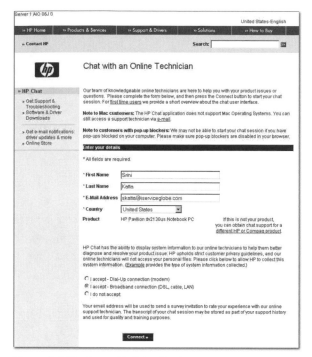

Figure 6.6 Starting a Chat Application

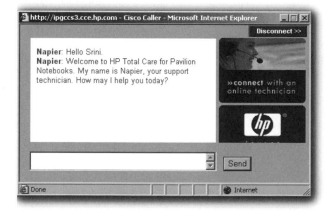

Figure 6.7 A Customer Chatting with the Customer Care Agent

When dealing with a large company that offers multiple product lines and a wide assortment of products per product line, customers can navigate via a structured product catalog to drill down through the hierarchy of products to identify the product they own (Figure 6.7).

So there you have a good look overview of the customer-facing tools and interfaces. Let's move on to review the capabilities of the SAP CRM interaction center.

SAP CRM Interaction Center Capabilities

The SAP CRM interaction center is an integrated solution providing access to all customer-facing SAP CRM Marketing, Sales, and Service functionality, as well as access to back-office SAP ERP functionality. The interaction center can be integrated with other SAP and non-SAP systems such as contact center software, standalone knowledge management and trouble-ticketing systems, ATP systems, pricing engines, and even legacy billing systems. The interaction center provides a complete 360-degree overview of your customers, allowing you to strengthen relationships and increase loyalty and profitability.

Until SAP CRM 2005, the interaction center was available in two options: the WinClient interface that runs in SAP GUI for Windows and the WebClient browser-based solution. As of SAP CRM 2006s and above, only the browser-based WebClient solution is offered.

Agent Desktop Productivity Tools

The SAP CRM interaction center provides a set of agent desktop productivity tools designed to increase the efficiency and effectiveness of interaction center agents. For example, text alerts can be used to remind agents of important customer-relevant information, such as the fact that a customer is a Gold customer or that the customer has an open order that hasn't shipped yet. Interactive scripts can be provided to step agents through difficult or complex procedures, providing the agents with guidance about what to say to the customer and what steps to take next.

Agent desktop productivity tools

Templates are also available for agents when creating emails or chat responses, allowing the agent to reuse standard greetings, signatures, and commonly asked questions instead of manually typing every email. And agents have access to a knowledge base, including automatically suggested solutions that can be inserted into an email or chat. The goal is to free agents from repetitive mundane tasks and to let them focus on value-added activities. Agents should spend their time helping customers or selling products, not cutting and pasting or constantly searching for the same documents all day long.

Multi-Channel Integration

Multi-channel integration via SAPconnect

Although it might sound counterintuitive, about half of SAP CRM interaction center customers don't currently have CTI or multi-channel integration enabled in their interaction centers. This doesn't mean that these companies don't accept telephone calls or email; instead, there is no connection between the company's telephone system and email server to the interaction center. For example, an incoming caller will get routed to an available agent by the company's telephone PBX switch, but the agent won't get a visual indication in the interaction center that a customer is calling. There will be no "screen pop" of the customer's data, and the agent will need to perform a manual search for the customer.

Similarly, a company can still receive and respond to customer emails without using advanced contact center software that performs real-time skills-based routing. Instead, the customer can use the SAPconnect interface to route emails from the company's exchange server to the agent inbox in the SAP CRM interaction center. Agents can manually pick emails out of the agent inbox and reply, in a fashion very similar to working with Microsoft Outlook or IBM® Lotus® Notes. However, there will be no real-time push of the email to an available agent, no skills-based routing, and no screen pop. To enable these features, multi-channel integration is required.

As discussed earlier in the chapter, contact center software — also known as Communication Management Software (CMS) — is required to enable real-time multi-channel integration in the SAP CRM interaction center. There are numerous options available on the market, including SAP's own Business Communications Management (BCM) solution as well as certified products from SAP partners such as Genesys, Avaya, Cisco, and others as mentioned earlier.

SAP CRM Marketing Integration

In the past, most marketing efforts focused mainly on customer acquisition. Marketing budgets were heavily dedicated to marketing activities designed to steal customers away from competitors, with less thought given to customer retention. At some point, however, marketers started to realize that it costs much more money — 5 to 10 times more — to acquire new customers than it does to sell to existing customers. Companies quickly realized that their existing customer base was one of their most valuable assets. So, marketing budgets were rebalanced to include a more appropriate distribution of efforts to retain and sell to existing customers — not just to target new customers.

Customer acquisition and retention capabilities

The SAP CRM interaction center supports both types of marketing efforts. Telephone campaigns and outbound telemarketing lists can be set up to target new prospects (as well as existing customers) with new promotions (see Figure 6.8.) The interaction center can also be used to qualify sales leads collected from websites, trade shows, and conferences, or external lists. In addition, the interaction center supports marketing efforts directed at inbound customers who contact the interaction center for service or support. After resolving the customer's issue, the system can propose relevant accessories or cross-sell items that complement the customer's existing product.

Real-time offer management functionality

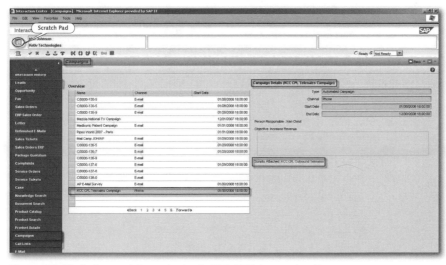

Figure 6.8 Marketing and Campaigning in SAP CRM Interaction Center

With SAP CRM 2006s, the interaction center is also integrated with SAP Real-Time Offer Management (RTOM), allowing for real-time, intelligent cross-sell recommendations, retentions offers, and targeted marketing messages.

 Tip

> SAP RTOM can be integrated with the interaction center as of release SAP CRM 2006s. RTOM helps you increase marketing conversion rates, customer satisfaction, and loyalty. Based on real-time customer information, RTOM filters through all relevant campaigns, promotions, and retention programs to find the most relevant cross-sell, up-sell, retention offer, or marketing message to deliver to the customer. RTOM is a separate product and is licensed and installed separately from SAP CRM.

SAP CRM Sales Integration

Although today's Web-savvy customers often order products and services online — bypassing the interaction center — there are still plenty of customers who place orders through the interaction center via telephone, chat, and even fax. Catalog retailers, for example, still process many orders via telephone, as do Telco companies. Telephone orders are also still very common in B2B sales models where a retailer or distributor orders products from the manufacturer.

Integrate with SAP ERP using middleware

The SAP CRM interaction center supports all of these scenarios and more. Interaction center agents can create new sales orders or pull up existing sales orders to provide customers with up-to-date shipping and delivery information, or even make a change to the order. Agents can also create quotations, or convert an existing quotation into an order. The SAP CRM interaction center sales processes are also integrated with SAP ERP — via SAP CRM middleware as well as through interaction center-specific RFCs (Remote Function Calls) and BAdIs (Business Add-Ins)— allowing orders and quotations to flow freely between the two systems. You can, for example, create orders in SAP CRM via the interaction center and then replicate the orders to SAP ERP. Alternatively, you can manage leads, opportunities, and quotations in SAP CRM but then create the actual orders in the backend SAP ERP application. In this case, it isn't necessary to use the sales order capabilities of SAP CRM. The entire order management process, including pricing, could be handled using SAP ERP logic — but accessed via the interaction center agents from SAP CRM (see Figure 6.9).

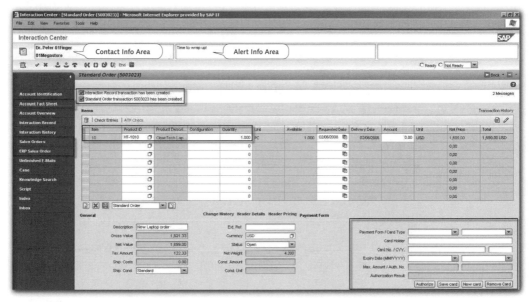

Figure 6.9 SAP CRM Interaction Center Sales with Backend ERP Integration

SAP CRM Service Integration

Customer service is one of the most important aspects of any business. In the past, companies relied on their products to impress customers and generate profits. In today's Internet economy, a customer can instantly find the lowest price available for your products — as well as the prices of competitor's products. Additionally, profit margins on physical products have been squeezed due to increased competition from high-volume retailers such as Wal-Mart, Cost-Co, and Sam's Club. Today, companies can often make more money selling service contracts because the profit margins are sometimes as high as 50% or more.

Provide world-class customer service
Increasingly, products are being seen as a commodity, and companies are forced to differentiate themselves — and generate profits — via customer service. Any customer can immediately go online and read reviews of what other customers think about a company, its products, and, most important, its customer service. Companies that provide bad customer service find themselves publicly bashed in Web logs (blogs) and online product reviews.

The SAP CRM interaction center can help your company provide world-class customer service. Interaction center agents have access to a customer's complete information and history and can quickly pull up an open order or trouble ticket to provide the customer with the most up-to-date status. Agents can also search for product information to answer customer questions. For technical issues or troubleshooting, agents can search a knowledge base of solutions and knowledge articles; solutions can also be automatically recommended to the agent based on the problem classification or product information.

To provide customers with the information they need via the communication channel they prefer, agents can send product information, solutions, and other documents via email or Web chat. For service issues that require installation, maintenance, or repair, agents can schedule appointments for the customer based on the customer's service contract and preferred dates and times. Finally, in the event that the customer has an issue with a shipment or an invoice, the agent can create a complaint on the customer's behalf and generate follow-on tasks such as returns, credit memos, or free-of-charge replacement deliveries. See Figure 6.10 for an overview of SAP CRM Service via the interaction center.

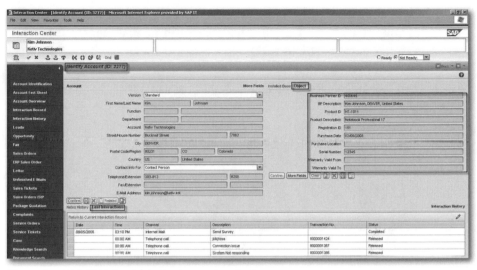

Figure 6.10 SAP CRM Service in the Interaction Center

Blended Business Scenarios

Many companies — especially large companies — organize their interaction centers so that dedicated groups of agents focus on different, specific business areas such as customer service, telemarketing, or sales order entry. Additionally, companies often separate their agents into groups based on which communication channels the agents are proficient at, for example, one queue of telephone agents who have good speaking voices and pleasant demeanors, and another group of email/chat agents who have good typing skills but perhaps have trouble communicating with customers due to a foreign accent. However, other companies — especially SMBs — tend to have just one group of agents who handle all forms of customer requests across all communication channels.

Blended customer service business role

In these companies, interaction center agents don't have a specific business focus such as customer service, telemarketing, or sales order entry but instead have a blended business role where they have access to all SAP CRM Marketing, Sales, and Service functionality. The SAP CRM interaction center can be easily configured to support such a blended business scenario. For example, agents can be assigned to a profile that provides them with access to Marketing, Sales, and Ser-

145

vice functionality and allows them to receive incoming communications of any type, including telephone calls, emails, and chat requests (see Figures 6.11 and 6.12).

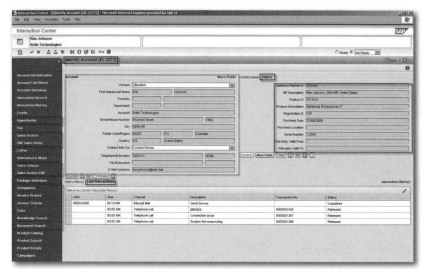

Figure 6.11 SAP CRM Interaction Center Sales and Service — Mixed Scenario

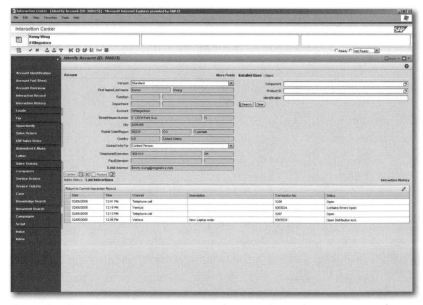

Figure 6.12 SAP CRM Interaction Center Marketing, Sales, and Service — Mixed Scenario

Shared Service Centers

Companies have known for some time that larger interaction centers are more efficient due to economies of scale. This knowledge led many large, global companies to consolidate their global interaction center operations into a single, centralized interaction center to reap cost savings associated with efficiency gains. However, more recently there is another trend again driving global consolidation of interaction centers; but, this time it's aimed at traditional "back-office" functionality.

This new trend is being driven by *Shared-Service Centers* (SSC). The concept is that companies should centralize their various back-office functions such as HR, IT management, finance and accounting, facilities management, and travel management to save money. However, this time around, the efficiency gains and cost-savings aren't just being economies of scale but also by business process re-engineering and elimination of redundancy. For example, rather than having several regional IT help desks and employee interaction centers, a company can consolidate its operations to a single (often low-cost) location and provide centralized HR and IT services.

Centralize back-office functions with Shared-Service Centers (SSCs)

The SAP CRM interaction center provides an out-of-the-box solution for both IT help desks and employee interaction centers (EIC). The IT help desk solution takes advantage of several features of the interaction center service ticket business transaction that were designed specifically for IT help desk scenarios, including multi-level categorization of trouble tickets, automatic suggestion of solutions based on the categorization, an auto-complete feature for easy-to-solve re-occurring issues such as password resets, and a dispatch/escalate feature that automatically re-assigns a trouble ticket to the appropriate second-level support technician or engineer based on configured business rules. The IT help desk can also be used with IT Infrastructure Library (ITIL) approaches.

SAP also offers an out-of-the-box solution for the EIC that allows HR professionals to provide consistent, personalized services. The key features of the solution include a custom employee search screen, an employee request business transaction that has features similar to the service ticket, and integration to backend HR screens from the SAP HCM (Human Capital Management) system. In addition to the out-of-the-box IT help desk and HR EIC solutions, consulting packages are available from SAP Consulting and SAP Custom Development for other SSC topics such as finance and accounting interaction centers.

Running Your Interaction Center: Operations and Administration

Running an efficient interaction center with real-time reports and dashboards

At its best, an interaction center runs like an expensive Swiss watch with all of the various little moving parts spinning, whirring, and humming — each doing its own job. However, a poorly managed interaction center is more like a broken cuckoo clock. A little bird comes out and makes a fuss every few minutes, but the clock never shows the correct time. To just keep things up and running, interaction center managers obviously need to know what the agents are doing and how many customers are waiting. But to really optimize and improve the interaction center, managers need access to historic analytics as well as the tools to adjust future performance.

The SAP CRM interaction center provides managers with real-time reports and dashboards to monitor things such as queue levels and agent behavior, as well as historic reports to analyze information such as service ticket volume and resolution times. Managers can see, for example, how many telephone callers are currently waiting in the queue to speak with an agent. Managers could also pull a report to see how many high-priority service tickets were reported last month and how many are still open. Additionally, companies can create their own reports and analytics using tools provided with SAP NetWeaver BI. Let's take a look at the analytics implemented by one high-tech manufacturer to gain greater insight into their service contract profitability – or lack thereof.

Case Study

It was no fun when customers complained about the delays in customer service to a U.S.-based sports company that manufactures and markets a complete line of sleds and ATVs (all-terrain vehicles). The company has annual sales revenues of $782 million in 2007 and employs 1,500 people, but they faced a number of challenges in their customer service department. They determined that they needed to:

> Replace an outdated nonintegrated call center application.

> Provide an integrated interaction center.

> Reduce the average wait time before an incoming customer/prospect call is connected to an agent.

> Use one interaction center application to support both customers and 1,000 or more dealers.

> Improve overall customer and dealer satisfaction.

> Implement a flexible, scalable, and user-friendly customer-centric SAP CRM system with phone integration.

The solution deployed was the SAP CRM interaction center with Genesys express software for telephony integration, self-service options to dealers, and a seamless integration to a backend SAP ERP application.

After successfully implementing the solution, the company has gained approximately 15% efficiency in the call center operations. It has also achieved 95% first call resolution rates when compared to 40% resolution rates, and less than 1% call abandonment rates when compared to 33 to 36% call abandonment rates prior to SAP CRM implementation.

The company achieved the complete return on investment (ROI) in 15 months after going live with SAP CRM. The company is now in the process of extending the self-service options to the customers and implementing a sales force automation (SFA) using SAP CRM and enterprise portals to support a field sales force.

The company is also looking ahead to upgrade the SAP CRM 4.0 system to SAP CRM 6.0 (SAP CRM 2007) and further implement and enhance the following business processes:

> Lead management

> Opportunity management

> Quotations management

> Installed base management
> Warranty management
> Channel management

Conclusion

In this chapter, you learned about the SAP CRM interaction center, which acts as the front door of a company, allowing customers to contact the company any time the customer wants, through whichever communication channels the customer prefers. You discovered how the interaction center provides full customer-facing SAP CRM Marketing, Sales, and Service functionality as well as integration to SAP ERP and other systems. The following are the key things you should remember about the CRM interaction center.

> To truly get the most out of your interaction center, it often makes sense to add CTI or multi-channel integration. Communication Management Software (CMS), also known as contact center software. This is available both from SAP — via the new SAP Business Communication Management (BCM) product — as well as from SAP partners such as Genesys, Avaya, Cisco, and others. SAP BCM — like similar solutions from SAP partners — is a separate product from SAP CRM and is installed and licensed separately.

> The interaction center provides agent desktop productivity tools that increase the efficiency and effectiveness of an agent by providing the agent with reminder alerts, interactive call scripts, auto-suggested knowledge-base solutions, access to a knowledge-base search, and integration of an email and chat editor for sending solutions and documents to customers.

> SAP CRM interaction center provides out-of-the-box solutions for some back-office Shared-Service Center (SSC) applications such as IT help desk and HR employee interaction center (EIC). Additional solutions are available from SAP Consulting and SAP Custom Development for other types of SSCs such as Finance/Accounting interaction centers.

> SAP Real-Time Offer Management (RTOM) is integrated with the interaction center as of release SAP CRM 2006s, providing agents with real-time, intelligent cross-sell recommendation, retention offers, and targeted marketing messages. SAP RTOM is a separate product from SAP CRM and is installed and licensed separately.

> Up until and including SAP CRM 2005, SAP offered two different user interface options for the interaction center: an SAP GUI for Windows application called WinClient, and a thin-client Web browser-based application called WebClient. As of release SAP CRM 2006s and above, the SAP CRM application has adopted the WebClient user interface, and SAP GUI transactions such as the WinClient are no longer supported or available. As of SAP CRM 2006s and beyond, only the WebClient option is available for the interaction center.

In the next chapter, we'll look at how the Web channel (formerly known as E-Commerce) allows companies to conduct business on the Internet using Web shops and customer self-service portals.

7

Web Channel Enablement Solution

In the early 1990s, there was considerable debate about the viability of conducting business over the Internet. At the time, companies worried that consumers wouldn't feel safe using their credit cards to buy goods and services online. Companies were also concerned that consumers, particularly in rural or low-income areas, wouldn't have adequate access to the Web because high-speed broadband access was still relatively expensive and not widely available. Additionally, computer prices were significantly higher than they are today, making computer access cost-prohibitive for many families.

Today, however, almost everyone does business on the Internet. Computer prices have fallen dramatically, so that you can buy a computer at Wal-Mart for under $200. High-speed Internet access is almost ubiquitous. Consumers are also feeling safe buying and selling products over the Internet. For example, a 2007 report from Jupiter Research found that over half of all consumers (52%) now books their personal travel entirely on the Internet. Similarly, retail online sales

Doing business on the Internet is here to stay

during the 2007 holiday season exceeded $28 billion USD, a 19% increase over the previous year. And, according to various reports, up to 1.5 million people supplement their income by selling products on online auction sites such as eBay©.

Every major business has a Web presence. The top e-commerce websites, which are measured by the number of unique visitors, include the expected big-name retailers such as Amazon, Wal-Mart©, Target©, JC Penny©, and Sears©. But even small "mom and pop" neighborhood businesses are setting up their own websites for everything from babysitting, to lawn mowing, and dog walking services.

However, the Internet is useful for more than just selling things. Companies both large and small are using the Web to communicate marketing messages and to reinforce their brand image. Companies also use the Web to provide customer service, allowing customers to check the status of their orders and deliveries, update their own account information, log complaints, and even search for FAQs or solutions to common questions and problems.

SAP's CRM Web Channel Enablement solution, formerly called E-Commerce or Internet Sales, allows you to increase your revenues and market reach by extending your sales process to the Web. It also allows you to reduce your Total Cost of Ownership (TCO) and your costs of sale and support — while empowering your customers — by providing customers with convenient, personalized tools for buying products and requesting service online. The Web Channel Enablement solution consists of E-Marketing, E-Commerce (formerly E-Selling), E-Service, and Web Channel Analytics (formerly E-Analytics) as shown in Figure 7.1. We'll look at each area in detail in the following sections of this chapter.

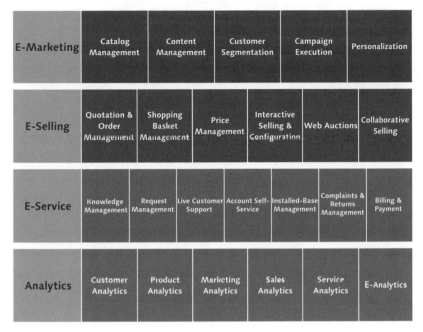

E-Marketing	Catalog Management	Content Management	Customer Segmentation	Campaign Execution	Personalization	
E-Selling	Quotation & Order Management	Shopping Basket Management	Price Management	Interactive Selling & Configuration	Web Auctions	Collaborative Selling
E-Service	Knowledge Management	Request Management	Live Customer Support	Account Self-Service	Installed-Base Management	Complaints & Returns Management	Billing & Payment
Analytics	Customer Analytics	Product Analytics	Marketing Analytics	Sales Analytics	Service Analytics	E-Analytics

Figure 7.1 SAP CRM E-Commerce Solution Map

 Tip

SAP CRM Web Channel Enablement (or Web channel for short) includes the following areas:

> E-Marketing

> E-Commerce (formerly E-Selling)

> E-Service

> Web Channel Analytics (formerly E-Analytics)

See OSS note 817119 for details regarding the Web channel naming conventions and changes.

To give you a practical understanding of the capabilities and benefits of the SAP CRM Web channel, throughout this chapter, we'll use an example of a B2C consumer named Alison Fisher who is shopping for a video game for her son's birthday from a fictitious company called Game Style. In each section of this chapter, we'll use this example to demonstrate how the different aspects of SAP CRM Web channels come into play during the customer's online experience.

E-Marketing

In some respects, doing business on the Internet is completely different from doing business in person or over the telephone. Obviously, in a well-automated Web experience, it's possible for a customer to order a product from your Web shop, pay online using a credit card, check the status of the order at each step of the process from pick and packing to final delivery, and return online to search for documentation or FAQs — all without ever talking to a person from your company.

Every sale begins with marketing

On the other hand, doing business on the Internet is no different from conducting business via any other channel; doing business on the Internet still requires companies to follow standard business processes of marketing, selling, providing service, and analyzing data. Whether doing business on the Web, in person at a retail location, or over the telephone via the interaction center, everything begins with marketing. To sell something, you typically first have to generate demand and inform potential customers about your products or services. After a customer or prospect is interested, you need to provide the customer with an organized catalog of products and services so he can find what he's looking for. To keep customers coming back to your site for repeat business rather than jumping ship to a lower-cost competitor, you need to provide the customer with a personalized, fun, value-added shopping experience.

E-Marketing allows companies to target customers and prospects with personalized, relevant offers. E-Marketing supports demand generation via targeted marketing campaigns, catalog management for organizing products, and personalized offers and recommendations.

Demand Generation

As mentioned, to sell things, you first have to inform prospective customers about the new product or promotion. Ideally, the offering should have some relevance to the prospective customer. This can be achieved through customer segmentation. For example, if a company wants to target customers via an email campaign for a new product, the company creates a target list of customers and prospects whose interests and marketing attributes are somehow related to the offered product. For example, using the video game company example, if the company was releasing a new game called *Samurai 3: Ganyru Island Duel*, it might target existing customers who had bought other games involving martial arts, combat, or Japan. However, the company might refrain from targeting customers who had maintained "family friendly" or "nonviolence" options in their online user profiles.

In a typical example, a customer who has been targeted as part of a marketing campaign might receive an email (or view a targeted message on a website after they have logged in) containing a campaign-specific promotion code, perhaps entitling the customer to a discounted price. When the customer clicks on the link in the email or Web page, the customer is sent to the Web shop where the appropriate product catalog and pricing are displayed (based on the campaign or promotion code). When the customer adds the product to the shopping basket and completes the sales order, the order will contain a reference to the campaign or promotion code, which can be used later to drive analytics.

Catalog Management

To purchase something, customers have to be able to locate what they are looking for in your Web shop. Catalog management gives customers the tools they need to find the products and information in which they are interested.

With catalog management, you can create multimedia product catalog hierarchies with detailed product information, image files, customer-specific pricing, and product availability information. You can maintain and publish multiple catalogs for different customer groups, regions, seasons, holidays, and so on. You can even include customer-specific catalog views, provide personalized product recommendations, and allow customers to do side-by-side comparisons of different products.

Create multimedia product catalog hierarchies

For example, if a customer was trying to decide between two video games — perhaps *Nascar Nextel Cup Points Champion 2007* and *Formula One Grand Prix World Champion 2008* — the customer could compare the two games side by side to see differences in product features, supported languages, and pricing.

Personalization

Customers are more likely to return to your website and do repeat business with you if you can provide them with personalization tools that add value and make their shopping experience easier and more enjoyable. This process is referred to as increasing the "stickiness" of your website, which means that customers will visit more often, stay longer with each visit, and hopefully buy more products and services.

Using information about the customer, including preferences and marketing attributes, the SAP CRM Web Channel allows companies to dynamically personalize the customer's Web experience. For example, product recommendations can be made based on customer analysis and customer segmentation, including personalized cross-sell and up-sell offers as well as recommendations of accessories and related or complementary products. In addition, customer-specific catalogs and customer-specific pricing is available. Using our example of the customer shopping for a video game for their child, you can imagine that the personalized product recommendations section of the company's website would probably show games geared toward a child rather than an adult. Additionally, the Web channel allows customers to find the nearest retail store location in case they want to buy something at a brick-and-mortar location rather than via the Web.

E-Commerce (Formerly E-Selling)

Driving traffic to your company's website is the hard part. Allowing customers to buy products and services after they are at your website should be the easy part. If it isn't easy for your customers to buy your products and services online, you're definitely doing something wrong, and they are probably not going to remain your customers for long. Studies have shown that customers who have trouble using your company's website are not only likely to stop using the website but are also likely to stop doing business with your company altogether.

E-Commerce helps a company model and run a complete end-to-end, order-to-cash sales process on the Internet. It includes support for interactive selling processes, such as configurable products and guided selling (on a project basis). E-Commerce also supports pricing and contact management, enabling companies to provide pricing tailored to each customer based on items, such as product, contracts, or quotes. Standard Web shop features such as shopping basket management are, of course, included as well. As of SAP CRM 2007, E-Commerce also supports selling via auctions.

E-Commerce helps your company with an end-to-end, order-to-cash process

 Note

Unlike most other SAP CRM component applications, E-Commerce does not use the SAP CRM WebClient user interface and Business Server Page (BSP) architecture. E-Commerce is delivered with Java Server Pages (JSP), and SAP NetWeaver Application Server (SAP NetWeaver AS), a component of SAP NetWeaver. E-Commerce is installed on a J2EE server.

Interactive Selling

A hundred years ago, buying a product was pretty simple and straightforward. Due to the advent of the assembly line, products became standardized — rather than made to order — and often available in only one model or color with few, if any options. As Henry Ford famously wrote in his autobiography, "customers could have a car painted any color as long as it was black."

Today, however, the trend has reversed, and products — including automobiles — are modular and configurable with more granular pricing. For example, when ordering a computer online, a customer can generally choose options such as memory size, CPU power, sound and video cards, monitor size, color, and so on. Although configurable products afford the consumer greater choice and flexibility, they also present a challenge in terms of pricing. Rather than having one set price for a product, pricing needs to dynamically be determined in real time based on a customer's selected product configuration. The E-Commerce component of SAP CRM Web Channel supports variant product configuration and variant pricing via the SAP Internet Pricing and Configurator (IPC).

Support for variant product configurations and pricing

E-Commerce also supports guided selling on a project basis by using a partner solution that allows companies to pose a series of questions to customers to determine which product (or product configuration) best suits the customer's needs. This prevents the customer from having to manually navigate through a large product catalog or fumble through difficult product configuration options.

So, now let's return to our example of Alison, the mother who is shopping for a video game for her son's birthday on the Game Style website (see Figure 7.2). Alison is overwhelmed by all of the different games available and doesn't know where to begin. However, by using a guided selling feature, she can answer a few simple questions, such as the age of her son, the type of video game hardware or console that he has (Sony PlayStation® III, Microsoft Xbox™ 360, Nintendo® Wii™, PC, etc.), and his interests (sports, fantasy, military, music, etc.).

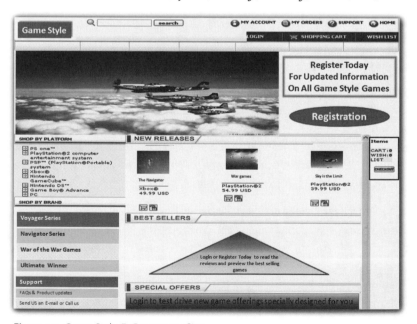

Figure 7.2 Game Style E-Commerce Site

If Alison indicated that her son was six years old and enjoyed music, the system might recommend *Guitar Hero III*. On the other hand, if Alison indicated that her son was 15 and enjoys fantasy games, the system might recommend a title from the *Voyager Series*.

SAP E-Commerce also provides standard shopping basket management tools. Following along with our example, Alison clicks on the *Voyager Series* to display all of the games that belong in this series. She is curious about the game *Challenging Voyager* for the Playstation 2 platform, so she clicks the link to the product title. This takes her to the product's detail page, which displays product information.

Standard shopping basket management tools

 Tip

The actual product details can come from either the SAP CRM system or the SAP ERP application, depending on where the product master data is maintained. (We'll talk about SAP CRM master data in Chapter 11.) See Figure 7.3.

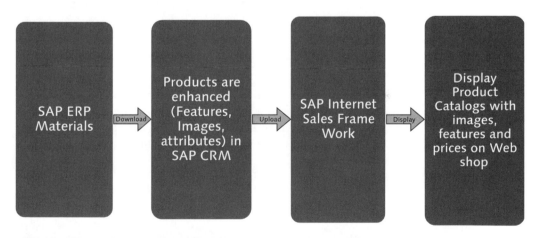

Figure 7.3 Integrated Product Master Data from Backend System to Web Shop

Alison decides to buy *Challenging Voyager*, and clicks Buy Now. The product is automatically added to her shopping basket. She can view the items in the shopping basket and optionally change the quantity, if desired. She could also move the item from the shopping basket to a wish list by selecting Add to Wish List, allowing her to decide to purchase the items later.

Pricing

E-Commerce supports both B2C and B2B scenarios. Pricing is generally relatively straightforward in B2C scenarios — at least when compared to B2B scenarios. In a B2C scenario, all customers generally pay the same price for a product. Certainly, you can have promotional discounts and perhaps even a "VIP" customer group who receive a discount (perhaps 5%) on all orders. However, you generally do not have customer-specific pricing or contract-based pricing like you do in B2B scenarios.

So far, we've only focused on the B2C scenario, using the example of Alison, the consumer who wants to buy a video game for her son from a company called Game Style. But, let's consider a B2B scenario for a moment where one company is buying products online from another company. Let's assume that our company, Game Style, wants to order a new video game title from a video game manufacturer. Game Style might log on to the manufacturer's website and create a request for quotation (RFQ) for 1,000 units of a new game. The manufacturer could then respond to the RFQ by generating a quotation with adjusted terms and pricing. Pricing could be determined, for example, based on a contract, customer group, product, or even customer-specific pricing.

 Tip

Internet Pricing and Configurator (IPC)

> Internet Pricing and Configurator (IPC) maintains the necessary pricing logic such as base price, discounts, and surcharges that are displayed on the order confirmation page. IPC supports variant product configuration and variant pricing. IPC is a separate component and is installed separately from SAP CRM.

Order to Cash

Now let's return to Alison. She's decided on the game *Challenging Voyager* and proceeds to the checkout. However, because she isn't already an existing customer, the system prompts her to create a new account by registering online. Alison enters all of her pertinent information, including billing address, telephone number, email address, and a personal password (Figure 7 4)

Real-time integration

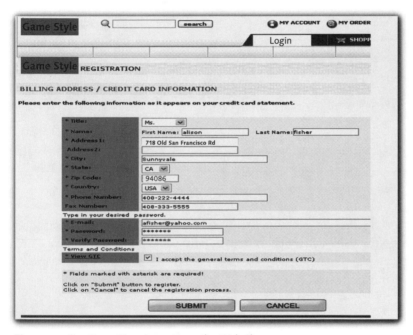

Figure 7.4 Creating a New Account on the Web Shop

At this point, a new customer record is created in the SAP CRM system in the background. Optionally, if an SAP ERP application were connected, the customer record would then upload to the backend SAP ERP application in real time (Figure 7.5).

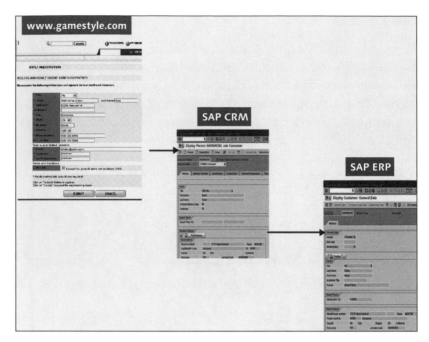

Figure 7.5 Integrated Account Management in SAP CRM Web Channel

After creating an account, an order confirmation page is displayed that shows the price of the item as well as any applicable taxes and shipping and handling cost (see Figure 7.6). As with all SAP CRM pricing, this information is provided by IPC.

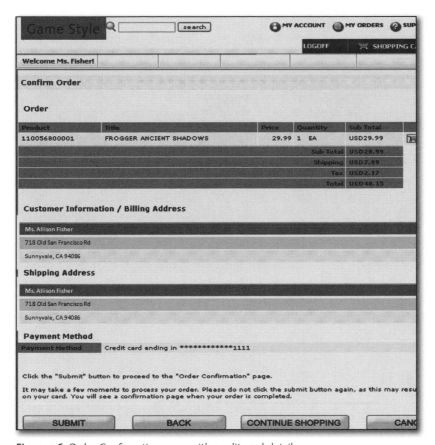

Figure 7.6 Order Confirmation page with credit card details

SAP CRM can be integrated with third-party credit-card clearing-houses, such as VeriSign or Paymetric. When Alison enters her credit card information and clicks the Submit button, the SAP CRM system sends an initial request to the clearinghouse with the total price and address information to validate Alison's credit limit and address. If the initial validation is successful, the SAP CRM system then sends the request to the clearinghouse to charge the card (see Figure 7.7).

Credit card verification

165

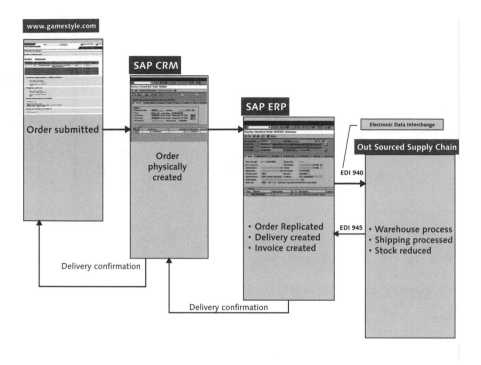

Figure 7.7 Payment process using Credit Card on Game Style Web Shop

➕ **Tip**

The SAP CRM system will display an error message such as "invalid credit card" if the credit card validation fails based on information received back from the third-party clearinghouse.

Integrated Order Management and Fulfillment

After the payment information is verified, the system displays a final confirmation screen. When Alison clicks the Confirm button, the order — that has already been created — is released into the backend SAP ERP application for processing and fulfillment. Game Style doesn't have the product in stock so the company needs to outsource the order to its supplier. Game Style uses SAP ERP procurement system electronically communicates with the supplier's computer system using standard transaction documents such as the EDI 940 shipment request form and the EDI 945 shipment confirmation form (see Figure 7.8).

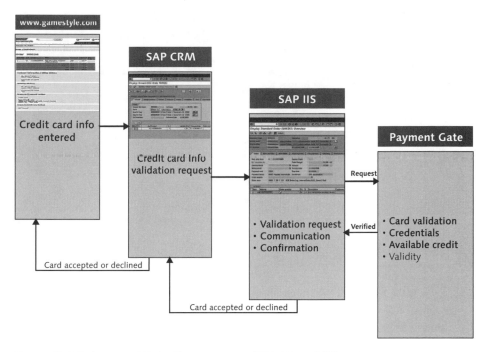

Figure 7.8 Fully Integrated Order Management and Third Party fulfillment

Alison can check the status of her order at any time by logging in to the company's website. The system provides a list of Alison's open and completed orders (Figure 7.9).

Order tracking

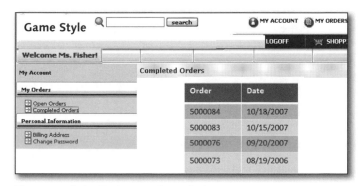

Figure 7.9 Order Tracking on the Web shop

All of the completed orders have a truck icon next to them indicating that they have already been shipped (Figure 7.10).

167

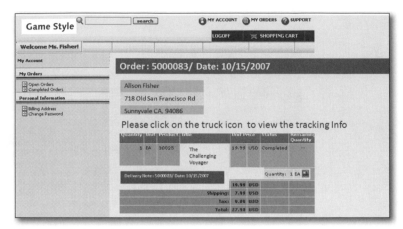

Figure 7.10 Delivery Tracking on the Web Shop

Alison can click on an individual order to view the delivery status. The shipping status of an order is stored in the SAP CRM system as part of the order via the "document flow," which is used across SAP software to display inter-linkages between business transactions and documents. If the E-Commerce application has been integrated with Web services from third-party shippers such as UPS, FedEx, DHL, or others, the system can pass the tracking number to the third-party website to pre-fill the tracking request (Figure 7.11).

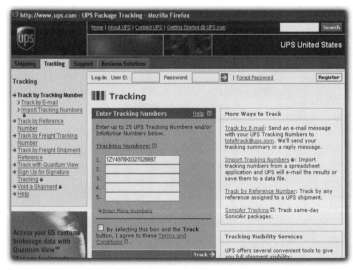

Figure 7.11 Launching UPS Tracking Info From SAP CRM Web Channel

The user can track the delivery status on the UPS website (Figure 7.12).

Figure 7.12 UPS Delivery Information Display Launched from SAP CRM Web Channel

After an order has shipped, the order-to-cash process wraps up with billing, accounting, and settlement with external financial institutions. For example, companies need to generate bills from invoices to collect payment. Similarly, credits and debits need to be entered correctly in the accounting ledgers for all transactions to keep the books balanced. Material movements have to be tracked and recorded. Finally, external financial institutions — such as merchant banks, clearinghouses, and card-issuing banks — all have to be paid when credit cards purchases are involved! However, all of this, including shipping, billing, accounting, and settlement, is handled via the backend SAP ERP application (Figure 7.13).

Billing and payment

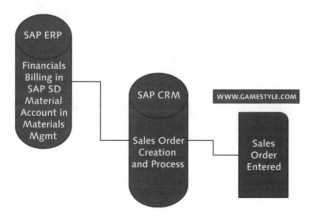

Figure 7.13 Material and Financials Accounting in SAP ERP

Web Auctions

As of SAP CRM 2007, the SAP Web channel also provides support for selling via Web auctions. Companies are increasingly turning to Web auctions as a way to get rid of surplus goods, excess inventory, and used assets online in a very time-sensitive manner. Web auctions are also becoming an increasingly popular way for companies to reach new audiences and to allow the market to determine an appropriate price. For example, many companies — such as Game Style — don't have large marketing budgets to spend on driving traffic to their websites. So, one alternative is for a company to sell products via auctions on eBay, and then try to bring the buyer over to the company's website to see additional products, check shipping rates, and so on. The E-Commerce functionality of SAP CRM Web channel supports both auctioning via eBay, as well as auctioning via the company's own Web shop.

Now that we've discussed E-Marketing and E-Commerce, let's turn our attention to E-Service.

E-Service

E-Service lets customers get service and answers quickly

The world is changing. Customers today aren't willing to wait for anything. They want answers, they want service, they want action — and they want it now! Customers are increasingly feeling empowered to search for information on the Internet rather than driving to the library to look for information or waiting on the telephone to speak with a so-called expert. Internet sites such as Google and Wikipedia have trained people to trust the Internet as a source of quick, reliable information.

People also like the fact that the Internet is open for business 24 hours a day, 7 days a week, every day of the year. Similarly, people now demand the same level of service and reliability from the companies they do business with. Customers expect that they can go to your company's website and find answers to common questions, search for solutions to problems, perform technical troubleshooting, request an installation or repair, check the status of any open service requests, view what products they have bought, file a complaint or a return, or locate the nearest retail store location.

Clearly, not every customer issue can be handled over the Web via Internet customer self-service. Some issues still require the trained service professional or call center agent. For example, problems that require detailed troubleshooting often require knowledgeable experts. Similarly, issues involving financial customer disputes, legal topics, or health matters may often still require a trained professional. Although the interaction center should still be a crucial part of any company's customer service strategy — especially for high-value customers or transactions of great monetary value — E-Service can supplement a company's service offerings by empowering customers to service themselves for easy-to-solve issues in a low-cost manner.

As we discussed, the SAP CRM Web Channel Enablement solution provides robust E-Service functionality, but it also provides knowledge management and service management capabilities. Customers can view answers to frequently asked questions and search for solutions to problems. They can request service — such as installation or maintenance of a product — and they can track open service requests through to completion. They can also create complaints and returns for problems with orders or deliveries. In addition, of course, customers can view their account balances and pay their bills online.

 Note

E-Service is also sometimes referred to as Internet Customer Self-Service (ICSS).

So let's look at knowledge management in a little more depth.

Knowledge Management

Visitors to a company's SAP CRM Web channel customer portal can find answers to frequently asked questions (FAQs) about products, either by doing a search by keyword or model number, or by browsing through a list of products. Returning to our example of the video game retailer, Game Style, customers might want to find out whether a particular game is available for their particular hardware console. Customers can also search for knowledge-based articles or solutions to technical problems. For example, if a user was having a problem with a game always freezing up at a particular point during the game, the user could do a search to see whether there was any known workaround solution. Additionally, the Web portal might also provide product fixes and downloads that the customer could access. But if not, the customer can take advantage of the service management functionality.

Service Management

Customer portals

Visitors to a company's SAP CRM Web channel customer portal can also request service and track the status of a service request through completion. Let's assume that Game Style not only sells video games but also rents out high-end gaming systems that come with free installation. A customer logs on to the Game Style Web portal and orders a system. A service request for installation is created on the customer's behalf. Similarly, a customer might log a service request for an existing system that needs to be repaired or upgraded. The customer can monitor the processing status of the service request online without having to call the interaction center every day to find out about the status. Customers can, of course, also report issues via other communication channels such as email, Web form, live text chat, click-to-talk, or Web callback — if these channels are supported. E-Service provides customer-facing email and chat integration; however, these channels must also be enabled in the interaction center via contact-center software such as SAP BCM or a third-party partner solution. See Figure 7.14 for an example of what a company's E-Service Web portal might look like.

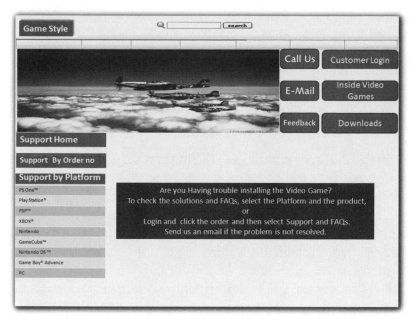

Figure 7.14 E-Service at Game Style

Now that we've discussed E-Service, let's look at the final functionality — Web Channel Analytics.

Web Channel Analytics

After you get your website up and running, you need to make sure that it keeps running. You need to know if any customers are visiting your Web shop and whether they are buying anything. You also need to know which products are selling best and which FAQs and solutions are being looked at or downloaded most often. SAP CRM Web channel provides out-of-the-box Web Channel Analytics, including sales analyses, technical analyses, and customer behavior analyses. Sales analyses indicate what your top 10 products are, who your top 10 customers are, and the percentage of quotations that are converted to sales orders and the total number of sales orders. Technical analyses show how many hits your website is getting and who your top referrers are. Customer behavior shows the number of viewed products,

Out-of-the-box Web Channel Analytics

number of ordered products, and the percentage of visitors who place orders. Using Web Channel Analytics, you can make sure that your customer Web portal or Web shop are functioning as intended, and you can make minor tweaks or major modifications as necessary.

Conclusion

Today, no one questions the role the Internet plays in business. Customers not only feel comfortable using the Web for business purposes, but they actually demand that companies provide Web access to most business functions. Yes, of course, there is still a need for call centers (or interaction centers) to provide high-touch personal service for important customers and high-value business transactions and to handle issues that require human involvement such as financial disputes as well as legal, regulatory, or medical issues. However, the Web channel should definitely also be a part of almost any company's business strategy. Today's empowered customers — let's call them *2.0 customers* — want tools to satisfy their own business needs, and they want 24/7 Web-based access. This fits well with the needs of businesses that want to keep both service costs and costs of sale as low as possible.

In this chapter, you learned about the capabilities of the SAP CRM Web Channel Enablement solution (Web channel for short), including E-Marketing, E-Commerce (formerly E-Selling), E-Service, and Web Channel Analytics (formerly E-Analytics). Throughout the chapter, we used an example of a customer conducting business with a video game retailer to illustrate the capabilities of the SAP CRM Web Channel Enablement solution. The most important things to remember about the Web channel are the following:

> The SAP CRM Web Channel Enablement solution was renamed from E-Commerce to better reflect the actual capabilities of the solution. (See OSS note 817119 for details.)

> E-Marketing allows you to send targeted email offers to customers or prospects as part of a promotion or campaign. The email can contain a direct link to your Web shop with an embedded promo-

tion code, or the customer can enter the promotion code manually to access special product catalogs and promotional pricing.

> The E-Commerce functionality of SAP CRM Web channel is unique from most of the rest of SAP CRM in that it has its own underlying technology based on JSP and runs on a J2EE server.

> As of SAP CRM 2007, SAP provides support for Web auctions — either selling via eBay or embedding auctions inside a Web shop — as part of SAP CRM Web channel's E-Commerce functionality.

In the next chapter, we'll look at Mobile CRM, including Mobile Sales and Mobile Service, which allows companies to support employees in the field via laptop, tablet PC, Smartphone, BlackBerry, PDA, and other mobile devices.

8

SAP CRM Mobile Applications

You might be wondering why mobile applications are even necessary: can't employees just connect to the SAP CRM system via the Internet from airports, hotels, homes, customer sites, or local coffee shops? Employees can always access SAP CRM applications over the Internet via their laptops when working outside of the office — whether working at home or from the road. However, some employees need to access SAP applications in an *offline mode* in places where even wireless Internet access is often still not always available, such as while sitting in a car or delivery truck in a customer parking lot, in factory shop floors, warehouses, farms, paper mills, lumber yards, and so on.

Additionally, some types of employees — such as service technicians — can't carry around laptops or tablet PCs and need to access SAP CRM applications and customer data from smaller, pocket-sized handheld devices, such as PDAs and smartphones. Some employees even require real-time, online access to SAP CRM data from their handheld devices.

Give your field sales people and service reps mobile SAP access

SAP CRM Mobile applications allow your field sales people and field service technicians to access SAP applications and customer data from

177

a variety of devices, including laptops and tablet PCs as well as smart-phones and PDAs, such as the BlackBerry. SAP CRM Mobile Sales is available in three options:

> Connected (offline) mode for laptop or tablet PC

> Connected (offline) mode for handheld devices such as PDAs and smartphones

> A real-time online version for select laptops and handheld devices such as the BlackBerry

SAP CRM Mobile Service is primarily only available via an occasion-ally connected (offline) mode for laptops and tablet PCs; an occasion-ally connected (offline) version for handheld devices is available with SAP CRM release 4.0, but this offering isn't available or supported with later SAP CRM releases.

All of the SAP CRM Mobile options allow field sales professionals and service technicians to access mission-critical customer informa-tion. Sales people can check the sales pipeline and forecasts from the airport, hotel, or customer site. Field service technicians can view appointments and schedules, check availability of service parts, and perform technical analysis and troubleshooting from an offline mo-bile device in the field — whether sitting in their van or in a crawl space of a customer building.

 Note

SAP CRM provides both a Mobile Sales and Mobile Service offering, including the following options:

> Mobile Sales Laptop (MSA LPT)

> Mobile Sales Handheld (MSA HH)

> Mobile Sales Online (MSOn)

> Mobile Service Laptop (MSE LPT)

> Mobile Service Handheld (MSE HH) — only available with release SAP CRM 4.0

Introduction to SAP CRM Mobile Technology

SAP offers various other mobile solutions outside of SAP CRM, as shown in Figure 8.1, including mobile asset management, direct store delivery, mobile procurement, mobile warehouse management, mobile Business Intelligence (BI), and mobile time and travel. These other mobile applications fall under the SAP NetWeaver product umbrella but are not part of SAP CRM. In this book, we'll only focus on those mobile applications that are part of SAP CRM.

Figure 8.1 SAP Mobile Applications

Note

> SAP provides various mobile applications under the SAP NetWeaver umbrella. Mobile Sales and Mobile Service are the only two SAP mobile applications available in SAP CRM. The following is the full list of SAP mobile applications:
>
> › SAP Mobile Sales (CRM)
>
> › SAP Mobile Service (CRM)
>
> › SAP Mobile Sales (ERP)
>
> › SAP Direct Store Delivery (ERP)
>
> › SAP Mobile Time and Travel (ERP)
>
> › SAP Mobile Warehouse Management (SCM)
>
> › SAP Mobile Procurement (SRM)
>
> › A full set of solutions from asset to warehouse management and time and travel
>
> › SAP Mobile BI (NetWeaver)

Develop your own mobile apps with Mobile Application Studio

The SAP CRM Mobile Sales Laptop solution and the SAP CRM Mobile Service Laptop solution were designed and developed using an SAP CRM tool called Mobile Application Studio (MAS), which customers can also use to develop their own custom SAP CRM mobile software applications or to make changes to the user interface of existing mobile applications.

When a mobile application is installed on a device such as a laptop or tablet PC, it's referred to as a *mobile client*. A mobile client has its own local database that is used to store data when the machine is running in the disconnected, offline mode until the user can connect to the company network and trigger an automatic bidirectional synchronization of data between mobile devices and the enterprise data using SAP CRM middleware. It's important to note that mobile applications designed with MAS — such as Mobile Sales or Mobile Service — use Microsoft .NET technology and can only run on laptops or tablet PCs using a Microsoft Windows 32-bit operating system. See Figure 8.2 for an overview of the landscape for mobile clients (i.e., laptops or tablet PCs.)

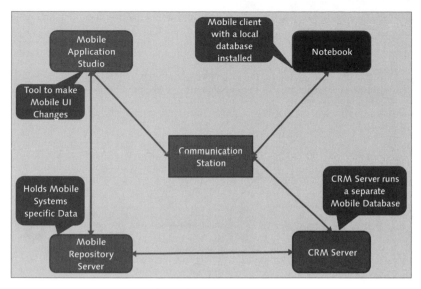

Figure 8.2 System Landscape for Mobile Clients

You can also run offline mobile applications — such as the Mobile Sales Handheld solution — on handheld devices such as PDAs and smartphones using SAP NetWeaver Mobile Infrastructure (MI), which will be discussed in more detail in Chapter 10. See Figure 8.3 for an overview of the landscape for offline mobile devices.

Run mobile apps offline on handheld devices

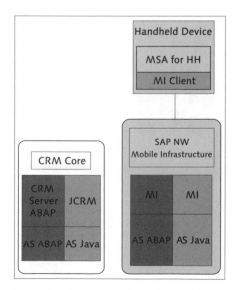

Figure 8.3 System Landscape for Mobile Handheld Devices

You can also run certain mobile applications online in real time. For example, the Mobile Sales Online solution allows you to access real-time SAP CRM sales data from select laptop and handheld devices, including the BlackBerry. See Figure 8.4 for an overview of how SAP CRM Mobile Sales Online works with BlackBerry devices.

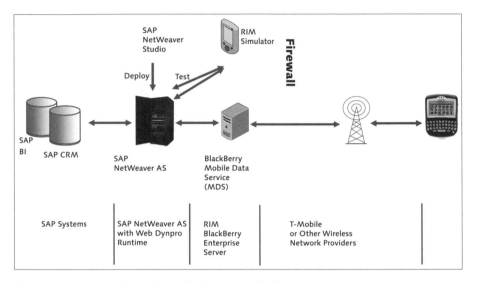

Figure 8.4 System Landscape for a BlackBerry Handheld Device

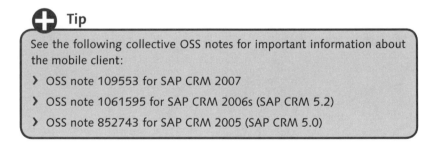

Tip

See the following collective OSS notes for important information about the mobile client:

> OSS note 109553 for SAP CRM 2007

> OSS note 1061595 for SAP CRM 2006s (SAP CRM 5.2)

> OSS note 852743 for SAP CRM 2005 (SAP CRM 5.0)

SAP CRM Mobile Sales

As mentioned, SAP CRM Mobile Sales can be run — either offline or online — on a variety of devices, including notebooks, tablet PCs, PDAs, and smartphones. Clearly, larger full-size devices such as laptops and tablet PCs offer larger screen real estate and greater depth of functionality; however, smaller, pocket-sized handheld devices can often be more convenient even though they provide less functionality. Let's take a look at the three options for running SAP CRM Mobile Sales: Mobile Sales Laptop, Mobile Sales Handheld, and Mobile Sales Online.

Mobile Sales Laptop

The SAP CRM Mobile Sales Laptop solution, also known as MSA LPT (and formerly known as xMSA LPT), provides a full-feature, offline SAP CRM Sales solution for notebooks or tablet PCs that are only occasionally connected to a network (see Figure 8.5.) The Mobile Sales Laptop solution provides the most comprehensive functionality of all three SAP CRM Mobile Sales options. Of course, it includes standard SAP CRM Sales functionality such as contact management and activity management.

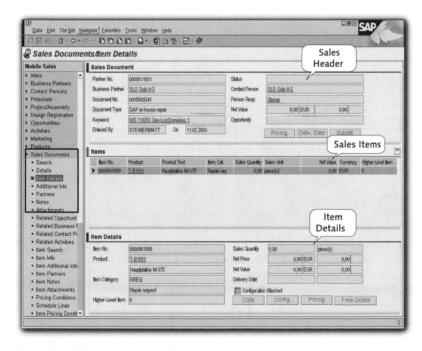

Figure 8.5 A Sales Document in the Mobile Sales Application

Monitor marketing retail efforts and perform shelf management

Contact management gives sales people a 360-degree view of customer details, order history, and other critical information. Activity management allows sales managers and sales people to allocate the right sales resources to help close deals as quickly as possible. A sophisticated visit planning tool is also provided that can help optimize customer sales calls by deciding in which order customers should be visited, along with a schedule of appointment times and durations; last-mile route optimization is available from third-party partners such as ServicePower, ClickSoftware, and others.

As you would expect from any sales solution, Mobile Sales Laptop also supports opportunity management as well as quotations and sales order management. Sales people can pull up current opportunities and view the most current information and status, including history, milestones, buying center, and progress. Mobile Sales Laptop also supports the complete sales order process:

> Check product availability

> Create proposals

> Perform pricing and credit checks

> Enter orders

> Manage contracts

Additionally, Mobile Sales Laptop provides advanced functionality such as field campaign management, field trade promotion management, and field territory management functionalities.

Ex Example

A company can include its mobile sales force in the same marketing campaigns as its direct sales force or interaction center sales agents.

Another functionality is Trade Promotion Management (TPM), which enables consumer product goods (CPG) companies to monitor retail performance of marketing efforts to ensure that promotions are achieving the desired goals; shelf management is also supported for retail accounts, allowing mobile sales people to perform compliance checks to ensure that the agreed-upon shelf plan with the retailer is being fulfilled. Finally, field territory management allows companies to include their mobile sales forces in organizational planning.

 Note

> The Mobile Client Companion to the SAP CRM Mobile Laptop solution allows sales people to synchronize data with a PDA for situations in which the laptop isn't practical. Although this solution was designed for the pharmaceutical industry to allow sales people to maintain data on drug samples, customers from other industries have adopted this solution as well, including high tech and consumer products industries.

The Mobile Sales Laptop solution offers the greatest depth and breadth of SAP CRM Sales functionality out of the three Mobile Sales options:

> Account management
> Account planning
> Activity management
> Calendar and task management
> Product search and display
> Opportunity management
> Contract management
> Sales order management
> Service order management
> Complaint management
> Campaign and trade promotion management
> Shelf management
> Visit planning and route optimization
> Territory management
> Time and travel management
> Sales analytics

Note

The SAP CRM Mobile Sales Laptop solution uses Microsoft .NET technology and Microsoft SQL Server, which can only run on laptops or tablet PCs using a Microsoft Windows 32-bit operating system.

Mobile Sales Handheld

The SAP CRM Mobile Sales Handheld solution, also known as MSA HH (and formerly known as xMSA HH), uses SAP NetWeaver Mobile Infrastructure (MI) and an IBM DB2e database installed on the mobile device. This provides field sales people with an offline tool they can use to quickly access and share business information on the fly using a PDA or smartphone. Unlike the Mobile Client Companion tool discussed as part of Mobile Sales Laptop, which is synchronized directly against a laptop and only runs on PDA devices, the Mobile Sales Handheld solution synchronizes with the SAP CRM central server when online and runs on a variety of handheld devices. Because Mobile Sales Handheld runs on SAP NetWeaver MI, it supports any handheld device that is compatible with NetWeaver MI, including most Microsoft Windows mobile devices.

 Note

Mobile Sales Handheld supports the following handheld devices:

> PDAs running Intel Strong Arm or xScale processors with a minimum of 64MB RAM

> PDAs running Microsoft Windows Pocket PC 2002 or Pocket PC 2003 OS

> PDAs, smartphones, and other devices running Microsoft Windows Mobile 5.0

Microsoft Windows Mobile 5.0 Phone Edition isn't supported, nor is Microsoft Windows 6.0.

Mobile Sales Handheld provides the necessary tools to retrieve customer account information, access product and pricing information, manage customer visits and calls, manage opportunities, and create quotations and orders. For example, see Figure 8.6 to get a feel for the user interface for the Mobile Sales handheld device using a sample process of a sales person searching for and updating customer account data.

Figure 8.6 Mobile Sales Handheld User Interface on a Handheld Device

Keep in mind, however, that due to the limited screen real estate, memory, and processing power, handheld devices support relatively light sales applications and do not offer the data processing functionalities of a laptop or tablet PC solution. See Figure 8.7 to get a feel for the simplified interface available on a handheld device using the Activity Menu as an example.

Figure 8.7 Activity Menu on a Mobile Sales Handheld Device

Get a 360-degree view of customers

With SAP CRM Mobile Sales for handheld devices, you can perform basic sales-related tasks, note, however, that there is no support for contract management or analytics.

> Account management
> Activity management
> Calendar and task management
> Product search and display
> Opportunity management
> Sales order management
> Service order management
> Complaint management
> Search for, display, and retrieve customer data
> Search for and display products from a product catalog

188

> **Note**
>
> Mobile Sales Handheld uses NetWeaver MI. We'll discuss NetWeaver technology, including NetWeaver MI, in more detail in Chapter 10.

Let's also look at the sales order creation details screen on a handheld device. Notice, in Figure 8.8, that although the user interface is obviously economized, the most important fields are all available, including the sales order transaction type.

Create sales orders on handheld devices

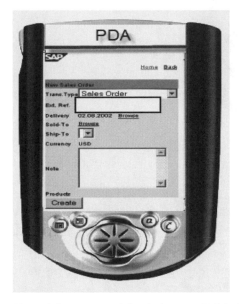

Figure 8.8 Creating a Sales Order on a Mobile Sales Handheld Device

Mobile Sales Online

The SAP CRM Mobile Sales Online solution, also known as MSOn (and previously referred to as xMSA Online), provides sales people with direct, real-time online access to SAP CRM functionality via smartphones such as RIM BlackBerry, Microsoft Pocket PC, Nokia Series 80, and Siemens SK65 (with built-in BlackBerry). In Figure 8.9, we see, that it's also possible to use smartphone devices — such as a BlackBerry — to access Mobile Sales Online handheld functionality.

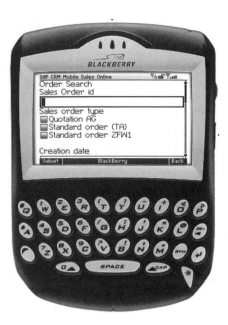

Figure 8.9 Sales Order Search on a BlackBerry Smartphone Device

 Note

For an up-to-date list of devices supported by SAP CRM Mobile Sales Online, please see OSS note 882945.

With SAP CRM Mobile Sales Online, you are able to perform basic sales-related tasks such as the following:

> Account management

> Activity management

> Opportunity management (header data only)

> Contract management (header data only)

> Sales order management (header data only)

> Analytics

SAP CRM Mobile Service

Many problems arise when field service technicians and engineers don't have immediate access to the SAP CRM system from the field. For example, instead of being able to immediately record the time and costs spent on an issue, engineers have to write it down and remember to enter it into the SAP CRM system later when they are back in the office. This obviously increases the likelihood of omissions, errors, and incomplete entries. Additionally, if service technicians don't have access to the SAP CRM system from the field, delivery of spare parts is delayed because the technician must wait until he is back in the office to place the order. Similarly, invoicing, collecting accounts receivables, and handling financial accounting can all be delayed as well. Even the most basic tasks, such as re-scheduling a repair or updating an appointment in the calendar, aren't possible without access to the SAP CRM system.

While there are several options for running SAP CRM Mobile Sales, the options for Mobile Service are more limited. Although a Mobile Service Handheld solution was offered in SAP CRM 4.0, the solution did not contain an online support option and was discontinued with later releases. SAP indicates that there are plans to reintroduce an SAP CRM Service Handheld solution; however, the solution is still not available with newer SAP CRM releases, up to and including SAP CRM 2007. Therefore, there is primarily only one option for running Mobile Service: the Mobile Service Laptop solution for laptops and tablet PCs.

Service management on the Mobile Service Laptop solution

Mobile Service Laptops

The Mobile Service Laptop solution, also known as MSE LPT (and formerly known as xMSE LPT), provides service reps and technicians with all of the information and tools they need to resolve a customer's onsite service issues and accurately record their work in the field using an offline laptop or tablet PC. Technicians can view a structured overview of all of the equipment and products installed at the customer site, which is referred to as installed base management. Technicians have access to their calendar and inbox to view appointments, emails, and pending work orders. They can search for product documentation, installation/repair guides, or technical procedures via the knowledge management tool. And, of course, they can pull up service contracts and service orders (see Figure 8.10). The service representative can perform all of these tasks directly while at the customer site via a laptop computer.

Figure 8.10 Service Order Management in Mobile Service

Sometimes, however, it isn't possible — or practical — to carry a laptop. In SAP CRM release 4.0, service reps can also access Mobile Service via a handheld device, as discussed in the next section. However, as mentioned, this solution isn't available in SAP CRM releases after 4.0.

 Note

Mobile Service can only run on laptops or tablet PCs using a Microsoft Windows 32-bit operating system.

Mobile Service Handheld (for SAP CRM 4.0)

It's often difficult for service technicians to lug around all of their tools and equipment plus a laptop computer when providing onsite support. The Mobile Service Handheld solution — available in SAP CRM release 4.0 but discontinued in subsequent releases — can be run on several handheld devices, making a service technician's life much easier. Using handheld devices, such as PDAs, service technicians can access the information they need to handle repairs and installations and accurately record their working time and costs. As with the laptop version of Mobile Service, technicians using handheld Mobile Service can also view customer data and installed base product information, manage service contracts, and view or update service orders. Service reps can also record their working time and costs, update their availability in the calendar, and record any breaks or absences. When a technician makes a change to the service order on the handheld device, it updates the main SAP CRM server (Figure 8.11).

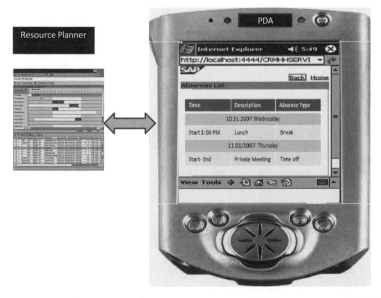

Figure 8.11 Synchronization of Service Technician Availability Between Handheld Device and the SAP CRM Central Server

Note

> SAP introduced the Mobile Service Handheld solution in SAP CRM 4.0 but discontinued it with later releases. SAP indicates that there are plans to reintroduce a SAP CRM Service Handheld solution again in the future.

With SAP CRM Mobile Service Handheld, you can perform basic service-related tasks such as the following:

> Search for, display, and update customer data

> Search for and display products from a product catalog

> Display and create service orders

> Access service confirmation

> Create complaints

> Compose emails

> Manage personal tasks and calendar

> Access the resource planning functionality

So there you have an overview of the mobile application of SAP CRM. Now let's take a look at a case study to see how it can resolve service issues for a medical instrument company.

Case Study

The company in this case study is the leading provider of medical diagnostic instruments for state-of-the-art patient-monitoring systems. The company employs 2,300 people and had a global presence with sales of $227 million in 2007.

The following are the business challenges for this company:

> Empowering the service technicians with up-to-date customer information, product orders, and service orders while away from the office

> Providing service technicians offline access to service applications to provide efficient service at hospitals and physician offices

The business objective for this company is to implement a solution that allows the field service technicians to stay tuned to the service request alerts and have access to the data to provide optimum customer service while away from the office.

To meet this objective, the company must face the technical challenge of creating an integrated service solution that seamlessly integrates with backend financial and logistics systems, the central customer relationship management system, and the mobile service application. The solution deployment will require SAP CRM Enterprise Sales, Enterprise Service, Mobile Service, SAP BW, and SAP R/3.

When the solution was deployed, the following values were achieved:

> Service technicians were empowered with Mobile Service applications on their laptops.

> Field service technicians were able to synchronize the Mobile Service application on their laptops with the main SAP CRM server at the beginning of the workday. They could then plan the workday per the assigned service requests and use the visit planning tool to optimize field visits.

> Field service technicians could update the service orders, including ordering spare parts from the customer location, by using the Mobile Service application.

 Tip

If you choose to implement SAP CRM Mobile applications, such as Mobile Sales or Mobile Service, you'll incur additional implementation effort, increased system complexity, and higher maintenance costs. So you should primarily consider mobile solutions only when offline access to sales and service applications is absolutely mandatory to conduct business efficiently. One company that underwent a costly offline Mobile Sales implementation because its sales force "absolutely had to have it," later discovered that 90% of the time, the sales people were connected to the company VPN (virtual private network) via wireless access at airports, hotels, or local coffee houses. In this case, the company spent a great deal of money and effort to implement an offline Mobile Sales solution that it probably could have done without.

Conclusion

This wraps up our coverage of SAP CRM Mobile applications. As you've learned in this chapter, SAP CRM provides mobile solutions for all types of business needs. SAP CRM Mobile Sales runs on laptops and tablet PCs as well as handheld devices, including the BlackBerry. In addition, Mobile Sales can be accessed in either an occasionally connected (offline) mode or via a real-time, online mode. Several flavors of Mobile Sales are available, including Mobile Sales Laptop, Mobile Sales Handheld, and Mobile Sales Online. SAP CRM Service also offers an occasionally connected (offline) mode for laptops and tablet PCs. SAP CRM Mobile applications provide a great way to conduct business when access to the main SAP CRM server is limited or when there is no connectivity.

The key things to remember from this chapter are the following:

> SAP CRM provides two sets of mobile applications: SAP CRM Mobile Sales and SAP CRM Mobile Service. In addition, various other mobile applications are available from SAP outside of SAP CRM as part of SAP NetWeaver, including mobile asset management, direct store delivery, mobile procurement, mobile warehouse management, mobile Business Intelligence (BI), and mobile time and travel.

> SAP CRM Mobile Sales can be run on either a laptop or tablet PC, or on a variety of handheld devices. SAP CRM Mobile Service can also be run on either a laptop or tablet PC.

> Mobile applications reduce paperwork and prevent information from being delayed, misplaced, or lost. If your company has field sales people or service technicians who spend most of their time in places without wireless Internet access, you should consider mobile applications.

> When field sales people and service technicians aren't able to connect directly to the SAP CRM system to access real-time data, they can access stored (but relatively up-to-date) information via mobile solutions.

> Before implementing Mobile Sales or Mobile Service, carefully consider whether a mobile solution is required. With increased availability of real-time SAP CRM access — via the pervasiveness of wireless Internet hotspots, increased support of wireless broadband technologies such as Wi-Fi and WiMax, as well as the increased availability of Web Services for cell phones — some companies find that they no longer actually require a mobile solution.

In the next chapter, we'll discuss SAP CRM Partner Channel Management.

SAP CRM Partner Channel Management

In earlier chapters of this book, you learned about the key components of SAP CRM: Marketing, Sales, Service, and Analytics. We also discussed the different business channels that allow your employees to interact with customers, including the interaction center, Web channel, and SAP CRM Mobile. In this chapter, we'll turn our attention to partner channel management.

Not all companies sell directly to their customers. Even companies that do sell directly to some of their customers, often also use channel intermediaries to reach some portion of their customers. *Channel partners* are the distributors, agents, dealers, value-added resellers, wholesalers, and retailers that bridge the gap between you and your customers. A 2006 study by AMR Research indicated that 70% of companies earn the majority of their revenue through channel intermediaries. The tricky thing about channel partners, however, is that they are neither employees nor customers, but a hybrid. For example, even though they sell your products, they are not on your payroll, so they're not exactly employees.

And although they contact you for product details, pricing information, and support questions, they're not the actual end users or customers of your products. Nonetheless, you need to provide channel partners with the same high-quality service as customers, while also giving them access to the same marketing, sales, and service tools your employees use.

Why Use Channel Partners?

Companies use channel partners for a number of reasons. One of the main reasons is that using channel partners allows a brand owner to reach more customers and prospects, including customers that the brand owner might not be able to reach on its own. For example, an automobile manufacturer would likely struggle if it tried to sell cars directly to consumers over the Internet, so instead, the manufacturer partners with local dealers that have established relationships in their local communities. Brand owners also often use channel partners when they want to enter new markets or new business segments. For example, a large SAP ERP software vendor that wants to make a push into the small and midsize business (SMB) market might choose to partner with existing vendors and system integrators, rather than trying to retrain and reorganize its own sales force. Finally, brand owners often discover that channel partners can result in lower cost of sales and increased revenue, despite the lower profit margins. For example, most brand owners of consumer electronics sell their products through big retailers such as Best Buy™, Circuit City®, Frye's Electronics®, and Wal-Mart®.

Managing your channel partners is key to successful customer relationships

Although most companies rely heavily on channel partners to market, sell, and service their products, many companies do a poor job of managing their channel partner relationships. When customers buy your products from channel partners, such as resellers or dealers, the customer's impression of your company is based solely on the customer's interaction with your channel partner. Not only don't you have control over these interactions, but also, in many cases, you might not even be aware that the customer has purchased your product unless the customer later contacts you for service. Because of the

200

very important role that channel partners play in influencing how customers perceive your company, you need to engage your channel partners very closely. You want your channel partners to provide the same quality of service that your company provides, so that your customers have the same buying experience as if they came directly to you.

SAP recognizes the importance of being able to properly manage your channel partner relationships and offers an innovative channel management application available since SAP CRM 4.0. This application has been continually strengthened and enhanced in new releases. Let's look at what it offers today.

 Note

Channel intermediaries are not just for SMBs that can't afford their own sales forces. Global leaders in industries such as insurance, financial services, automotive, and high tech also use channel partners. By 2010, 65% of the revenue of Global 2000 companies such as Citigroup™, General Electric™, and Toyota Motor™ will be driven by partner networks.

Channel Management and SAP

SAP first recognized the need to provide channel management functionalities even before SAP CRM was available, beginning with the first releases of SAP's ERP products R/2 and R/3. The SAP ERP Sales and Distribution (SD) component provided reporting capabilities, allowing companies to see which of the company's distribution channels, including channel partners, were generating the most sales. Companies wanted to extend access of these reports to their channel partners but were only partially successful because an out-of-the-box solution was not available at the time. To address this issue, SAP developed the SAP CRM partner channel management component, which is a robust solution that greatly strengthens the channel management functionality of SAP. In this chapter, we'll review the SAP CRM partner channel management solution map to see what it offers and explore how it can benefit your company.

The solution map in Figure 9.1 shows, in detail, the components that are available to help you manage your partner relationships.

Partner Management	Partner Recruitment	Partner Training & Certification	Partner Networking	Partner Compensation	Partner Planning & Forecasting	Partner Lifecycle Management
Channel Marketing	Content Management	Catalog Management	Campaign Management	Lead Management	Channel Marketing Funds	Partner Locator
Channel Sales	Accounts & Contacts	Opportunity Management	Pricing & Contracts	Interactive Selling & Configuration	Quotation & Order Management	POS & Channel Inventory Tracking
Channel Service	Knowledge Management	Service Order Management	Live Support	Complaints & Returns	Installed Base	Warranty Management
Channel Commerce	Collaborative Showroom	Distributed Catalog & Content Management		Distributed Order & Inventory Management		Hosted Partner Sites

Figure 9.1 Channel Management Solution Map

As you can see in the solution map, partner channel management is divided into various areas:

> **Partner management**
> Helps you find and train partners, and enables you to build and manage partner relationships.

> **Channel marketing**
> Helps you engage your partner's strengths to gain better market penetration through joint collaborations.

> **Channel sales**
> Allows you to make the right sales tools available to your partners so they can manage sales to the end customers effectively.

> **Channel service**
> Helps brand owners educate their partners about the brand owners' products to get the partners quickly up to speed so they can provide customers with the right level of service.

> **Channel commerce (also known as partner order management)**
> Allows brand owners to take advantage of SAP CRM Sales tools such as hosted websites, collaborative Web shops, and distributed order management. In addition, partner and channel analytics are available to help brand owners better understand how their channel activities are affecting operations in terms of inventory turns, pricing, and sales revenue.

Let's take a more detailed look at each of these, beginning with partner management.

Partner Management

Due to the critical role that your channel partners play in interacting with your customers, you don't want to allow just anyone to become a partner. SAP CRM partner channel management provides partner lifecycle management tools to manage recruiting, registering, profiling, and segmenting channel partners. In addition, you want to make sure that your partners stay current and up to date on your latest offerings and have the necessary knowledge and skills to sell your products and implement your solutions. Partner channel management also provides tools to enable online management of training and certifications to track partner competencies. Sometimes, your partners may need to collaborate with other complementary partners. Partner channel management provides tools to help complementary partners find each other and share information. And, of course, you also need tools to plan and forecast channel partner sales and to design and administer partner compensation plans. SAP CRM partner channel management also provides these tools.

Partner Recruitment

SAP CRM partner channel management provides tools for locating and recruiting potential channel partners. One option is to use SAP NetWeaver BI to analyze your existing database of B2B customers to find customers that might be a good fit as channel partners. Another option is to import and analyze external customer lists using SAP's external list management (ELM) functionalities to find good potential channel partners. You can also use the SAP marketing campaign management feature to solicit potential partners, or you can advertise on your corporate website.

Recruit partners effectively

After you've attracted interested potential partners, the partner recruitment functionalities of partner channel management allow interested prospective partners to fill out an online application on your company's corporate website using a Web form that you can customize. After the prospective partner fills out the Web form, providing data such as company name, address information, contact person name, company profile, and so on. The request is then forwarded via automated email workflow to the responsible channel manager at your company. The channel manager can then either approve or reject the application. In either case, the prospective partner is then informed via email about the outcome of the decision. See Figures 9.2 and 9.3 to see what a channel partner application could look like, in this case using SAP's own partner application website as an example.

 Note

The channel manager is the person from a brand owner's company who is responsible for overseeing all partner-related activities. The channel manager is typically responsible for activities such as recruiting and approving new channel partners, routing leads and opportunities to the right partner, setting up campaigns for channel partners, and so on.

Figure 9.2 SAP's Partner Website

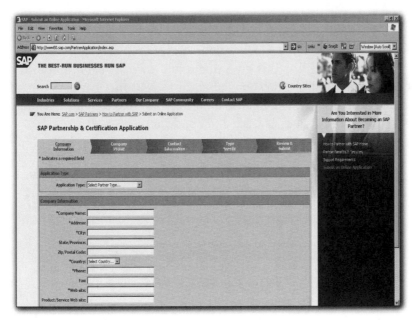

Figure 9.3 Online Partnership Application on the SAP Website

Partner Profiling and Segmentation

SAP CRM partner channel management also provides tools that give the brand owner a 360-degree overview of each channel partner, allowing the brand owner to classify channel partners based on who they are, what they sell, to whom they sell, and on which industries they focus. This allows the brand owner to profile partners and monitor their activities. Brand owners can dispatch sales leads and opportunities to the best-suited channel partner based on factors such as geographic region, industry, size, and sales conversion success rates.

Partner Training and Certification

After a prospective channel partner has been approved by the channel manager of the brand, the partner is given access to a partner portal that provides access to all of the tools and functionality the partner needs to do business on behalf of the brand owner's company. Through the partner portal, channel partners can access training courses and online evaluations. For example, a brand owner may require that all partners obtain certification for a product before being allowed to sell the product. Additionally, partners can maintain and update their skills and qualifications using a self-service solution as shown in Figure 9.4. This gives the brand owner visibility into the certifications and qualifications of all of the channel partners. Brand owners can also use this information to determine to which channel partners to dispatch sales leads and opportunities.

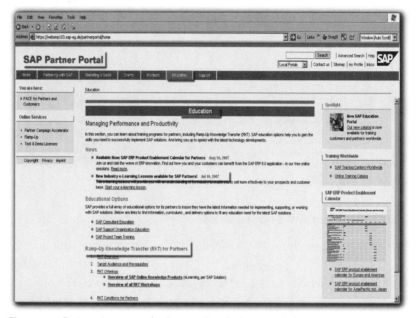

Figure 9.4 Partner Access to the Partner Portal eLearning Solution

 Note

Companies can give their channel partners access to everything the channel partner needs to properly sell to and interact with end customers through a partner portal. Through the partner portal, the brand owner provides channel partners with access to sales tools, business transactions, product information, technical documentation, self-service functionalities, and powerful analytics — everything the channel partner needs to successfully do business with customers on behalf of the brand owner.

Note

> You can use the SAP eLearning solution to make online training classes available to channel partners via the partner portal. However, this requires additional licensing and implementation of the SAP Learning Solution.

Partner Networking

Sometimes, a channel partner isn't able to close a deal on its own and needs to work with a complementary partner or initiate a joint sales engagement with the brand owner. SAP CRM partner channel management provides a set of online collaboration tools for joint marketing and sales efforts by complementary partners, as well as by brand owners and partners (see Figure 9.5). Partners can leverage a tool called the SAP Partner directory and work on projects together using a resource called the collaboration room.

Give your partner's complete access through the SAP Partner Portal

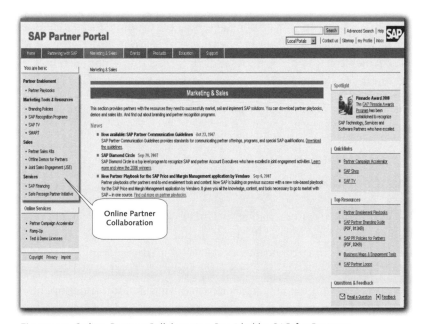

Figure 9.5 Online Partner Collaboration Provided by SAP for Partners

Partner Compensation

This tool, using SAP incentive and commission management (ICM), enables the setup of partner compensation planning for different partner types and individual partners. It also calculates compensation based on posted sales data and offers a compensation simulator to demonstrate how much compensation partners can earn, if a deal is closed. This simulator can also provide a look at compensation settlements in which partners can view the earned compensation and payment dates.

Partner Planning and Forecasting

With partner planning and forecasting, brand owners can set sales goals for channel partners and then track and measure the partner's progress toward the goals. This tool supports both collaborative channel forecasting as well as pipeline forecasting. With collaborative channel forecasting, the channel partner can plan and forecast sales by individual partner, partner segment, or product line, including "what if" analysis. Pipeline forecasting can be done by region, product, partner type, and so on, including forecasting channel revenues and funnel analysis.

This wraps up our coverage of partner management. Next, let's discuss channel marketing.

Channel Marketing

Drive demand for your products through your channel partners

Recruiting and training channel partners is the first step. When your partners are up to speed, it's time to put them to work. The channel marketing functionalities of SAP CRM partner channel management enable brand owners to better drive demand for their products through channel partners. Partner communication functionalities allow brand owners to publish personalized, targeted marketing information to channel partners. Catalog management tools can be used to deploy centrally managed product and pricing information to channel partners. The campaign management functionality enables collaborative marketing with channel partners. Lead management features allow brand owners to route sales leads to the best-suited channel partner. Marketing funds can be managed and distributed to partners via marketing channel funds functionalities. And, a partner locator tool allows your end customers to find your nearest channel partner, such as a dealer, retailer, or service provider.

Partner Communication

Brand owners can take advantage of partner communication tools, enabled by the SAP Enterprise Portal (EP), to publish product information, news, and upcoming events directly to targeted channel partners. However, it's not just a one-way communication. Channel partners can also search for information, and subscribe to products and topics of interest to keep abreast of the latest news, and even provide feedback and rate published documents. Using the SAP Sales and Marketing Library, channel partners can search within a repository of downloadable marketing documents, presentations, templates, sales tools, product information, price lists, and so on.

Catalog Management

Catalog management provides channel partners with up-to-date access to personalized product information, pricing, and availability. Channel partners can view side-by-side comparisons of multiple products from the product catalog to compare features and make better purchasing decisions. Channel partners can also download marketing collaterals or access rich, multimedia presentations in various languages. Brand owners can import and export product catalogs using XML and can edit catalogs in stages to prevent in-process or not yet approved portions of the catalog from being exposed to customers.

Campaign Management

Campaign management allows brand owners to involve channel partners in marketing campaigns. Brand owners can set up a new campaign using the standard SAP CRM Marketing tools discussed earlier, such as the marketing planner, marketing calendar, and campaign automation. After a campaign has been created, the brand owner can

Manage your campaigns, catalogs, leads, and marketing funds effectively select and assign relevant channel partners using the marketing segment builder tool. For example, during the launch of a new product, the responsible channel manager at the brand owner's company might decide that only channel partners who have Gold certification should be allowed to participate. Campaigns can be executed through any supported channel including email, telephone, letter, fax, SMS, or even face-to-face. And, of course, the brand owner can monitor campaigns using the standard SAP CRM Marketing functionality.

Lead Management

Lead management allows the responsible channel manager at the brand owner's company to create, qualify, and dispatch sales leads to appropriate channel partners. Leads can be created using any standard SAP CRM Marketing channels, including external lists, third-party service providers, Web forms on the corporate website, call centers, and so on. After the lead has been created and qualified — either manually or automatically via questionnaire/survey integration — the channel manager can dispatch the lead to the most suitable channel partners. The channel manager can do this manually based on the analysis of the partner profiles and data, or by using business rules via the SAP CRM rule modeler tool. The partner is then able to accept or reject the lead and begin working on the sales opportunity on behalf of the brand owner.

Channel Marketing Funds

The channel marketing funds functionality helps brand owners to better manage and allocate their budget for channel marketing activities, as well as to better understand the effectiveness of their channel marketing expenditures. Channel marketing funds was revamped by SAP in SAP CRM 2007 to include enhancement of the marketing development funds (MDF) functionality such as integration with SAP CRM rule-based claims management and SAP ERP financial liability management. However, even the basic channel marketing funds functionality available in earlier releases enables brand owners to manage their channel marketing budgets, as well as to plan and monitor channel marketing activities (see Figure 9.6). The responsible channel manager at the brand owner's company sets the marketing budget and planning. The brand owner and channel partner then jointly execute the marketing and campaign activities, while the finance controller of the brand owner's company monitors the marketing events and reimburses the channel partners according to the agreed upon terms and conditions.

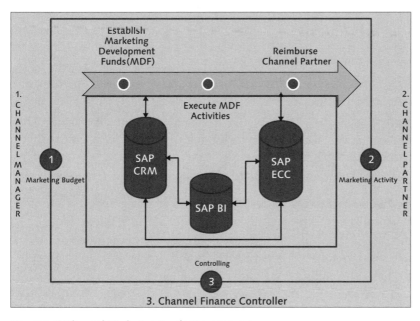

Figure 9.6 Channel Marketing Funds Management

Partner Locator

The channel marketing functionality of SAP CRM partner channel management also contains a partner locator tool that allows customers to find the nearest channel partner of a brand owner — such as a dealer, retailer, or authorized service provider — while visiting the brand owner's website.

Find new partners with the partner locator tool

This concludes our coverage of channel marketing. Next, let's talk about channel sales.

Note

> To better illustrate the partner channel management processes, in the following section, we'll provide examples using an automobile parts company called Auto Inc. as the brand owner, and a spare parts dealer named Xllent Parts as the channel partner.

Channel Sales

Give channel partners access to the same tools your internal sales people use

In the previous section, we discussed that brand owners need to involve their channel partners in marketing processes to better drive customer demand for the brand owner's products. Similarly, brand owners need to involve their channel partners in the sales process to close deals with customers who don't buy directly from the brand owner. Channel partners need to have access to all of the same sales tools and knowledge that internal sales people have access to.

Additionally, it's very important to establish clear guidelines and rules of engagement to prevent overlaps and conflicts between your internal sales force and your channel partners. Nothing alienates channel partners faster than when the brand owner's own sales people try to steal established customers from channel partners. The channel sales features of SAP CRM partner channel management allow both the brand owner and channel partner to jointly manage accounts and contacts, activities, and opportunities, including support for partner-specific pricing and point-of-sale (POS) inventory tracking. Analytics are also provided to allow brand owners to identify gaps and overlaps in the sales process and better support the selling efforts of their channel partners.

 Example

> The brand owner, Auto Inc., gave its channel partner, Xllent Parts, Web access to manage Auto Inc.'s end customers and contacts, product catalog, and order processing (see Figure 9.7).

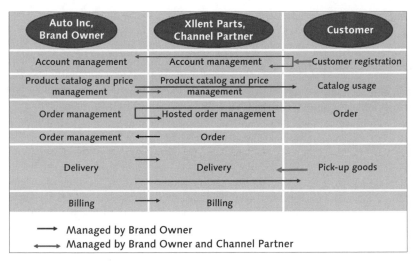

Figure 9.7 Channel Sales Management

Account and Contact Management

One of the biggest challenges that brand owners face when selling through channel partners is getting access to customer information owned by the channel partner. The account and contact management functionalities of SAP CRM partner channel management allow brand owners and channel partners to share information about customers to give both the brand owner and the channel partner an up-to-date view of the customer. Of course, it's also possible to restrict the channel partner's view of customer data to only provide access to information that is relevant to the channel partner. For example, as a brand owner, you may only want a channel partner to be able to view accounts that channel partner has a relationship with, rather than letting the channel partner view information about all of your customers, including customers who are serviced by other channel partners.

Activity Management

Every sales opportunity involves various activities: sales calls, appointments, and other tasks. Activity management allows brand owners and channel partners to collaboratively manage, execute, and document these sales-related activities. It's possible to route tasks and

Share information about customers between the brand owner and the channel partner activities back and forth between the brand owner and the channel partner as necessary using status management, which, for example, allows you to set the processing status of a document to a status such as "in partner processing." As with account and contact management, it's also possible in activity management to only provide partners with visibility into those activities that they are personally responsible for.

Opportunity Management

Opportunity management allows brand owners to stay involved with sales leads and opportunities that have been handed over to channel partners. After a brand owner identifies an opportunity and sends it to a channel partner, the brand owner maintains complete insight into the opportunity's history, milestones, buying center (involved parties), and current status. Opportunities can be distributed to channel partners automatically, manually, or semi-automatically (using a list of partners proposed automatically by the system). Notification tools allow the brand owner to notify the partner of new opportunities and also allow the partner to notify the brand owner of opportunities that have been returned, downgraded, or rejected.

Channel Sales Analytics

Channel sales analytics allow brand owners to identify gaps in the sales process and to better support sales efforts of channel partners. Standard reports are available for both brand owners and channel partners. The channel manager at the brand owner's company can monitor the overall channel performance as well as the performance of individual channel partners. Channel partners can also monitor their own channel performance in relation to the brand owner. Out-of-the-box reports are also available for account analysis, activity analysis, and opportunity analysis.

Partner Order Management

Involving channel partners in your marketing and sales activities is wonderful. However, the real payoff comes when your channel partners start taking sales orders from customers, which generates revenue for you, the brand owner. The partner order management functionalities of SAP CRM partner channel management allow brand owners to optimize the partner ordering process and incorporate channel partners into the brand owner's e-commerce strategy. Partner order management includes quotation and order management, which provides channel partners with the online pricing and order functionalities necessary to allow the partner to create orders on behalf of customers. Partner order management also enables interactive selling and product configuration, enabling channel partners to customize products to suit customer-specific needs.

Brand owners can centrally manage and deploy personalized pricing and contracts to their channel partners, including partner-specific pricing and discounts. In addition, POS and channel inventory functionalities are available, allowing brand owners to easily capture and reconcile POS data from retailers and distributors as well as to track inventory held by channel partners. Another nice feature of partner order management is that brand owners can host collaborative showrooms allowing customers to check pricing and availability of products across the brand owner's entire partner network. Finally, distributed order management allows brand owners to distribute orders out to channel partners for fulfillment. Brand owners can also host the order-management process for channel partners who don't have their own order-management system, providing the partner with an infrastructure to receive, process, and fulfill customer sales orders.

Optimize partner ordering processes

Quotation and Order Management

Quotation and order management provides channel partners with online quoting and order functionalities, allowing channel partners to create orders on behalf of customers and to track the order across the entire fulfillment process. SAP CRM partner channel management provides support for three out-of-the-box quotation and order management scenarios: Business to Business (B2B), Business on Behalf (BoB), and collaborative selling. In the B2B scenario, the partner orders directly from the brand owner and then later resells the product to an end customer. In the BoB scenario, the channel partner creates an order directly on behalf of a specific customer. And in the collaborative selling model, an end customer might order from a partner using the brand owner's collaborative partner showroom that allows the customer to see product availability and pricing across the brand owner's complete partner network. Pricing and contracts functionality allows brand owners to centrally manage and deploy pricing and contracts, including partner-specific pricing and contracts, to all channel partners.

Interactive Selling and Configuration

Provide customer-centric solutions

Interactive selling provides your channel partners with rich, real-time online tools that allow them to configure and customize products to match customer requirements. Product configuration helps brand owners provide customer-centric solutions, allowing channel partners to tailor a brand owner's product to the precise customer needs. Online tools guide channel partners through the various steps of configuring a product, shortening the order process, and potentially eliminating inquiry calls and errors in the order. And, because the interactive selling and configuration tools work in real time, partners always have access to the most up-to-date product model and configuration options.

POS and Channel Inventory

POS and channel inventory functionalities allow brand owners to capture and reconcile POS data from retailers and distributors and to track inventories held by channel partners. Brand owners can also execute "what-if" scenarios to analyze the impact of pricing changes, including considerations of existing price protection programs.

Collaborative Showrooms

Using partner order management, brand owners can host partner e-commerce websites, such as collaborative showrooms and distributed catalogs. A *collaborative showroom* is a website that provides a single face to customers of the brand owner and the brand owner's channel network. The showroom typically provides a complete listing of all channel partners, including the products they carry and pricing. To access the showroom, customers log on using the customer portal. Channel partners can also access the collaborative showroom by logging on through the partner portal.

Ex **Example**

> As a brand owner, Auto Inc. maintains a collaborative showroom where customers can purchase auto parts from any channel partner that carries the inventory the customer needs. The collaborative showroom has both B2B and B2C access for channel partners and customers. See Figures 9.8 and 9.9.

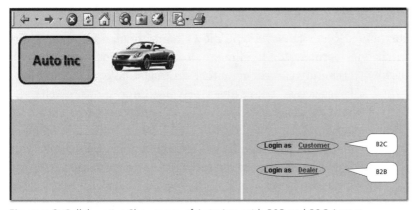

Figure 9.8 Collaborative Showroom of Auto Inc. with B2B and B2C Access

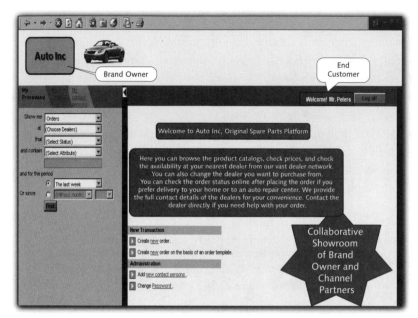

Figure 9.9 Using the Collaborative Showroom to Buy Spare Parts from a Dealer

Distributed Order Management

Get orders to channel partners who also manage your inventory

Distributed order management allows brand owners to send orders to channel partners for fulfillment in situations where the channel partner stores and manages inventory for the brand owner. The brand owner still has access to the inventory, but the responsible channel partner processes the orders. Even though the channel partner is processing the order, brand owners will often host the order-management process for channel partners. This is convenient for channel partners that don't have their own order-management system, allowing the partner to receive, process, and fulfill customer sales orders using the brand owner's infrastructure. This also ensures a consistent customer experience (and consistency in branding) for the brand owner because the customer logs on to the brand owner's Website and may not even be aware that a third party is servicing or fulfilling their order (see Figure 9.10).

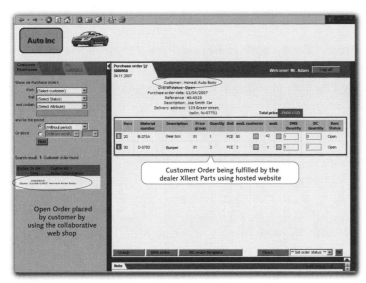

Figure 9.10 Hosted Order Management by a Channel Partner

Ex Example

Channel partner Xllent Parts representative, James Adam, can log into the hosted website to retrieve a customer order that needs to be fulfilled by his company (see Figure 9.11).

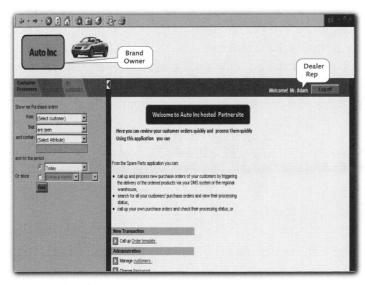

Figure 9.11 Brand Owner Hosting Channel Partner Website

Channel Service

After a customer buys a product from a channel partner, the customer will often return to the channel partner — rather than the brand owner — when the customer has a question about the product or when the customer requires service, maintenance, or repairs. This is the case in the automotive industry, for example, where customers take their cars in to the local dealer for routine service and maintenance; customers don't go to the corporate headquarters in Detroit, Japan, or Germany every time they need an oil change or a tune-up. Because of the crucial role that customer service plays in retaining customers and driving repeat business, brand owners need to make sure that their channel partners can provide the same high-quality customer service that the brand owner's internal service employees provide. Thus, channel partners need to have access to the same service tools, knowledge repositories, and internal expertise that internal employees can access.

Provide timely and satisfactory service

The channel service functionalities of SAP CRM partner channel management empower channel partners with service tools and problem resolution functionalities, so that channel partners can provide timely, satisfactory service to the end customers. Channel service gives channel partners access to all of the standard SAP CRM Service functionalities, such as the ability to view installed base information, the ability to create and monitor service requests; to access knowledge repositories, including solutions and FAQs; and to create complaints and returns. In addition, channel service also provides additional functionalities such as live support, providing the channel partner with immediate assistance from the brand owner's Website.

Refer to Figure 9.12 for a good overview of how the channel service process works between the brand owner and channel partner as supported by SAP CRM partner channel management.

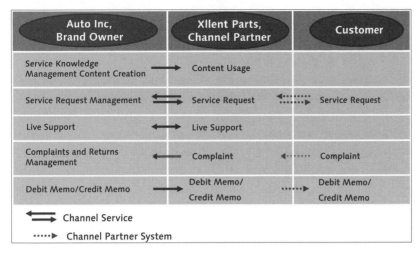

Figure 9.12 Channel Service in SAP CRM Partner Channel Management

Knowledge Management

Knowledge management allows channel partners to research and resolve customer issues. For example, partners can access knowledge repositories maintained by the brand owner, such as the Solution Database (SDB), to search for solutions, FAQs, how-to-guides, technical documents, and so on using natural language search or advanced search options. Partners can also subscribe to service bulletins, engineering change orders (ECOs), or recall notices published by the brand owner to keep current on service-related issues.

 Note

SAP CRM includes a knowledge repository structure called the Solution Database and a set of knowledge authorizing, maintenance, and knowledge base administration tools. The SDB is delivered empty without any problem descriptions, solutions, or FAQs because these would obviously differ by company, industry, and so on. However, standard SAP tools, such as the SAP NetWeaver Exchange Infrastructure (SAP NetWeaver XI), which was recently renamed, SAP NetWeaver Process Integration (PI), can be used for migrating content from external knowledge bases into the SDB.

Let your channel partners research and resolve customer issues

221

Live Support

Live support enables channel partners to request immediate support from the brand owner via either email or Web chat using the brand owner's website. With the live Web chat (LWC) solution, partners can communicate directly in real time with an employee from the brand owner's interaction center. Partners can also push URLs or files to the interaction center agent. With the email solution, partners have access to a Web form that collects the necessary information and then forwards the email request to the appropriate interaction center agent. It's also possible to leverage the SAP email response management system (ERMS) solution to send auto-acknowledgment emails to the partner or even to automate simple request that don't necessarily require a live interaction center agent.

Service Order Management

Service order management allows channel partners to create and monitor service requests. Partners can initiative service processes and perform service activities. Using out-of-the-box functionality, partners can create, update, and maintain service requests on behalf of themselves; on a project basis, SAP customers can implement a solution that allows partners to also create, update, and maintain service requests on behalf of end customers. In addition, channel partners can also view the installed base information of customers, perform warranty and entitlement checks, and create complaints and returns (Figure 9.12).

 Note

The out-of-the-box service functionalities of SAP CRM partner channel management are based on the Internet Customer Self-Service (ICSS) application component and, therefore, only allow partners to create service requests, complaints, and returns on behalf of themselves; enabling channel partners to create service requests, complaints, and returns on behalf of customers can be implemented on a project basis with manageable effort.

Complaints and Returns Management

Complaints and returns management allows partners to create complaints and returns online and to monitor the status of complaints and returns through to completion. Complaints can be created with reference to an existing product by entering the serial number of the product. Based on the product serial number, it's possible to see whether the product is under warranty and whether the product is allowed to be returned. As with service orders, out of the box functionality only supports the creation of complaints and returns by the channel partners for products that the partner has ordered. Project-specific work is required to enable the creation of complaints and returns by the channel partner on behalf of an end customer.

Now let's move on to talk about the analytics capabilities in partner channel management.

Partner and Channel Analytics

As a brand owner, you want to know how much sales revenue you are generating through your channel partner. You want to know whether the resources you are devoting to your channel network are being used optimally. Are your channel partners performing as expected? Is the money you spend on channel marketing expenditures generating the expected return on investment? How are inventory levels and price protections programs affecting your profitability? Partner and channel analytics help you answer these questions.

Monitor, analyze, and act on channel business trends quickly

The partner and channel analytics functionality of SAP CRM partner channel management enables brand owners to monitor, analyze, and act on channel business trends. Out-of-the-box analytical reports are available to analyze channel partner coverage, determine channel marketing effectiveness, analyze channel sales, and scrutinize inventory flow and price protection programs. For example, brand owners can check their partner network to find any regions, product lines, or markets that are not currently being served by any channel partner. Brand owners can also break down marketing activities to determine the effectiveness of their marketing expenditures. Sales analysis allows brand owners to gain insight into their channel inventory and channel

223

pricing to better understand how sales efforts affected revenue. In addition, brand owners can also provide their channel partners with access to reports and analysis to gain insight into their relationship with the brand owner.

This completes our discussion of the functionalities of SAP CRM partner channel management, so let's look at a quick case study to see it in action.

Case Study

A large high tech services company that provides services to branded PC manufacturers and financial institutions is implementing SAP CRM channel management with Interaction Channel (IC) WebClient to better service end customers and improve the operational efficiency of channel service partners. The company also manufactures and sells printers and high-end office automation equipment.

This tech service company thrives on an ecosystem of 500 plus channel service partners and delivers excellent services to the end clients. The company is a brand owner and also serves other brand owners using the support of an excellent network of service channel partners. The company provides services ranging from cell phones to ATM machines. Some of the services provided by the company are listed here.

Field Support Services:

> Repair
> Upgrade

Customer Contract Management:

> Customer call registration, creation, and assignment of service tickets to appropriate channel partners and closure
> Technical support via telephone
> Asset management
> Warranty management

The business challenges facing this company include the following:

> Disparate systems and lack of integration between the legacy channel management system and the SAP ERP application

> Limited or no visibility on channel service partner business transactions for loan parts and parts sold

> Manual parts planning at the channel service partner level

> Manual channel service partner claims management

> No integration between call center operations and the backend SAP ERP application

> Manual and cumbersome SLA compliance and tracking

The company's business objectives are listed here:

> Support business expansion by using an automated and extendable system

> Create an integrated solution for channel service partners

> Prevent revenue leakage

> Optimize inventory planning

> Enhance the brand owner relationship

To meet these objectives, the company is faced with creating an integrated, easy-to-use user interface for the channel service partner that provides the following:

> Auto replenishment of dealer stocks

> Workflow for channel service partner claims processing

> Inventory management to handle channel service partner loan stocks and purchased stocks separately

> Management of the channel service partner as vendor and customer

The solution requires the deployment of SAP CRM partner channel management with an integrated phone supported IC WebClient, E-Commerce channel, and seamless integration to the backend SAP ERP application. This solution will provide the following:

> An SAP CRM system that is truly integrated with the backend SAP ERP application

> Automated assignment of channel partners to a service request based on the customer address

> Warranty tracking

> Warranty cost analysis and improved warranty profitability

> Spare parts management and accountability for channel service partners

> Defective parts accounting

> Integrated channel partner claims processing

> Email alerts sent to channel partners when a ticket is assigned

> Channel partner access to the ticket information via a channel portal

> Ability for channel partners to check the spare parts availability before scheduling a service visit to the customer site

> Viewable invoices via channel portal for the channel partner

> Channel partner access to brand owner knowledge management via the channel portal

> Inventory integrated with service order management

> SLA (Service Level Agreement) maintenance for the product

> Product performance analysis

> Part consumption analysis

With these capabilities the company will be much more efficient and effective at managing large numbers of partners.

Conclusion

In this chapter, you learned about partner channel management, a key functionality of SAP CRM. With partner channel management, brand owners can jointly market products and sell collaboratively with channel partners. For companies that work with channel partners — which includes the majority of all companies — partner management tools are absolutely critical for ensuring that your end customers receive the products, service, and information they need when they do business with your partners.

The key things that you should know about SAP CRM partner channel management are:

> Partner management helps brand owners find and train partners, and enables brand owners to effectively build and manage their partner relationships.

> Channel marketing enables brand owners to engage the strengths of their channel partners to achieve greater market penetration through joint collaboration with channel partners.

> Channel sales guides brand owners in their quest to increase sales revenue through their channel partners by jointly managing accounts, activities, and opportunities while preventing conflicts and overlaps between the brand owner's internal sales force and channel partners.

> Partner order management allows brand owners to incorporate channel partners into the brand owner's e-commerce strategy through tools such as collaborative showrooms and distributed catalogs where the brand owner lists all of the channel partners in the brand owner's partner network, including the products each partner carries and pricing.

> Channel service provides channel partners with access to all of the necessary tools and research to resolve customer-related service issues. Channel partners can search for FAQs, solutions, or other documents in a knowledge repository maintained by the brand owner. In addition, channel partners can request immediate assistance from experts in the brand owner's organization via either Web chat or email.

> Partner and channel analytics enables brand owners to analyze whether the resources they have invested in their channel network activities are generating the expected results and return on investment.

In the next chapter, we'll move on to the topic of technology and discuss the tools and architecture beneath SAP CRM.

The Technology and Tools Behind SAP CRM

Any technology book would be incomplete without teaching you about what's under the hood. This chapter makes it simple to understand the various technical components of the underlying SAP CRM engine. With this in mind, we'll discuss the technologies used across SAP applications in general, as well as within SAP CRM specifically. Let's start by looking at the SAP NetWeaver technology stack, which provides the underlying framework on top of which all SAP applications run. Then we'll turn our attention to the SAP CRM-specific tools and technologies. Finally, we'll conclude with a few words about ABAP (Advanced Business Application Programming), arguably the most famous of all SAP technologies.

SAP NetWeaver Introduction

SAP NetWeaver is the technology platform that supports all of SAP's applications, including SAP CRM. SAP NetWeaver is essentially a collection of different tools and applications that enables SAP's products to run. The main component of SAP NetWeaver is the SAP

SAP NetWeaver is a collection of tools and applications that enable SAP's products to run

NetWeaver Application Server (formerly known as SAP Basis), which provides the foundation on top of which most SAP application run. However, SAP NetWeaver also includes other components. SAP NetWeaver Exchange Infrastructure (SAP NetWeaver XI), which is now called Process Integration (PI), enables SAP systems and non-SAP systems to communicate with each other using different technologies (such as ABAP and Java). The SAP enterprise portal allows customers to access applications, information, and services from one central tool. SAP NetWeaver Master Data Management (SAP NetWeaver MDM) helps consolidate and cleanse master data objects from disparate systems. SAP NetWeaver Mobile enables enterprise mobility, providing the technology for SAP Mobile applications. And, SAP Business Information Warehouse (BI), formerly known as BW, provides analytical reporting functionalities across SAP applications, including SAP CRM.

 Note

SAP NetWeaver consists of different SAP applications including the following:

> SAP NetWeaver Application Server (SAP NetWeaver AS)
> SAP NetWeaver Process Integration (PI) (formerly SAP NetWeaver Exchange Infrastructure (SAP NetWeaver XI)
> SAP Enterprise Portal (SAP EP)
> SAP NetWeaver Master Data Management (SAP NetWeaver MDM)
> SAP NetWeaver Mobile
> SAP NetWeaver Business Intelligence (SAP NetWeaver BI)
> SAP NetWeaver Auto-ID Infrastructure
> SAP NetWeaver Identity Management

SAP NetWeaver also provides various SAP tools:

> Adaptive Computing Controller
> SAP NetWeaver Composition Environment
> SAP NetWeaver Developer Studio
> SAP NetWeaver Visual Composer
> SAP Solution Manager
> TREX search engine

Enterprise Service-Oriented Architecture (Enterprise SOA)

Just as Microsoft Windows is the technical foundation on which you likely run your daily productivity applications, SAP NetWeaver is the technology stack on which SAP applications run. SAP NetWeaver provides tools to consolidate and cleanse data, enable disparate applications and technology to work together, and facilitate Web Services and composite Web applications. More than 13,000 new SAP customers adopted SAP NetWeaver in 2006. The increasing popularity of SAP NetWeaver reflects the many tools and features it provides.

Although SAP NetWeaver provides an enterprise with many tools and features, it's primarily a technical foundation for service-oriented architecture (SOA). As such, it allows you to create new Web Services and enhance existing Web Services to make your IT infrastructure fit your business strategy.

SAP NetWeaver and enterprise SOA

 Note

> A *Web Service* is basically any computer application that can be accessed via the Internet. For example, stock tickers, online weather forecasts, or PayPal and credit card verification services are all examples of Web Services.
>
> *Service-oriented architecture* (SOA) refers to computer software infrastructures that allow users to find and access Web Services to support business processes.
>
> SAP uses the term *enterprise service-oriented architecture (enterprise SOA)* to describe the functionalities provided by SAP NetWeaver for enabling Web Services to support the business processes of an enterprise.

Although we won't discuss enterprise SOA in depth here, it's important to at least understand the basics. Enterprise SOA is an architecture that uses Web Services to support business processes. Think about a typical business process that is made up of one or more Web Services, such as performing a credit card check, billing the customer, and then creating a sales order when a customer orders a product from your website. If you want to make a change to the process, you don't need to re-code an entire software application; rather, you simply add a new Web Service or replace an existing one. Therefore, if your order

Enterprise SOA is an architecture that uses Web Services to support business processes process currently involves a credit check, but you decide to stop including a credit check for every order, you simply remove the credit check service to modify your business process.

SOA makes building and modifying business processes much easier and less expensive than writing and modifying custom software code. What does SAP bring to the mix for SOA? SAP's enterprise service-oriented architecture (enterprise SOA) gives Web Services access to enterprise data to create processes that address enterprise business functions.

For example, to make Web Services more robust and useful for the business world, you also need to integrate aspects of enterprise software, such as data dictionaries, which introduce standards for how data is organized and stored. Enterprise SOA crosses all boundaries of your organization to integrate enterprise functionality in a standards-based environment. Concisely, it's a blueprint for adaptable and flexible services-based IT architecture that enables enterprise-scale business solutions.

SAP NetWeaver Integration

SAP NetWeaver provides a way to integrate people, information, and processes by leveraging an application platform that helps people communicate, organize and access data, and perform business processes. One way in which SAP NetWeaver acts as an integrator is by taking advantage of your existing IT investment, whether it's made up of third-party products, SAP products, or a mixture of the two. In fact, part of the strength of SAP NetWeaver is that it's supported by a host of independent software vendors (ISVs) that develop "Powered by SAP NetWeaver" applications to integrate and work seamlessly with SAP applications.

If you have business processes that span different systems and data stored in various applications, SAP NetWeaver can help you access all of those systems and all of that data; SAP NetWeaver also helps you reduce the complexity inherent in your business processes by consolidating the complexity one level higher in your technology stack — where it can be more easily managed. In addition, SAP NetWeaver enables all of SAP's products and tools to function together and communicate with each other. You should note that all of SAP's products are built on and ship with SAP NetWeaver as their base.

> **Tip**
>
> In addition to providing tools for developing new applications, SAP NetWeaver also comes with business content, built-in templates, and industry-specific applications that you can use out of the box.

SAP NetWeaver enables the integration of people, information and processes using a single, consolidated technology platform: the SAP NetWeaver Application Server (SAP NetWeaver AS) (see Figure 10.1). Let's discuss these areas in detail.

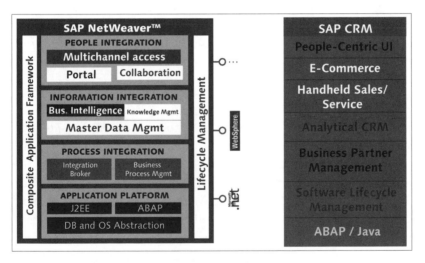

Figure 10.1 SAP NetWeaver Integration Functionalities

People Integration

SAP NetWeaver allows people to access and share information across the enterprise by providing collaboration tools and by allowing employees to access data via a variety of devices. Multi-channel access via mobile laptops and handheld devices is provided by SAP NetWeaver Mobile. In addition, SAP NetWeaver Enterprise Portal facilitates collaboration by allowing employees to share documents and calendar items. The portal provides a unified and role-based single point of access to all relevant businesses and IT systems.

Information Integration

Access and share information across the enterprise using collaboration tools

SAP NetWeaver provides employees with access to the information they need to do their jobs — including analytical data and reports — regardless of where the information resides in the system. SAP NetWeaver BI allows you to integrate, analyze, and disseminate information from both SAP and non-SAP systems in a timely manner. SAP NetWeaver MDM provides all of the systems within your IT landscape with access to consolidated master data. In addition, the knowledge management functionality provides a single point of access to SAP application content management and a host of third-party content servers, including full-text search functionalities with several search modes.

Process Integration

The SAP NetWeaver PI (formerly XI) enables both SAP and non-SAP systems to communicate with each other using different technologies (such as ABAP and Java) via standard XML/SOAP protocols. The technical runtime component of SAP NetWeaver — the Integration Broker — supports XML (Extended Markup Language)/SOAP (Simple Object Access Protocol) communication between different systems. SAP NetWeaver also supports business process integration by allowing business processes to be modeled and created using Web Services from both SAP and non-SAP IT environments.

Example

If you are planning to use key performance indicators (KPIs) to measure and compare performance in terms of meeting strategic and operational goals, SAP NetWeaver Business Process Management provides a set of industry standard KPIs and templates that you can use. For instance, the KPIs for customers include the following:

> Delivery Performance to Customer by date

> Delivery Performance to Customer by Quantity

SAP NetWeaver Business Process Management also provides a set of modeling tools, and you can find more information on these at *http://www.bpx.sap.com*.

Application Platform

As discussed earlier, SAP NetWeaver provides an application platform called the SAP NetWeaver Application Server (SAP NetWeaver AS), formerly known as SAP Basis. The SAP NetWeaver AS is the underlying technology for almost all SAP applications and includes native support for protocols such as HTTP, HTTPS, SMTP, and other Internet protocols. The SAP NetWeaver AS also supports server-side scripting in both ABAP and JavaScript. In addition, a development environment for Web applications is integrated into the SAP ABAP Workbench. You can use the SAP NetWeaver AS to develop Internet applications such as online Web shops and portals, which are displayed using Business Server Pages (BSP). SAP NetWeaver gives you the tools to compose new business applications built on top of your existing systems using Web Services, Java, or any other industry standards. For example, you can create portals to provide end users with access to the functionality and data they need to do their jobs, and you can build composite applications that string together services into useful business processes.

SAP NetWeaver also provides a Virtual Machine Container (VMC) designed to allow Java applications to be run with the same stability as applications developed using ABAP — with the goal of avoiding any unnecessary restrictions regarding development environments. The SAP NetWeaver AS is operating system and database indepen-

String useful business processes together

dent and supports common databases such as Oracle Database, IBM DB2, and Microsoft SQL as well as standard operating systems such as UNIX, Linux, and Microsoft Windows.

 Note

For more detailed information about SAP NetWeaver functionalities, visit *http://www.sdn.sap.com*, and choose SAP NetWeaver Capabilities.

SAP NetWeaver for SAP CRM

As mentioned, SAP NetWeaver provides various tools and applications that enable other SAP applications, including SAP CRM, to run. For example, the SAP NetWeaver AS provides the non-application-specific coding (formerly called SAP Basis) on which business applications such as SAP CRM are built. In addition, SAP NetWeaver tools are tightly integrated within SAP CRM. For example, SAP CRM leverages SAP NetWeaver TREX to perform high-speed customer searches in the interaction center and to enable high-speed segmentation of customers in the marketing campaign planner application.

Access both SAP and non-SAP applications from a single location

The SAP NetWeaver EP allows SAP CRM users to access both SAP and non-SAP applications from a single location. SAP NetWeaver BI provides SAP CRM users, such as sales executives, with historical reports and analytics, including customer sales history or Customer Lifetime Value (CLTV). In addition, SAP CRM imports and exports data to SAP and non-SAP systems using the SAP NetWeaver Process Integration (PI) interface. Finally, the SOA offered by the SAP NetWeaver AS enables communication between SAP CRM and other non-SAP systems using Web Services (e.g., via Adobe Forms). We'll discuss Web Services in detail in the next section.

SAP NetWeaver Web Services for SAP CRM

As mentioned, a Web Service is simply a computer software application that has been made available over the Internet or intranet. Web Services communicate using Internet standard protocols, such as

XML/SOAP messages. A Web Service is a self-contained, self-describing, modular software application that can be published, discovered, and invoked through open Internet standards.

Web Services are available in SAP CRM, as early as SAP CRM 2005. Using SAP NetWeaver 2004s, it's possible in SAP CRM 2005 to expose any RFC-enabled function component as a Web Service by using the SAP NetWeaver Web Service creation wizard. In SAP CRM 2006s, with support packages 04 and 05, SAP provides execution-ready enterprise services for the main SAP CRM business objects, including the business partner, service order, service confirmation, lead, and quotation. Customers and partners can use the Web Services provided by SAP, or they can create their own Web Services using the Web Service Tool available with SAP CRM release 2006s and above.

The Web Service Tool provides wizard-based guidance to help users create and deploy new Web Services on the fly without any coding. The tool automatically generates the underlying Web Service Description Language (WSDL) file and is integrated with the SAP NetWeaver testing environment. The Web Service Tool hides all technical complexity from the business user, allowing for rapid and easy deployment of Web Services that can be consumed by any service-enabled technology, such as Adobe Interactive Forms.

Use the Web Service Tool's wizard-based guidance to create and deploy new Web Services

Ex **Example**

Zee Computers is a brand owner who uses the SAP CRM system. Several customer leads are created in Zee's SAP CRM system. Zee computers converts the leads into an Adobe Interactive Form using a Web Service. The leads are then sent as PDFs via email to the appropriate channel partners. One such lead — "1122" — was emailed to the channel partner Geek Computers. A lead qualifier at Geek Computers opened the Adobe Interactive Form and noted the lead contents. Geek Computers qualified the lead by contacting the prospective customer and updating the form. The updated form was sent as an email attachment to the SAP CRM system. The system updated the lead based on the updated Adobe Interactive Form. The entire lead qualification process was done by a channel partner without logging into the SAP CRM system (see Figure 10.2). What a flexible way of doing lead management!

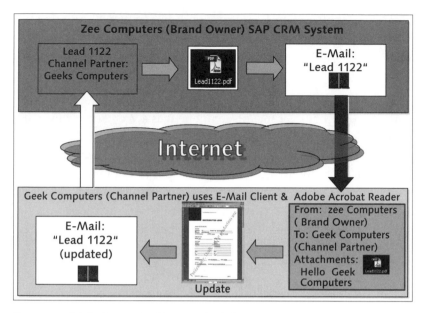

Figure 10.2 Adobe Interactive Form as a Web Service

SAP NetWeaver Mobile for SAP CRM

SAP NetWeaver Mobile Infrastructure provides the technical foundation for SAP mobile applications, empowering so-called cross-application composite applications (formerly referred to as xApps), such as SAP CRM Mobile Sales and SAP CRM Mobile Service. SAP CRM mobile applications are designed to allow sales and service applications to run on offline laptops as well as offline and online handheld devices. For more information on SAP CRM mobile applications, refer back to Chapter 8.

SAP NetWeaver Process Integration (PI) for SAP CRM

SAP NetWeaver Process Integration (PI) (formerly SAP NetWeaver XI) is an integration platform based on Java and XML standards that enables integration and data sharing between SAP and non-SAP systems. In the past, before SAP NetWeaver, when it was necessary to integrate two systems, the systems were generally connected directly to each other on a rigid one-to-one basis. Using such a paradigm, the complexity of system integration grew exponentially as the number of required systems increased. SAP NetWeaver PI solves this problem by acting as an Integration Broker — a central hub or middleman connecting all other systems. SAP NetWeaver considerably reduces the cost of mapping disparate systems together. In the old one-to-one paradigm, if 10 applications were sending customer master data to 4 systems, you needed 40 separate mappings. Using SAP NetWeaver as the Integration Broker to transfer data, the number of mappings is reduced to only 14.

SAP CRM can take advantage of SAP NetWeaver PI in a number of ways. For example, SAP CRM provides a knowledge repository called the Solution Database (SDB) that is used in several SAP CRM Service scenarios. Although SDB provides a standardized format for storing and retrieving problem descriptions and related solutions, the actual database is delivered to customers without any content. Customers can, of course, manually add problems and solutions to the database by hand. However, this is often time-consuming and labor-intensive. Instead, if the customer has already maintained the content in another database or knowledge repository, the customer can leverage SAP NetWeaver PI to automatically import the data from the customer's old database into SAP CRM SDB.

Reduce the cost of mapping disparate systems together with SAP NetWeaver Process Integration (PI)

Ex Example

A large high-tech enterprise implemented SAP CRM to handle customer service requirements. The implementation team overcame a challenge in integrating the enterprise's monster homegrown Central Master Data (CMD) system with SAP CRM. CMD is used to centrally manage customer data and product registration data and to distribute the data to other connected business systems, including SAP CRM. The CMD system receives master data updates from several systems, using timestamps to manage which records to update. On average, the CMD generates 100,000 messages per day for new and updated records, which are sent to the SAP CRM system. The SAP CRM system generates about 50,000 messages per day for new and updated customer records, which are sent back to the CMD system. The data updates need to happen in near real time. This was an obvious challenge. The design team found SAP NetWeaver PI as the best fail-safe Integration Broker to handle the challenging message transfers between SAP CRM and CMD (see Figure 10.3).

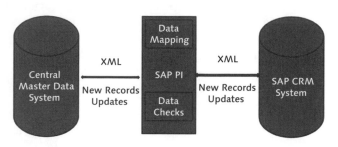

Figure 10.3 SAP NetWeaver PI as an Integration Broker with SAP CRM

SAP NetWeaver Java for SAP CRM

SAP NetWeaver also provides complete support for Java technology including Java 2 Platform Enterprise Edition (J2EE), Enterprise Java Beans (EJB), Java Message Service (JMS), Java Database Connectivity (JDC), and so on.

 Note

> Java is an object-oriented programming language similar to C++. Java source-code files (with a .java extension) are compiled to byte-code format (with a .class extension). The compiled code can be run on most computers running Java Virtual Machine (JVM), because JVM's exist for almost all operating systems, including Windows, UNIX, Mac, and so on. Java is a general-purpose, open source programming language with features that are well suited for the Internet.

Internet Pricing Configurator (IPC)

In the past, SAP CRM also leveraged Java-based technologies, offering various J2EE-based applications, including E-Commerce and the interaction center. As of SAP CRM 2005 (SAP CRM 5.0), the interaction center was migrated back to a standard ABAP server solution. As of SAP CRM 2007, the E-Commerce (Internet Sales) portion of the SAP CRM Web channel application still runs on a J2EE server. In addition, SAP CRM uses another J2EE-based application for all SAP CRM-related pricing functions: the SAP Internet Pricing Configurator (IPC).

Build custom applications for the portal with business packages

SAP NetWeaver Enterprise Portal for SAP CRM

The SAP NetWeaver Enterprise Portal (EP) is a Web-based application that provides users with role-based, personalized access to SAP and non-SAP systems from a single, secure application. Different types of portals can be made available to your customers, partners, and employees. Portals provide users with a single, unified view of information coming from various sources and facilitate greater collaboration and sharing of information because users can find everything they need in one location.

SAP CRM leverages SAP NetWeaver Enterprise Portal. In SAP CRM 3.1, SAP CRM 4.0, and SAP CRM 2005, an Enterprise Portal-based user interface called People-Centric User Interface (PCUI) became available. PCUI delivers standard business roles in Enterprise Portal, such as Lead Qualifier, Lead Manager, Sales Manager, and so on, with predefined portal content called *business packages*. These business packages are configurable, so you can build custom applications for the portal. However, it's necessary to have knowledge of various Java and Internet technologies such as HTML, Java, Java Servlets, Java Server Pages (JSP), and SAP Java Web Dynpro (see Figure 10.4). SAP discontinued the PCUI with SAP CRM 2007, replacing PCUI with the new SAP CRM WebClient user interface. Nonetheless, Enterprise Portal itself is still supported in SAP CRM 2007 and can still be used as a launch pad for accessing SAP and non-SAP functionality.

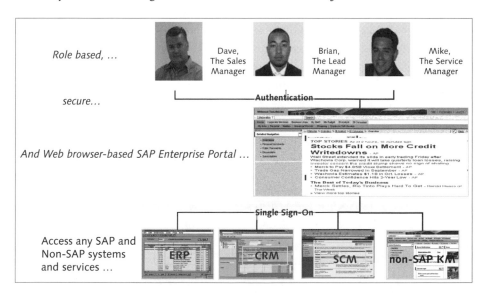

Figure 10.4 SAP NetWeaver Enterprise Portal for SAP CRM

SAP CRM Technology

SAP NetWeaver provides the underlying plumbing and the tools that allow business applications such as SAP CRM to run. However, SAP CRM also has its own technologies in addition to SAP NetWeaver technology. For example, the SAP CRM middleware is responsible for replicating, synchronizing, and distributing data across all relevant components of the SAP CRM landscape, including SAP NetWeaver BI and SAP ERP. SAP CRM groupware integration enables user of SAP CRM activity management to synchronize their SAP CRM calendars with industry-standard groupware packages such as Lotus Notes or Microsoft Outlook. SAP CRM also has its own tools for mobility, such as the Mobile Application Studio (MAS). In addition, SAP CRM has its own business objects, business object model, and user-interface technologies, including the People-Centric User Interface (PCUI) available from SAP CRM 3.1 to SAP CRM 5.0, and the SAP CRM WebClient user interface available as of CMR 2006s and SAP CRM 2007.

SAP CRM Middleware

SAP CRM middleware is an SAP-proprietary tool used to synchronize data between SAP CRM and other systems, including both SAP and non-SAP systems. SAP CRM middleware allows you to manage data from various types of applications within your SAP CRM landscape, including mobile clients, SAP ERP backend systems, SAP NetWeaver BI, and so on. For example, you can use the SAP CRM middleware to replicate customer data, product information, and sales orders back-and-forth between SAP CRM and SAP ERP. The SAP CRM middleware downloads the master and transaction data from the backend SAP ERP to SAP CRM as an initial download and then performs delta downloads of new and changed objects as necessary.

You can also use the SAP CRM middleware to synchronize data between the central SAP CRM server and mobile clients — typically, offline laptops running SAP CRM Mobile Sales or Mobile Service. The SAP CRM middleware initiates an initial download of data from the SAP CRM server to the mobile client, and then the middleware receives and sends updates from the mobile clients to and from the

SAP CRM server. The data may include information about customers, contact persons, products, installed base objects, sales orders, service orders, and so on.

Groupware Integration with SAP CRM

SAP CRM provides groupware integration that allows customers to synchronize groupware packages such as Microsoft Outlook and Lotus Notes by linking the SAP CRM server with the Microsoft Exchange Server or Lotus Domino Server for synchronization of email, calendar availability, and appointment functionality (see Figure 10.5). For example, when an employee receives an email in his personal email account from a customer, the employee could send the email over to the SAP CRM system with a click of the Synchronize with SAP CRM button in their Microsoft Outlook or Lotus Notes application. The email would then be replicated over into the SAP CRM system via the SAP CRM middleware.

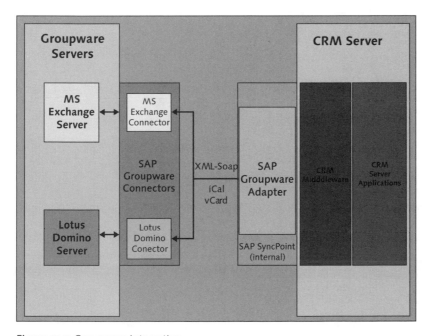

Figure 10.5 Groupware Integration

SAP CRM Mobile

Although SAP CRM leverages SAP NetWeaver Mobile for some mobile applications, SAP CRM also provides an SAP CRM-specific tool called Mobile Application Studio (MAS) that can be used to change the look and feel of the screens, enhance mobile client applications, and create new mobile application (see Figure 10.6). MAS provides wizards to create new user interface elements such as tiles and tile sets, as well as new business objects and new business queries.

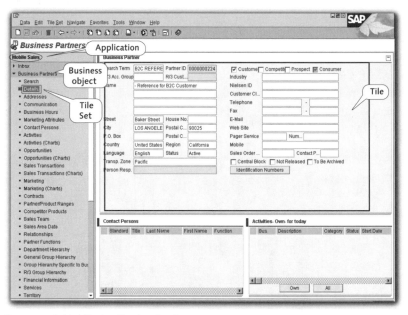

Figure 10.6 Mobile Application Studio

In addition, the MAS visual modeling tool minimizes manual coding and provides effortless generation of new mobile applications. MAS also supports the multi-language and translation functionality needs of mobile applications (see Figure 10.7).

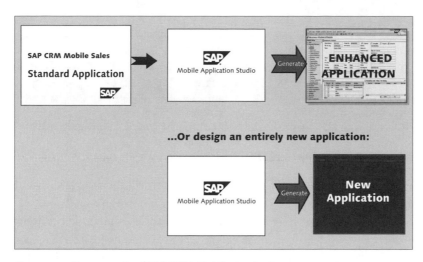

Figure 10.7 Components of SAP CRM Mobile Application

People-Centric User Interface (PCUI)

SAP introduced the People-Centric User Interface (PCUI) in SAP CRM 3.1. PCUI was designed as a thin-client, Web-based interface to provide SAP CRM functionality in a Web browser via SAP Enterprise Portal, rather than in the standard thick-client SAP GUI for Windows interface. The underlying concept behind PCUI was that all SAP CRM application components — from Marketing to Sales to Service — should have a consistent look-and-feel and use similar design elements.

All PCUI screens, therefore, used a consistent pattern, with three main screen areas. The top area is used to search for the desired object, the first detail area (located beneath the top area) is used for displaying the important attributes of the chosen object, and the second detail area (located at the bottom of the screen beneath the first detail area) is used for showing additional details that are hierarchically dependent on the object in the first detail area. Because all PCUI screens use the same design pattern, PCUI is sometimes also referred to as a "pattern-based" user interface.

Note

PCUI is delivered with and runs inside SAP EP and is available with release SAP CRM 3.1 to SAP CRM 2005 (SAP CRM 5.0). PCUI is replaced by the SAP CRM WebClient with release SAP CRM 2006s and SAP CRM 2007. Hence, PCUI is no longer supported after release SAP CRM 2005 (SAP CRM 5.0)

Business Server Pages (BSP)

Business Server Pages (BSP) is the technology behind both PCUI and the new SAP CRM WebClient user interface. BSP is the ABAP counterpart of JSP. BSP uses HTML pages with dynamically embedded content — typically JavaScript or ABAP fragments provided by SAP NetWeaver AS via server-side scripting. With BSP-based applications, the data displayed in the Web browser is sent via HTTP from the SAP NetWeaver AS to the Web browser client. BSP programming follows the widely accepted Model View Controller (MVC) modular-programming paradigm for object-oriented user interfaces, allowing business logic to be separated from the user interface. SAP provides tools, such as the BSP Component Workbench, to allow customers to make UI changes with minimal or no coding (see Figure 10.8).

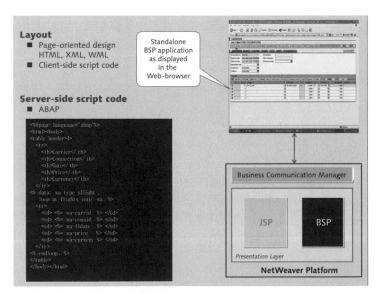

Figure 10.8 BSP Application Structure

SAP CRM WebClient (New with SAP CRM 2006s and SAP CRM 2007)

Perhaps one of the most important SAP CRM technologies is the SAP CRM WebClient user interface, originally developed for the interaction center WebClient in SAP CRM 4.0 and recently rolled out to the rest of SAP CRM in release SAP CRM 2006s and above. Unlike PCUI, the SAP CRM WebClient does not require Enterprise Portal. The SAP CRM WebClient is a thin-client, browser-based solution that allows SAP CRM business applications to run in a standard Web browser without the need for the Enterprise Portal or SAP GUI. The SAP CRM WebClient relies on Business Server Pages (BSP), which is discussed later. One of the advantages of the new SAP CRM WebClient user interface is that it comes with one set of tools that can be used for adding new fields, moving or removing fields from the UI, changing field labels, and so on. You no longer need multiple tools sets — with separate skill sets — for making changes to different SAP CRM components. Another advantage of the new SAP CRM WebClient user interface is the inclusion of Web 2.0 features such as end-user personalized screens, fields, UI skins, and layouts.

 Note

As of SAP CRM release 2006s and above, all SAP CRM business applications are delivered with the SAP CRM WebClient user interface. The SAP CRM WebClient is a thin-client, browser-based solution that has a zero footprint and requires no installation of special software such as SAP GUI. Older user interface technologies such as SAP GUI and PCUI are no longer offered or supported for SAP CRM business users. Consultants and IT users will still access SAP GUI for administration and configuration activities.

SAP CRM Business Object Layer (BOL)/ Generic Interaction Layer (genIL)

The SAP CRM WebClient, like the interaction center WebClient on which it was based, uses a multilayer architecture consisting of three layers:

> **Presentation layer**
  Based on BSP

> **Business layer**
  Based on the Business Object Layer (BOL) and generic Interaction Layer (genIL)

> **Business application/business engine layer**
  Consisting of database tables and application programming interfaces (APIs)

The SAP CRM WebClient uses a multilayer architecture.

Let's look at the business layer quickly. The Business Object Layer (BOL) is designed to store business objects that are being used in the current user session. For example, if an interaction center agent is working with a customer who wants to register a product, the BOL will be used to store both the customer ID (in the customer business object) and the product ID (in the product business object). The generic Interaction Layer (genIL) handles the transfer of the data from the BOL to the APIs of the application logic and database tables to access the functionality of the SAP CRM business engine.

So far we've discussed the technologies approved by SAP NetWeaver as well as the SAP CRM-specific technologies. However, no discussion of SAP technology would be complete without a word about ABAP.

ABAP

ABAP is the programming language developed by SAP in the 1980s.

ABAP (Advanced Business Application Programming) is a proprietary fourth-generation programming language developed by SAP in the 1980s. ABAP is the main workhorse behind SAP's engines. ABAP began as a reporting tool in the SAP R/2 release. ABAP was originally an abbreviation of *Allgemeiner Berichts Aufbereitungs Prozessor*, which means "generic report preparation processor in English." It was later renamed to Advanced Business Application Programming (ABAP) and used in the development of SAP R/3. ABAP is one of the first 4GL languages to include logical databases (LDBs), which provide a high-level abstract at the database level. In 1999, SAP released an object-oriented extension to ABAP called ABAP Objects that allows object-oriented programming on the basis of classes and interfaces. ABAP is extremely flexible and adaptive and has become the preferred Web application programming language of programmers in the SAP ecosystem. The ABAP development story is an amazing journey and transformation from a classic reporting tool to a modern Web UI tool.

This concludes our look at the technology behind SAP CRM. Now let's see how it works in the real world.

Case Study

In this case study, we'll consider a large public-sector water resource department with $8 billion in revenue and 2,600 employees. The company implemented SAP Interactive Forms to provide a paperless, easy-to-use user interface to employees.

Following are the business challenges the company faced:

> Continuing to use the existing manual operation logging method using a static Word template could lead to errors.

> Maintaining data accuracy is critical for taking timely action concerning flood control, public water safety, and dam safety operations.

> Providing an easy-to-use, interactive application that updates the backend SAP ERP plant maintenance system seamlessly is very important.

> Using high data encryption, enhanced security and authorizations, and data integrity is necessary.

The company has two main business objectives it wants to meet by implementing SAP Interactive Forms:

> Have a simple to use and easy-to-understand operational report form that requires minimal training

> Be able to send the midnight reporting to the plant maintenance system using an Internet connection

Creating these easily customizable interactive forms that support "Midnight Conditions" reporting must come out of 29 plants with different equipment and configurations that are operated by 70 operators. To meet this technology challenge and meet the business objectives, the company deployed the SAP ERP application with SAP Interactive Forms. The result of this deployment is a huge maintenance cost savings and improved operational efficiency because the reporting data is directly transferred into the SAP ERP application.

The company now looks forward to implementing SAP Interactive Forms with workflow to automate the employee travel expense approval process.

Conclusion

In this chapter, you learned about all of the different technologies used across SAP applications. We looked at SAP NetWeaver, which provides the underlying technology platform on top of which all SAP applications run. We discussed the SAP NetWeaver enterprise service-oriented architecture (enterprise SOA) that allows organizations to use Web Services to support their business processes. Then we talked about SAP NetWeaver's integration functionalities, which allow you to integrate people, information, and processes on top of a single application platform.

After discussing the general SAP NetWeaver technology functionalities, we looked at how SAP NetWeaver technologies could be integrated into SAP CRM applications and business processes. Then we shifted gears and focused on the SAP CRM-specific technologies such as SAP CRM middleware, SAP CRM Mobile, BSP, PCUI, and the SAP CRM WebClient. Finally, we concluded with a discussion of ABAP, the first and still the most famous SAP technology.

The most important things to remember from this chapter are the following:

> SAP NetWeaver provides the technology platform to satisfy your technology needs and business requirements in any SAP environment. SAP customers like SAP NetWeaver's open architecture, scalability, and robustness. They also like the fact that SAP NetWeaver helps reduce TCO for a company's IT infrastructure.

> SAP NetWeaver provides the technology platform on which all SAP applications run. SAP NetWeaver enables enterprise SOA and allows you to integrate people, information, and processes on a single application platform.

> SAP NetWeaver Process Integration (PI), formerly known as Exchange Infrastructure (XI), enables data sharing between SAP and non-SAP systems and can be used, to import data from third-party systems into SAP systems such as SAP CRM.

> SAP CRM middleware allows you to continually synchronize and replicate data between your SAP CRM system and other SAP (or non-SAP) systems in your IT landscape, such as SAP NetWeaver BI, SAP ERP, and so on.

> SAP CRM Groupware Integration enables you to synchronize groupware packages such as Microsoft Outlook and Lotus Notes with SAP CRM. For example, you can import emails from a personal email account into SAP CRM or download SAP CRM tasks and appointments into your groupware calendar.

> The SAP CRM WebClient user interface, introduced with SAP CRM 2006s and SAP CRM 2007, replaces SAP GUI and PCUI for business users. The SAP CRM WebClient comes with a single set of tools that can be used to make user interface changes across all SAP CRM application components, and allows end-user personalization of screens, fields, UI skins, and layouts.

In the next chapter, we'll turn our attention to master data, one of the most important but most overlooked aspects of any SAP CRM project.

Master Data

Customer Relationship Management (CRM) is all about identifying your most valuable customers and providing differentiated levels of service to increase customer satisfaction, loyalty, and profitability. To do this, you need a complete 360-degree view of your customers. This can be difficult in today's business environment where consolidations and acquisitions tend to leave companies with a variety of software products from different vendors — each product with its own database and master data.

If, for example, your company stores customer product-registration information in one computer system, customer sales orders in another, and customer trouble tickets in yet another, chances are that you aren't easily able to get an accurate overview of your customers. And, without an accurate picture of your customers, you don't know very much about the health of your relationship with them, or the value they bring to your organization. However, with an integrated CRM product such as SAP CRM, all customer data is available in one system, providing you with a consolidated overview of your customers.

All customer data is available in one system.

Poorly managed customer data is one of the most common reasons for CRM project failure

Yet, even with a single CRM system and a consolidated database, data challenges still remain. Duplicate records can exist for the same customer with slightly different spellings of the customer's name or with outdated addresses. Keeping your customer database up to date might seem like a simple task, but it often proves to be very difficult. Companies frequently comment that poorly managed customer data is one of the most common reasons for the failure of CRM projects, right along with other well-known mistakes, such as lack of top management support or attempting to do too much with too few resources.

To make things even more difficult, customer master records aren't the only type of data that you need to worry about. You need to keep track of all kinds of master data records including:

> Customer master records

> Product master records

> Data about the organizational structures in your company

> Product and customer-specific pricing data

Master data is the foundation on which your CRM system is built; so the design and execution of your master data management policy will greatly influence the success of your CRM project.

 Note

The challenge of providing a consolidated view of data stored in disparate systems across an enterprise has given rise to master data management software. SAP offers an MDM solution called NetWeaver Master Data Management (MDM) that leverages various SAP NetWeaver capabilities, including SAP NetWeaver BI, SAP NetWeaver Process Integration (SAP NetWeaver PI – formerly XI), and SAP master data server to provide data consolidation and synchronization across your IT infrastructure. However, we won't discuss MDM in detail here because this book is about CRM, so we'll only focus on the master data management capabilities provided by SAP CRM.

SAP CRM master data generally falls into four areas, as shown in Figure 11.1:

> **Business partners**
Such as customers, prospects, contact persons, employees, and so on

> **Products**
Such as materials, equipment, service products, warranty products, and financial products

> **Organizational data**
Such as sales organizations, service organizations, sales offices, sales groups, and positions

> **Pricing**
Such as customer-specific pricing, product pricing, and so on

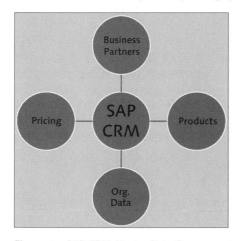

Figure 11.1 SAP CRM Master Data Components

Let's look at each of these in a little detail.

Business Partner (BP) Master Data

SAP uses the term *business partner (BP)* to refer to any type of company or person with whom you conduct business, including customers, partners, employees, and so on. The success of your company's marketing, sales, and service efforts are highly dependent on the way your BP master data is designed, collected, stored, and retrieved in your CRM system. Your BP master data is very personal to your organization; no one understands your customers like you do. Therefore,

How your business partner master data is designed, collected, stored, and retrieved affects your success your BP master data strategy needs to be aligned with your organization's business processes.

Business Partner Design in SAP CRM

In this section, we'll talk about BP categories, roles, and relationships, or the concepts specific to SAP CRM BP management. We'll explain each of these concepts in detail and show you how they can be used to design a BP master data strategy that best supports your enterprise.

Business Partner Categories

BPs in SAP CRM are categorized as either natural persons (private individuals), organizations (legal persons or entities), or groups of either natural persons or organizations. When creating a new BP, the first thing you must do is select the appropriate category.

The natural person category can be used to represent contact people, employees, and citizens, etc. The organization category is useful for modeling BPs, such as companies, vendors, suppliers, and so on. And the group can represent families, and joint proprietors.

SAP CRM BPs are categorized as natural persons, organizations, or groups

Depending on which business partner category you are working with, you'll access different screens and enter different data. For example, when creating a new BP of category organization, you can maintain the relevant industry and legal form, which is obviously not relevant for a natural person. On the other hand, when creating a new BP for a person, you would maintain attributes such as gender, marital status, and nationality, which aren't relevant for legal entities such as organizations.

The BP categories include:

> Natural Persons (private individuals)

> Organizations (legal entities)

> Groups (collection of related persons or organizations, such as a married couple or shared living arrangement)

After selecting the BP category, the next level of granularity is determined by the BP role, which allows you to specify the business function of the BP. Let's have a look.

Business Partner Roles

Different types of BPs serve different purposes and support different processes within your business. And, one BP may support more than one business process. For instance, a private individual who orders a product from your company would likely play the role of sold-to party, ship-to party, bill-to party, and payer. On the other hand, it's possible that one individual person might buy a gift for a friend or relative, in which case, the person buying the product would be the sold-to party, bill-to party, and payer but not the ship-to party. So, a BP master record in the system can have one or more roles (see Figure 11.2).

BPs can support more than one business process

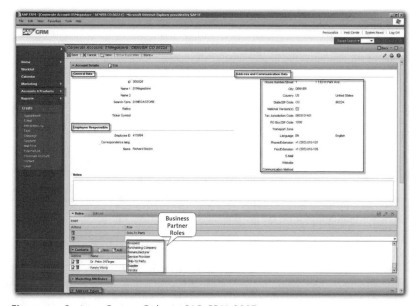

Figure 11.2 Business Partner Roles in SAP CRM 2007

It 's important to note that all BPs have the general role of Business Partner (Gen.) in addition to any other more specific roles.

A partial list of BP roles includes:

> Business Partner (Gen.)

> Consumer

> Account

> Prospect

> Contact Person

> Sold-to party

> Ship-to party

> Bill-to party

> Payer

> Employee

When working with a BP for whom more than one role is maintained, the BP role provides a specific view of the BP master data based on the selected role — even though all of the data for all maintained BP roles are stored in the same physical master record based on the BP's ID.

 Tip

All BP records, regardless of the BP role, have general data such as title, name, address, and communication information. This information is stored and viewed under the Business Partner (Gen.) default role. Every BP has the general role and may have additional roles as well.

BP Classification

Assign customer account groups to control the properties of your customer

BP classification indicates how a BP is used within the SAP CRM system, although classification is primarily of importance when distributing or replicating customer master data from SAP CRM to SAP ERP. The SAP CRM BP classification is used by SAP ERP to assign the relevant customer *account group*, which controls properties of the customer in SAP ERP, including number ranges, master data fields, and available SAP ERP Sales and Distribution (SD) functionality.

Note

SAP CRM uses *BP* objects to represent customers, vendors, employees, and other entities that an organization conducts business with. But the BP object isn't available in SAP ERP, which instead uses *customer objects*. However, it's possible to synchronize customer data between SAP CRM and SAP ERP via the SAP CRM middleware, which handles the technical mapping between the SAP CRM BP object and the SAP ERP customer object.

SAP CRM has four BP classifications:

> Customer

> Consumer

> Prospect

> Competitor

The classifications are automatically determined at the time the BP is first created and saved based on the role assigned to the BP (see Table 11.1). For example, if one of the four roles — sold-to party, ship-to party, bill-to party, or payer — is assigned to the BP, then the BP is classified as a customer. If the consumer, prospect, or competitor role is assigned, then the BP is respectively classified as a consumer, prospect, or competitor. Because it's only possible to assign one role to a BP before saving the BP master record, only one classification will be set based on the first role selected.

BP Roles	Customer	Consumer	Prospect	Competitor
Sold-to party	X			
Ship-to party	X			
Bill-to party	X			
Payer	X			
Consumer		X		
Prospect			X	
Competitors				X

Table 11.1 BP Classifications Determined by BP Role Assignment

BP Relationships

Model how your
BPs are connected
to each other.

SAP CRM provides you with the power to flexibly model how your BPs are connected to each other. A BP relationship represents the business connection between two BPs. Although you might not have many relationships between customers in straightforward Business to Consumer (B2C) scenarios, you'll often have many complicated relationships between BPs in Business to Business (B2B) scenarios. For example, you might have a main account or parent company called "ABC Company" with more than 100 different contact persons. When you receive a call from one of the contact persons in your call center, you need to be able to pull up the master data record of the main account as well.

In most cases, BP relationships are bi-directional; for example, if BP ABC Company has the relationship "Has Contact Person" with BP Cathy, then BP Cathy has the relationship "Is Contact Person For" BP ABC Company (see Figure 11.3). It's possible to maintain validity dates on each BP relationship, causing the relationship to cease after a specified "valid to" date, which is typically otherwise set to 12/31/9999 by default.

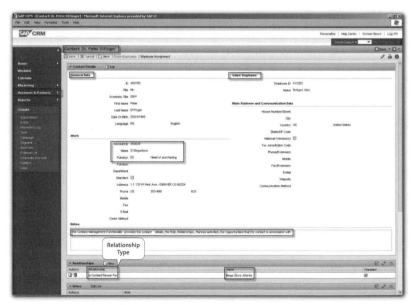

Figure 11.3 BP Relationships in SAP CRM 2007

Let's assume that your company is promoting a new product at a trade show. When an attendee visits your booth, your employees can scan the attendee's badge to electronically collect their data. The data may contain information about the person's name, employer, company address, corporate phone number, email address, and office telephone and fax number. Based on the information you capture, the SAP CRM system can create two BP records. The data of the attendee's employer will be used to create a BP with category *organization*, role *prospect*, and classification *prospect*. The data of the attendee will be used to create a second BP with category *person*, and role *contact person*, with the relationship "Is Contact Person For" the BP that was created for the organization.

Ex Example

John Doe, who recently attended a trade show, works as a purchasing manager at XYZ Company located in Milwaukee, WI. John has expressed interest in one of your newly launched products, but his purchase time frame isn't within the next six months. Because he isn't looking to purchase in the short term, you aren't sure if XYZ company should be created as an immediate prospect or not. Instead of creating XYZ as a prospect, you create XYZ with role Business Partner (Gen.) with the relationship "has purchasing manager" to John Doe, who would be created as a BP with role Contact Person and the relationship type "Is Purchasing Manager of" (see Figure 11.4).

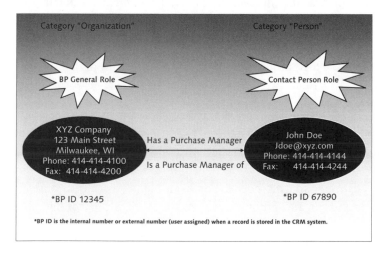

Figure 11.4 BPs, Categories, Roles, and Relationships

This concludes our discussion about customer master data. Now let's turn our attention to product master data.

Product Master Data

In SAP CRM, product is used to refer both to physical products and service products

In SAP applications, the term *product* is used to refer both to *physical* products (such as widgets) and *service* products (such as widget installation and repair); the term *product master* refers to a set of reusable information about the product that is maintained in the SAP CRM system. SAP CRM offers great flexibility in how you design, model, and implement your product master data. At the detailed product level, you can define attributes such as size, weight, and units of measure (e.g., is the product sold by piece, by weight, or by volume?). SAP CRM also supports configurable products, allowing you to offer different variants of your products to suit different customer needs. Products can also be modeled in product hierarchies or catalogs, allowing users to drill down through a navigable, intuitive structure to find the products they need. All of these decisions about how you design and organize your product master data will ultimately impact your business processes. So, planning your master design strategy is critical. Your product master data design needs to support all of your marketing, sales, and service business processes. For example, product information is available in a variety of SAP CRM business documents and transactions, including customer inquiries, product catalogs, contracts, sales orders, service orders, complaints, returns, and so on.

Let's look at the SAP product master design options in detail.

SAP CRM Product Master Data Design

SAP products recognize the need for product master-data design options that are flexible enough to accommodate a variety of different industry sectors (e.g., high tech, telecommunications, retail, etc.) as well as customer-specific needs. For example, in certain industries such as high-tech and automotive, products are often configurable with different options and accessories. In industries such as telecommunications (Telco), products are typically sold in bundles (e.g., a mobile phone and a two-year service agreement, or a bundle consisting of cable television, broadband Internet access, and long-distance telephone service). See Figure 11.5.

Figure 11.5 Product Master Data in SAP CRM 2007

SAP CRM provides you with the flexibility to design a product structure that captures the product attributes and product relationships that are important for your business. The product master contains general data such as attributes, product descriptions, features and attachments, and sales area data, such as the sales organizations and distribution channel combinations that are permitted to sell the product. In the product master, you can define relationships between one product and other related products such as accessories, spare parts, or competitor equivalents of the product.

Product Types

In the SAP CRM systems, products are broadly grouped into the following *product types:* Material, Service, Warranty, Financing, Financial Services, and Intellectual Property. The product type describes the

Products are grouped into product types and categories

263

basic characteristics of the product and determines to which *product categories* a product can be assigned (product categories will be explained shortly).

The following product types are available in SAP CRM:

> **Material**
Goods that can be produced, traded, used in manufacture, or consumed.

> **Service**
An action that can be performed for the customer, either at the customer site or by the service provider onsite.

> **Warranty**
A guarantee from the manufacturer or vendor that a product is free from defects and will be serviced (usually free of charge) for a specific period of time.

> **Financing**
An agreement about the payment terms and payment due date for a particular product (such as an automobile or other high-cost product).

> **Financial Services**
A financing arrangement, such as a consumer loan or mortgage loan, where money is lent and needs to be repaid on a schedule.

> **Intellectual Property**
A media product, such as a film, soundtrack, song, photograph, and so on, for which usage rights can be licensed and sold.

Product Attributes and Attribute-Set Types

A *set type* is a group of product *attributes* that can be used to define a new product. SAP software provides standard set types such as Descriptions, Units of Measure, Taxes, Basic Data on Materials, Default Value for Service Contracts, Warranty, Financing Set Types, and so on (see Figure 11.6). For example, the Warranty set type contains the standard attributes appropriate for a new warranty product such as whether the warranty is a customer warranty or a vendor warranty, as well as on what basis the warranty is evaluated (period of time such as 3 years, odometer reading such as 100,000 miles, etc.). Of course, if you don't want to use the default set types, you may also define your own set types using whatever attributes you think are appropriate for your products.

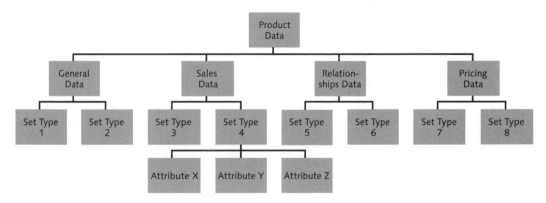

Figure 11.6 Set Types and Attributes

Set types aren't assigned directly to products, but rather set types are assigned to categories, which are assigned to products. In this manner, you can make all of the data you need to describe products available with minimum effort and in a reusable manner. When you create a new product with the appropriate category, set type, and attributes, you'll have access to all of the necessary fields required to create your products.

Product Categories and Hierarchies

Product categories and hierarchies are used for grouping products together according to various criteria (see Figure 11.7). *Categories* define which attribute set types and relationships are allowed for your products. *Hierarchies* allow you to model your products in a logical structure. The nature of the hierarchy depends on your business processes, of course. The important thing to know about product hierarchies is that the lower-level products inherit the attribute set type and product type of the higher-level category. As you move down the hierarchy, you can assign additional attribute set types to products, creating a structure with general products on top and the more specifically defined products at the bottom.

Figure 11.7 Product Hierarchy, Categories, and Sub Categories

Group your products together according to categories and hierarchies

For example, an automotive dealer might have a hierarchy with "automobiles" at the top of the hierarchy, followed by the categories "cars" and "trucks" at the next level. Beneath "trucks," there might be several categories such as "SUVs" and "pick ups." And beneath "SUVs," there might be categories such as "light SUVs," "full-size SUVs," and "hybrid SUVs."

 Tip

In SAP CRM, it's mandatory to select the product type and product category to create a product in the system.

Product Relationships

SAP CRM supports the concept of *product relationships*, allowing you to model how one product is related or connected to another product, or how a product is connected or related to other objects such as a customer. For example, you might define product sets or bundles, where each product in the bundle is related to each other. You can also use relationships to define accessories, spare parts, or service parts for a product. Take a laptop computer for example, in this case you might define accessories such as an optical mouse, a carrying case, and a flat panel monitor. Similarly, for a product such as a photocopier/printer/fax machine, you might define spare parts and service parts such as replacement toner or ink cartridges. You can also model relationships between products and customers to indicate that a certain customer owns a particular product.

 Example

> A high-tech computer company might define the product "optical mouse" as an accessory of the product "notebook computer." In this example, "optical mouse" is an accessory product, "notebook computer" is the main product, and "is an accessory of" is the relationship.

Organizational Master Data

In the SAP CRM system, you can create organizational master data to represent the way your company's sales, service, and marketing departments are organized and conduct business. The purpose of SAP CRM *Organization data (Org. data)* is to support the assignment of people and reporting structures. The SAP CRM *Organizational structure (Org. structure)* — sometimes also referred to as the Org. model — depicts the hierarchy of organizational units (such as departments) within your company according to task and function. The SAP CRM Org. structure will almost certainly differ from the *personnel structure* in your company, which is organized to support administrative tasks such as payroll accounting. The SAP CRM Org. structure can include relationships between positions in your company and other dependent objects, such as tasks, jobs, or work centers (Figure 11.8).

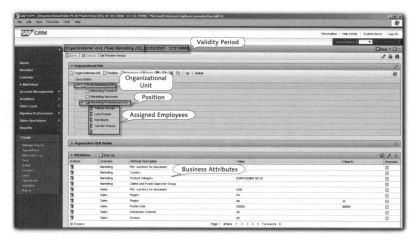

Figure 11.8 Marketing Organizational Structures Using SAP CRM

Organizational Objects

Use organizational master data to represent how your departments are organized

In the SAP CRM system, you model your Org. structure using two types of organizational objects: organizational units (Org. units) and positions. The Org. units form the basis of your Org. structure, representing the functional units of your company, such as departments, groups, or project teams. Organizational objects in SAP CRM include service organizations, sales organizations, and marketing organizations, as well as something called *business place*, which is only used for local tax reporting purposes in countries such as Brazil and South Korea.

Positions are used to describe functional tasks within an organization, including purchasing manager, sales manager, marketing specialist, call center agent, and so on. In the SAP CRM system, positions are assigned to employees and other SAP CRM users who are referred to as position "holders." You can assign "valid from" and "valid to" dates to an org. unit. You can also assign addresses to an org. unit. Org. units are also created as BPs with the role of Org. unit in the SAP CRM system (see Figure 11.9).

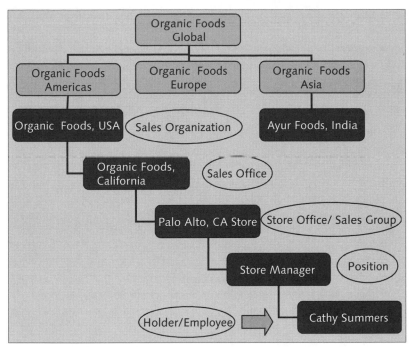

Figure 11.9 Plan for a Global Grocery Store Company

Organizational Attributes and Business Attributes

Attributes can be assigned to org. units when maintained in a specific scenario, such as service or sales, to define the type of Org. unit or the responsibilities of the Org. unit. Attributes are always used in conjunction with a specific scenario: either sales or service. There are two types of attributes: organizational attributes and business attributes. Organizational attributes define the *type* of organization, indicating, for example, whether it's a sales organization, a service organization, or a marketing organization (Figure 11.10).

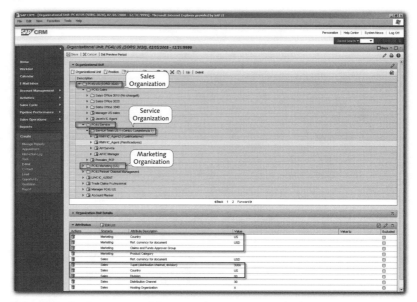

Figure 11.10 An Organizational Structure that Supports Multiple Organizational Units

Organizational attributes include objects such as sales organizations, sales offices, and sales groups. Business attributes define the *responsibility* of the Organizational unit, indicating, for example, products or distribution channels the Org. unit is responsible for. Business attributes include distribution channels, divisions, address information (such as region/state, ZIP code, and country), product attributes (such as product category, product ID), and BP attributes (such as BP ID). Business attributes assigned at the highest level of the Org. unit are inherited by the subordinate Org. units. However, you can manually overwrite the inherited business attributes if desired (Figure 11.11).

Organizational structure is flexible, time-independent adaptable, and extendable

Organizational master data can be integrated with backend SAP HR master data (positions and position holders) as well as with backend SAP ERP sales area data (sales organization and distribution channel with optional divisions.)

270

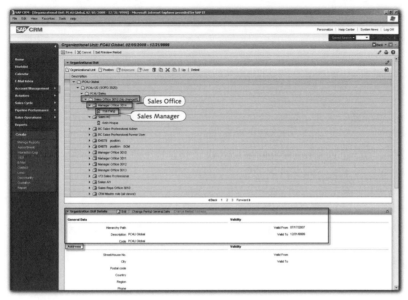

Figure 11.11 Sales Organizational Structure in SAP CRM 2007

> ▶ **Note**
>
> Organizational management allows you to display a company's functional organizational structure as a current organizational plan. Organizational units (sales organization, service organization, etc.) can be characterized by organizational and business attributes (Figure 11.12).

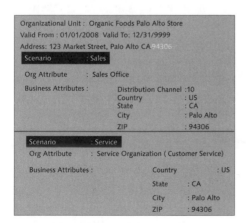

Figure 11.12 Designing an Organizational Structure for Sales and Service for Business and Customer Touch Points

Example

> The business benefit of maintaining the Organizational structure is that an incoming customer sales call can be routed automatically to a responsible sales group or sales person based on the customer address attributes such as ZIP code/postal code, and region/state. These attributes are assigned as business attributes to a sales office or sales group to which the sales person is assigned in the Organizational structure.

Pricing Master Data

Offer customer-specific and contract-based pricing

Pricing has become more important than ever. Companies are realizing that the one-price-fits-all static pricing model of the past is less relevant today and limits profitability. Pricing has gradually shifted from product-specific pricing — where all customers pay the same set price for a specific product — to customer-specific pricing and contract-based pricing. Customer-specific pricing involves charging different customers different prices for the same product, typically by offering discounts to certain customers based on their value to the company, their purchase history, or the volume of products they buy. Contract pricing allows you to specify different prices based on agreed-upon purchase volumes and time frames. For example, you might offer a lower price to a customer who agrees to buy a certain number of units every month. In addition, products today are more complicated and configurable than in the past, and configurable products require configurable (variant) pricing. Regardless of how you look at it, static, product-based pricing is obsolete.

 Tip

> Companies that operate globally should define their pricing strategy centrally and then adapt it locally.

SAP Internet Pricing and Configurator (IPC)

SAP recognizes the need for pricing flexibility and has developed a rule-based dynamic pricing engine called the Internet Pricing and Configurator (IPC) that performs all SAP CRM-related pricing and includes support for variant pricing. IPC has two important components: the Sales Pricing Engine (SPE) and the Sales Configuration Engine (SCE). IPC is capable of providing channel specific prices (Figure 11.13).

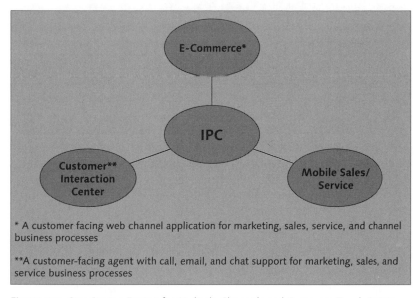

Figure 11.13 One Pricing Engine for Multiple Channels and Customer Touch Points

The SPE handles pricing, including variant pricing for configurable products via the *condition technique*, which relies on *condition records*. A condition record is a database table entry that defines the input and output values for price determination. Essentially, condition records are rules that define the appropriate price based on data such as customer group, customer, product, channel, date, and so on. We cover condition technique in more detail in a separate section of this chapter. It's important to note that IPC condition technique works similarly to the pricing condition technique of SAP ERP; however, whereas SAP ERP pricing conditions are implemented in ABAP, the pricing conditions in IPC are Java based.

The SCE is used to support *variant configuration* of configurable products and materials. Increasingly today, products are becoming more complex and more configurable. For example, in the automotive in-

The condition technique allows for variant pricing

273

dustry, cars are often sold as configurable products where customers choose the color, options, and accessories they want. Similarly, in the high-tech industry, computers are often sold as configurable products where the user chooses options such as the type of processor, amount of RAM and hard disk space, and so on.

Ex Example

> Most airlines charge a booking fee if you call the airline agent to make a reservation. The booking fee is waived if you make the reservation online. In this case, the airline pricing engine is performing customer-specific pricing based on the customer's interaction channel.

Increase profit margins by dynamically optimizing the prices of products

In addition to IPC, SAP Price and Margin Management is a process-driven price and margin management solution that helps you determine and enforce optimal pricing. The solution is offered in conjunction with an SAP partner named Vendavo. Unlike IPC, the Vendavo solution is a separate product and is licensed separately from SAP CRM. However, the solution is integrated with SAP CRM. The goal of price and margin management products such as the Vendavo solution is to increase profit margins by dynamically optimizing the prices of products based on factors such as inventory levels, customer type, customer, product, and so on, as well as enforcing the prices and preserving margins by limiting rogue sales activities and inappropriate price discounts.

Condition Technique and Condition Records

Pricing master data is maintained in the IPC via condition records, which are database table entries that define the input and output values for price determination. Condition records are basically rules that specify different pricing combinations based on input values such as the customer group, customer, material, customer/material, ship-to party/material, and so on. The condition records are accessed by the IPC using pricing logic and condition techniques to determine the particular price, discount, and surcharges to a customer. The condition technique incorporates a number of concepts, including condition types, condition tables, access sequences, and pricing procedures (Figure 11.14):

> **Pricing procedure**
This is a kind of cookie jar that holds the condition types and defines which condition types are permitted and in what sequence.

> **Condition types**
Condition types define the characteristic and attributes of a condition. For example, a specific condition types might be used to represent a base price, discount, surcharge, freight cost, and so on.

> **Condition Tables**
Condition tables define the key combination of fields that identify an individual condition record.

> **Access sequences**
Access sequences provide the search strategies for condition tables, determining in which sequence the conditions should be evaluated.

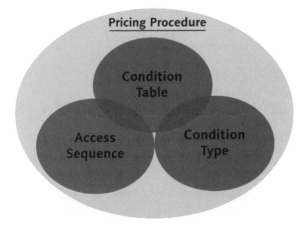

Figure 11.14 Condition Technique Used in the CRM Pricing Engine

This wraps up our discussion of SAP CRM master data.

Case Study

The company for this case study is a world leader in Electronic Design Automation (EDA) software and services that are used by global semiconductor and electronics industries to design complex integrated circuits (IC), systems-on-chips (SoCs), and electronic systems. The company's products enable its customers to improve performance, increase productivity, and achieve predictable success from systems to silicon. The company generates global revenue of more than $1 billion and has operations all around the globe.

This company has accelerated its technology strategy and innovation by technology gained from a series of mergers and acquisitions. In the process, the company ended up with 16 legacy CRM systems on different standalone systems. This raised a business challenge of merging the customer records, consolidating, and moving the master data (customers, products, and organizational data) into a single CRM system.

Therefore, the business objective for this company is to provide one CRM system for the entire enterprise to provide an efficient customer service and sales engagement process.

The challenge was developing a master data cleansing and merging strategy that extracts the data from 16 legacy CRM systems and transfers the data into one CRM system.

The company is already running SAP ERP software and has embraced innovative SAP technology to improve business efficiency.

The solution was to use a SAP CRM 3.1 system, which was later upgraded to SAP CRM 4.0 with SAP BW 3.5 and Enterprise Portal 6.0.

The solution gave the company the following benefits:

> Huge maintenance cost savings and increased operational efficiency by retiring the legacy CRM systems
> Easy corporate metrics using SAP NetWeaver BI with SAP CRM
> Accelerated customer service with increased visibility into service requests created in one system versus several systems
> Reduced turnaround time for issue resolution
> Greater visibility into sales activities and sales process with one system

The company is now looking forward to upgrading the current SAP CRM 4.0 system to SAP CRM 2007/SAP CRM 7.0.

Conclusion

In this chapter, you learned that master data is a critical component of your SAP CRM strategy and business processes. Without consolidated, accurate customer data, you don't have a complete overview of your customers and can't accurately determine the appropriate level of service to provide each customer based on that customer's value to the organization. Without well-organized and clearly structured product master data, customers can't find the products they are looking for. If your organizational data isn't well planned and carefully mapped, you won't have a clear picture of your sales, service, and marketing organizations and distribution channels. Finally, without the flexibility to define dynamic, optimized pricing, including customer-specific and contract-based pricing, you'll risk leaving money on the table and giving products and product features away for less than they are worth.

In this chapter, we looked in detail at the four areas of SAP CRM master data: BP master data, product master data, organizational master data, and pricing master data. The most important things to remember from this chapter are the following:

> SAP NetWeaver Master Data Management (SAP NetWeaver MDM) leverages various SAP NetWeaver capabilities, including SAP NetWeaver Business Intelligence (SAP NetWeaver BI), SAP NetWeaver Process Integration (SAP NetWeaver PI), and SAP master data server to provide master data consolidation and replication across your SAP IT landscape. However, MDM isn't within the scope of SAP CRM.

> SAP CRM master data falls into four categories: business partner (BP) master data, product master data, organizational master data, and pricing master data.

> SAP CRM uses a technical object called the business partner (BP) to represent customers (as well as other types of people you do busi-

ness with such as employees, vendors, and so on), whereas SAP ERP uses a technical object called customer. It's possible to map the two objects and replicate data using SAP CRM middleware.

> All pricing in SAP CRM is provided by the SAP Internet Pricing and Configurator (IPC), which is installed separately from SAP CRM. IPC relies on condition technique and condition tables for pricing, similar to how pricing is modeled in SAP ERP. However, IPC is based on Java, whereas SAP ERP pricing is based on ABAP. It's possible to migrate conditions tables from ABAP to Java.

> SAP CRM supports variant configuration of configurable products, as well as variant pricing for configurable products.

In the next chapter, we'll turn our attention to SAP CRM industry vertical solutions such as high-tech, telecommunications, utilities, public sector, life sciences, pharmaceutical, automotive, consumer products, retail, apparel and footwear, and more.

12

Working with SAP Industry Vertical Solutions

Now it's time to investigate the industry vertical solutions offered by SAP CRM. We first discussed industry verticals in Chapter 1, so as a quick reminder, an industry vertical is a particular market or group of companies in which similar products and services are developed, marketed, and sold using similar methods to customers with similar needs. Industry verticals are also referred to as vertical industries or vertical markets. Some common examples of industry verticals include high-tech, telecommunications, utilities, automotive, public sector (government), financial services, retail, and so on.

Obviously, the business software needs of each of these industries might differ, but SAP has a long history of providing support for industries, dating back to its early R/2 and R/3 ERP applications that were well tailored for manufacturing industries. Since then, SAP has added support for many other industries. SAP has worked very closely with customers in numerous different industries, accumulating a great deal of industry-specific knowledge along the way. SAP understands the pain points that different industries experience, and SAP specializes in providing industry-specific best practices that address those pain points.

SAP has a long history of supporting a variety of industries

Solutions for the manufacturing and service industries

Today, SAP CRM supports more than 25 different vertical industries. In this chapter, we'll look at the SAP CRM industry-specific capabilities for some of the most common manufacturing industries and service industries. SAP offers tailored SAP CRM solutions for a variety of manufacturing industries such as automotive, chemical, consumer products (CP), engineering and construction, high-tech, oil and gas, pharmaceuticals, and life sciences.

SAP CRM also offers solutions tailored to the needs of service industries, including insurance, banking, financial services, leasing, media, retail, professional services, public sector (government), telecommunications, and utilities. In the following sections, we'll provide a brief overview of each of the solutions to give you an idea about the options related to your business's industry.

Automotive

In today's market, the automotive industry is faced with growing global competition, falling prices, disconnected communication between automotive original equipment manufacturers (OEMs) and dealers, increased supply chain costs, and knowledgeable customers who conduct substantial pre-purchase Internet research. The answer to these automotive challenges is an integrated SAP CRM system that supports OEMs, suppliers, dealers, and sales and service organizations. SAP CRM supports a variety of automotive-related business processes including the following:

> Vehicle marketing
> Vehicle sales and distribution
> Leasing and asset management
> Vehicle management
> After-sales follow-up
> Customer-vehicle relationship management with the automotive interaction center

See Figure 12.1 for a breakdown of the automotive solution.

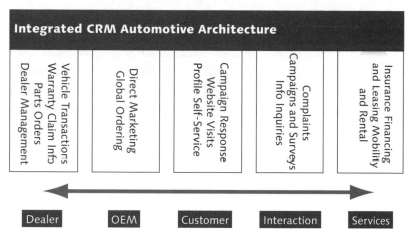

Figure 12.1 SAP CRM Automotive Solutions

Chemical Industry

SAP has more than 30 years of experience delivering enterprise solutions to the chemical industry. In fact, the top 10 chemical companies in the United Sates are all SAP customers. The chemical industry today, like most industries, faces many challenges. This is true for both the commodity chemicals industry (which includes generic chemicals that are produced in bulk) and the specialty chemicals industry (which includes unique chemical products that are custom ordered) as well as for the consumer chemical-products industry (e.g., personal care items, cleaning supplies, paints, etc.). The challenges facing companies in the chemical industry include the following:

> Optimizing excess capacity

> Handling high-energy costs

> Addressing the fluctuating costs of raw materials (feed costs)

> Fulfilling the need for a diverse product mix

> Dealing with globalization issues and regulatory compliance issues

SAP has 30 years of experience delivering solutions to the chemical industry

Manufacturers of commodity chemicals typically focus on producing a single high-volume, low-cost, basic bulk chemical, for example, ethanol, chlorine, and caustic soda. Because commodity chemicals are sold in bulk based on cost, manufacturers try to reduce production costs by using specialized plants that are optimized to produce just one type of chemical and that run year-round with only a few days downtime per year for maintenance. Specialty chemicals, (sometimes also known as performance chemicals), on the other hand, are usually produced on-demand in small quantities (known as batches) as needed, based on orders from customers. These chemicals are much more expensive (and more profitable) than commodity chemicals. Not surprisingly, most SAP customers are specialty chemical producers.

Because most of SAP's chemical customers produce specialty chemicals, and specialty chemicals are produced in small batches, SAP introduced batch management functionality in SAP CRM 4.0. Batch management supports the management and processing of small batches of chemicals across all of a company's business processes. For example, you can assign a unique ID to each batch and track that specific batch of chemicals from the production floor to the warehouse to the customer. You can even locate and recall batches of chemicals from customers, if necessary. The batch management application allows customers to reserve and order a specific batch, which the customer can even test before accepting.

Use price to market to determine your best price

As shown in Figure 12.2, the SAP CRM offering for the chemical industry also supports demand-driven distributed order management, price-to-market functionality, integration of handheld sales and service devices, as well as document management. Distributed order management allows sales orders to be entered centrally in the SAP CRM system and then distributed to the SAP Supply Chain Management (SCM) system for actual processing and fulfillment. Price-to-market functionality helps specialty chemical manufacturers determine the right price to charge for a particular batch based on the market conditions. Integration of handheld sales and service devices allows field sales people and field service people to access SAP CRM sales and service functionality from handheld mobile devices. Integration with SAP Document Management capabilities allow chemical factory workers and emergency personnel to quickly search for and locate Material Safety Data Sheets (MSDS) that describe the proper procedures for handling or working with a particular chemical substance.

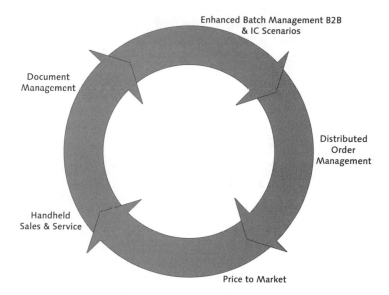

Figure 12.2 Chemical Industry Solutions Powered by SAP CRM

In addition, SAP CRM offers sample management, consignment processes, and the ability to track excess inventory, which are all critical for the chemical industry.

Consumer Products (CP)

SAP has built up an installed base of approximately 3,900 consumer products (CP) companies over the past 30 years in the various segments of the consumer-products industry, including consumer durables, home and personal care, food and beverage, and apparel and footwear. SAP CRM delivers a fully integrated CP tool that includes the following:

> Brand management

> Trade promotion management

> Category management

> Sales and service operations

> Coupon management

> Digital asset management, including support for marketing collaterals

In addition, the CP solution comes with tools to help enhance customer loyalty and increase market share (see Figure 12.3). We already talked about trade promotion management, sales, and service operations in earlier chapters, but we didn't cover brand marketing or categorization, so we'll cover those here.

Figure 12.3 CP Industry Solution as Supported by SAP CRM

Brand Management

Brand management tools

SAP CRM includes brand management tools that help you develop your brand strategy, create marketing campaigns to communicate your brand message to consumers, and analyze how your brand is performing in terms of profitability. In the CP industry, brand owners (manufacturers) typically spend a significant portion of their net sales revenue (around 20 – 30%) on marketing activities to drive brand awareness and performance among consumers. CP companies evaluate the success of their brand marketing efforts partially by sales revenue and market share increases (of course) but also by increases in brand awareness and brand recognition. Using the analytical tools provided with SAP CRM, brand owners can track the success of their brand — and their marketing efforts — using any of the described criteria.

Category Management

SAP CRM provides category management functionality that allows brand owners to organize their products in product groups based on how consumers use or perceive the products. For example, a brand owner in the food and beverage segment of the CP industry might create categories such as sodas, snack foods, family purchases, party supplies, and so on. At the heart of the functionality is the consumer decision tree (CDT), which models (or approximates as best as possible) the consumer's decision-making process when shopping for products in a specific category.

To see how this works, let's return to the example of the food and beverage brand owner. When a consumer goes to the store to purchase a product from the soda category, the decision tree might indicate that the customer is most likely to first have a particular product in mind (perhaps diet cola) and to then make a decision about size or quantity based on factors such as price or the presence of an in-store promotion. Based on point of sale (POS) data that is collected from the retailers, the brand owner can use analytics to analyze whether the CDT is accurate and to further refine the product assortment, in-store promotional marketing efforts, and pricing. Category performance analysis (CPA) can be performed to analyze consumer, market, retailer, and vendor data to identify opportunities. The CPA can also influence joint goal setting between manufacturers and retailers, and assist with pricing and promotion decisions for key accounts and retail stores.

Consumer decision tree

Engineering, Construction, and Operations

The offering for this vertical is used to satisfy the business processes and challenges of the machinery and equipment industries, as well as residential and commercial construction companies and contractors. This solution supports the many options that companies have for equipment purchasing in terms of the standard sales business process, including leasing, renting, and financing.

Rental and service solutions

In particular, the SAP CRM Rental solution supports contracts for rental and leasing agreements, logistical processes, and asset management for rental objects, billing, and settlement of the relevant financial processes. The SAP CRM Service Parts Management functionality provides a Web-based, self-service option that allows customers to create service requests, order spare parts, view technical documentation, and keep track of their orders online.

High-Tech

For the high-tech vertical, SAP CRM provides the following:

> Enhanced channel management
> Warranty management
> Marketing development fund management
> Usage-based billing, digital asset management
> Price and Margin Management by Vendavo (licensed separately from SAP CRM)

Price optimization is extremely important in the high-tech industry — particularly in the software industry — due to the tendency of sales people to heavily discount products to make a sale. Unlike a manufactured product, such as an automobile, which has clearly defined production costs, sales people often don't realize the true production costs of software and thus tend to sell it below value. Price and Margin Management by Vendavo prevents inappropriate price discounting by your sales team with the information they need to negotiate profitable contracts and provide accurate quotations. The product consists of the Price Manager that provides pricing guidance across the organization, and the Profit Analyzer that provides real-time pricing insights for decision makers.

In addition, SAP's CRM call center offering, known as the interaction center, also contains functionality originally designed for the high tech industry. For example, a special variant of the SAP CRM service order is available called the service ticket that provides features such as multi-level categorization of problems as well as automatically suggested solutions based on the problem categorization.

By allowing interaction center agents and second-level service technicians to record the precise nature of defects and causes of problems, the system can propose the most appropriate resolution. In addition, the detailed problem diagnoses can drive analytics to help the engineering department locate and resolve engineering defects and performance problems.

Oil and Gas

SAP CRM functionality for the oil and gas industry helps oil and gas companies manage their downstream marketing and retailing processes. With SAP CRM, you can control the quality of service offered at your retail outlets, manage the services used by you refineries, and optimize sales through your website or call center. SAP CRM provides crucial functionality that is specific to the oil and gas industry, such as support for consignment stock and consignment orders where the actual product (e.g., fuel) is located on premise at the customer site but is still owned by the supplier. For example, gas stations often sell gasoline on consignment — receiving a share in the profits after the gasoline is sold to consumers — rather than purchasing the gasoline upfront from the gasoline supplier. SAP CRM also supports other required oil and gas functionality such as the following:

> Commodity pricing

> Time-specific and location-specific pricing

> Transport and loading information

Consignment stock and order management

Life Sciences (Pharmaceutical)

The life sciences industry consists of several industry segments, including pharmaceuticals, biotechnology and biopharmaceuticals, and medical devices and scientific instruments. Pharmaceutical companies design, manufacture, test, and market over-the-counter and prescription drugs. Biotechnology (biotech) companies provide medical technologies such as genetic testing and gene therapy, whereas biopharmaceutical companies produce medicines that are made synthetically rather than extracted from compounds found in the living tissue of plants, roots, flowers, and so on. In general, SAP CRM supports all three of these industry segments; additionally, industry-specific functionality is available for the pharmaceutical industry segment.

Support for pharmaceutical, biotechnology and biopharmaceutical companies

It's estimated that 18 of the top 20 pharmaceutical companies run SAP software. The pharmaceutical industry is highly regulated and faces many legal and regulatory requirements, especially in the United States, from regulatory agencies such as the following:

> Food and Drug Administration (FDA)

> Drug Enforcement Agency (DEA)

> Environmental Protection Agency (EPA)

Some of these regulations and requirements include the Sarbanes-Oxley Act, the FDA's Title 21 Code of Federal Regulations (CFR Part 11), the U.S. Health Insurance and Portability Act (HIPAA), and the various FDA Good x Practices (GxPs), including Good Laboratory Practices (GLP), Good Clinical Practices (GCPs), and Good Manufacturing Practices (GMPs). SAP CRM allows pharmaceutical companies to build compliance into their core business processes and provides integrated support for compliance manufacturing, product safety, and lot and serial number tracking. SAP software also delivers a mobile client companion solution — discussed in Chapter 8 — that allows a PDA device to be synchronized with a laptop computer running the Mobile Sales laptop pharmaceutical solution to provide offline access to SAP CRM data via a PDA. The contract management solutions provide methods to construct incentive and discount programs for sales (see Figure 12.4).

Figure 12.4 Incentive Management in Pharmaceutical Solutions

Financial Services (Banking and Insurance)

The banking industry and the insurance industry are closely related and are collectively referred to as part of the broader financial services industry. Banks today are facing a dilemma. The old business models with which they have grown comfortable are no longer working. Customers rarely walk into their bank branch office anymore and apply for a loan. Instead, customers often shop online for the lowest rate, comparing various banks, credit unions, and other lending agencies. Banks today — whether they are retail banks, investment banks, or diversified financial service providers — need to focus on developing strong customer relationships. SAP CRM provides you — as a banking company — with a complete overview of your customers, which allows you to offer products that match the needs of your customers at every stage of their lives from student loans, to home loans, to retirement savings and life insurance.

In the past, SAP's strengths have traditionally been in SAP CRM industries outside of banking and insurance. However, in recent years, many banking and insurance customers have started to adopt SAP CRM, and SAP is passionate about meeting the needs of both the banking and insurance industries. We already discussed the banking industry, so now let's turn our attention to the insurance industry.

Incentive and Commission Management (ICM) tool

As you know, most insurance companies have an army of agents who work on commission. So it's important for an insurance company to motivate its agents by providing accurate information about the potential commissions the agents will earn if they close out the opportunities they are currently pursuing. To address this requirement, SAP provides the SAP Incentive and Commission Management (ICM) tool that works together with SAP ERP to calculate, simulate, and project commissions. SAP CRM provides industry-specific functionality for handling customer acquisitions, selling products and services, processing claims, as well as caring for and retaining customers. In addition, SAP provides robust integration between SAP CRM and third-party claims management and policy management systems. In other words, SAP CRM offers a fully integrated solution for the insurance industry (see Figure 12.5).

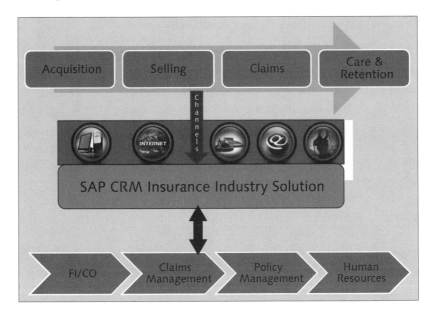

Figure 12.5 SAP CRM Insurance Industry Solution

Leasing

For a number of reasons, companies sometimes prefer to lease equipment — such as computers, office furniture and equipment, or industrial manufacturing machinery — rather than own it outright. This is particularly the case with SMBs, although large companies also lease products. There are a number of advantages to leasing a product rather than owning it. For startups and small businesses, it makes more sense to finance equipment rather than purchase it, which helps contribute to positive cash flow. Also, for small companies without their own IT departments, it's often more convenient to lease equipment that is maintained by the lessor. Even large companies may choose to lease certain products, such as computers, that have a short shelf life — allowing the company to upgrade products every few years.

SAP supports the leasing industry via the SAP Leasing (formerly SAP Leasing and Asset Management) solution, which leverages both SAP CRM and SAP ERP. SAP originally developed Leasing and Asset Management (LAM) together with IBM Global Finance as a strategic development project. Leveraging the SAP Leasing functionality, SAP CRM enables leasing companies to sell leases, offer various financing options, monitor contracts, remarket used equipment after a lease expires, and analyze profitability. SAP CRM provides a single end-to-end solution for the complete lease process from customer engagement to contract accounting. Some of the supported functions include the following:

Single end-to-end solution for lease processing

> **Quotation and contract management**
> You can use this functionality to manage the entire contract management process from the initial quotation to the end of the lease.

> **Pricing and financial mathematics**
> You can use this functionality's set of rules for mapping complex financing models.

> **Vendor integration**
> By integrating the systems of your equipment vendors, you can process vendor purchase orders and check vendor invoices.

> **Processing of third-party business relationships**
> You can also integrate manufacturers and dealers into the leasing process.

> **Asset management and accounting**
> Via integration with SAP ERP Financials, you can access all SAP contract management and accounting functionality, including accounting, cost allocation, and depreciation (see Figure 12.6).

➕ Tip

To leverage the full SAP Leasing functionality, you need SAP CRM and SAP ERP — either SAP ERP 6.0 Enhancement Package 3 (see SAP Note 786590), SAP ERP 2005, SAP ERP 2004, or SAP R/3 4.70 Enterprise Extension 2.00 (see SAP Note 786590).

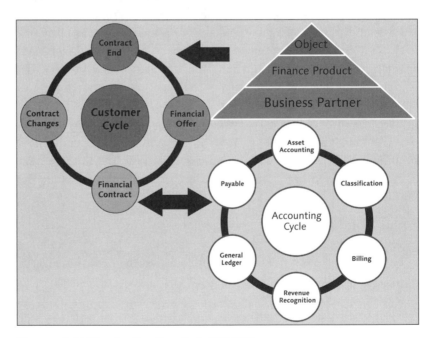

Figure 12.6 SAP Leasing Functionality in SAP CRM

Media

Companies in the media industry — such as newspaper, magazine, and special interest publishers — face a number of unique challenges. Increased Credit Risk Management and Collections Management competition, particularly from online sources and other nontraditional content providers, has eroded the subscriber base of most traditional media companies, resulting in reduced subscription income and stagnated advertising revenues. In addition, the costs of acquiring content continue to rise. As a result, media companies are getting squeezed. More than ever, media companies need to use SAP CRM to understand their customers and offer targeted marketing campaigns and personalized communication.

SAP CRM enables you, as a media company, to tailor products and services to the needs of your customers and to provide sales support and customer service, regardless of whether you provide traditional or online content, whether you sell subscriptions or single copies, or whether you sell advertising or content-usage rights. SAP CRM includes the following functionality to empower companies in the media industry:

> **Account and contact management**
> Allows you to capture and track critical customer information.

> **Campaign management**
> Helps you design and execute targeted marketing campaigns across communications channels, including direct sales, call center, postal mail, email, fax, or the Internet.

> **Advertising sales management**
> Empowers you to sell various forms of advertising, including both traditional print inserts as well as online advertisements.

> **Subscription sales**
> Enables you to offer variable pricing and online self-service to increase customer subscription sales.

> **Customer service**
> Lets you rapidly respond to customer requests received through any communication channel, including telephone, email, or mail.

Tailor products and services to meet your customer's needs

Call center representatives can update customer or order data, provide invoice details, or process complaints. Customers can also use Web self-service to update their own data online.

The success of the SAP CRM media offering is partly due to the fact that SAP software addresses important industry challenges such as Intellectual Property Management (IPM), as well as acquisition and licensing of media rights, contract management, and integrated license and royalty accounting (see Figure 12.7).

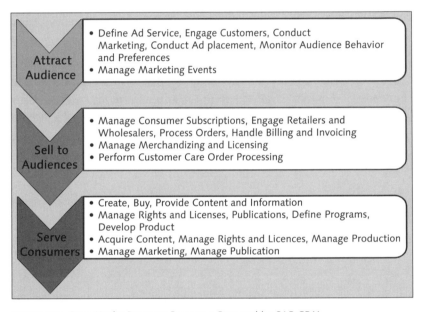

Attract Audience
- Define Ad Service, Engage Customers, Conduct Marketing, Conduct Ad placement, Monitor Audience Behavior and Preferences
- Manage Marketing Events

Sell to Audiences
- Manage Consumer Subscriptions, Engage Retailers and Wholesalers, Process Orders, Handle Billing and Invoicing
- Manage Merchandizing and Licensing
- Perform Customer Care Order Processing

Serve Consumers
- Create, Buy, Provide Content and Information
- Manage Rights and Licenses, Publications, Define Programs, Develop Product
- Acquire Content, Manage Rights and Licences, Manage Production
- Manage Marketing, Manage Publication

Figure 12.7 Core Media Business Processes Powered by SAP CRM

Professional Services

SAP CRM supports the professional services industry, helping service providers retain existing clients and gain new business. In theory, "professional services" can apply to any company that provides some kind of unique service offered by skilled or certified professionals. For example, law firms, recruiting and staffing agencies, accountants, auditors, engineers, physicians, real estate agencies, and architects all may consider themselves part of the professional services industry. And, SAP does have professional service customers in many of these professions. However, the majority of SAP's customers who use the SAP CRM Professional Services functionality are involved in auditing or consulting, particularly IT consulting.

Professional services companies who deliver project-based services to a broad spectrum of customers need to have a complete overview of their sales opportunities, prospects, customers, and customer projects. SAP CRM supports the professional services lifecycle, which consists of five phases as shown in Figure 12.8 and listed here:

Five phases of the professional services business lifecycle

> Strategy and planning

> Business development

> Service delivery

> Engagement management

> Performance management

Figure 12.8 The Five Phases of the Professional Services Business Lifecycle

Let's have a look at each phase in detail.

Strategy and Planning

Professional service companies need to be able to analyze their portfolio of service offerings to develop a strategy and begin planning. The SAP CRM solution for the professional services industry supports the strategy and planning phase by providing service providers with analytical tools such as customer analytics, services/offerings analytics, and customer support analytics. The solution also provides much-needed planning and simulation tools for marketing planning, sales planning, and forecasting.

Business Development

Increased competition in the market space is driving service providers to deliver more cost-efficient and value-driven services. The SAP CRM solution for the professional services industry offers tailor-made, industry-focused business analytics for marketing and lead management, opportunity management, and sales management.

Service Delivery

The most demanding tasks of a service provider are project management, resource and allocation management, and customer service. Although SAP CRM provides complete customer service functionality, project management and resource planning can be done by integrating SAP CRM with other SAP products. For example, service provides can use Collaborative Projects (cProjects) — part of the SAP cProject Suite belong to the SAP Product Lifecycle Management (PLM) product — to do advanced project planning. For example, a sales opportunity in SAP CRM could be used as the trigger to start project planning in cProjects. SAP's resource planning tool, SAP xApp Resource and Portfolio Management (xRPM), can be used to track availability and skill sets of consultants. Integration between SAP CRM and standard groupware products can be used to book consultants' time on projects.

Engagement Management

Engagement management involves tracking project time and expenses by using either an online laptop or an offline or online mobile device. Time and expense management can be handled via integration with SAP ERP components such as the Financial Accounting component (FI) and the Controlling component (CO). Service providers can bill customers for work done, materials used, and other costs involved in a project using resource-related billing, provided by the SAP ERP Sales and Distribution component (SD).

Performance Management

SAP CRM can be used together with SAP NetWeaver Business Intelligence (SAP NetWeaver BI) to provide business analytics that cover project profitability and planned versus actual comparison. Service providers can track the profitability at the project level or consultant level, enabling informed decision making.

Public Sector

SAP has made heavy investments in the public sector, and government agencies around the world have responded by adopting the SAP CRM solution. Public-sector agencies can no longer afford to ignore or mistreat their constituents. Taxpayers have started to demand to be treated like valued customers. And in today's Internet-enabled world, your constituents also expect to be able to reach you through a variety of communication channels, including the Web, at anytime and in multiple languages. The most recent versions of SAP CRM, including SAP CRM 2006s and SAP CRM 2007, come with full support for e-governance, constituent services, and case management, and updated Grantor Management functionality (see Figure 12.9).

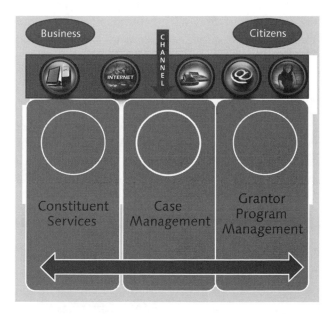

Figure 12.9 Important Components of the SAP Solution for the Public Sector

Constituent Services

Constituent services are the services that public organizations offer to their constituents and businesses. This functionality allows online registration for services by businesses and citizens — enabling service renewals, requests for permits or licenses, and periodic billing functionality.

Case Management

Case management ties all of the information, forms, and legal documents related to a particular issue into a case. The case can then be assigned to a case processor, who reviews the case and assigns tasks and activities to the appropriate team members working on the case. Case management also allows you to link together similar or related issues.

Grantor Program Management

Grantor Management provides government agencies with a toolkit for managing financial assistance for programs and services such as public transportation, agriculture, low-income housing, education, and so on. Grantor management includes capabilities to support program management, application processing, automated assessment of application, agreements, claim processing, case management, and monitoring.

Retail

Retail solution meets the needs of all types of retailers

SAP CRM, part of the SAP for Retail set of solutions, enables companies in the retail industry, such as department stores, fashion retailers, grocery stores, warehouse clubs, catalog retailers, and so on, to sell products to consumers through a variety of channels, including the telephone, Web, electronic kiosks, or brick-and-mortar stores. SAP CRM provides retailers with consistent information about customers at every touch point to enhance customer service and customer satisfaction. SAP also provides workforce management capabilities that help companies create optimum employee schedules by using historical workload data captured daily, weekly, or monthly. In addition, the tight integration between SAP CRM and SAP SCM enables retailers to conduct forecasting and replenish inventory merchandise more efficiently. SAP CRM also helps retailers adjust the marketing campaign and programs by continuously analyzing customer buying behavior and loyalty data (see Figure 12.10).

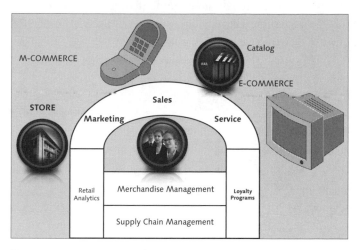

Figure 12.10 SAP CRM Retail Solution

Telecommunications

SAP supports many telecommunications (Telco) companies that offer services such as traditional local and long-distance telephone service, wireless calling, cable television, and dial-up and broadband Internet access. With SAP CRM 2006s and SAP CRM 2007, SAP enhanced an already robust Telco solution (see Figure 12.11). For example, SAP strengthened the product data management capabilities of SAP CRM by enhancing support for product bundles (e.g., offering several separate products such as wireless service, cable television, and broadband Internet as a single product package) and introducing product-modeling capabilities. SAP also extended the sales order management capabilities, which already include the dealer channel, to now also support e-commerce and the interaction center.

Additionally, SAP enhanced the contract management functionality available in the interaction center to allow customers to easily extend contracts, move their service from one residence to another, change their telephone number, and so on. Credit card management integration to external systems (via SAP NetWeaver) was also enhanced,

Enhanced support for bundled products

as were dispute resolution and sales analytics. These enhancements nicely complement the already existing functionality from SAP CRM 2005, which includes order management, service management, dealer management, customer financials management, network cycle management, and business management, in addition to the standard SAP CRM Marketing, Sales, and Service capabilities.

Figure 12.11 SAP CRM Telecomunications Industry Solution

Utilities

Utility-enabled version of the interaction center

Utility companies need to respond to competitive market challenges by offering tailored service offerings to become more customer-centric. At the same time, utility companies need to deploy state of the art, integrated IT systems to improve quality and efficiency and to reduce Total Cost of Ownership (TCO). SAP CRM delivers powerful utility-specific functionality, including a utilities-enabled version of the interaction center and support for utilities-specific processes such as meter reading. However, utilities companies can also benefit from many of the same SAP CRM features and functions that are available to non-utility companies such as the SAP CRM Sales functionality as well as the SAP CRM marketing campaign management capabilities. Let's have a look.

Interaction Center

The interaction center is of critical importance to utility customers because this is the primary means by which customers interact with the company. The utilities version of the interaction center contains important, utilities-specific functionality such as the move-in and move-out process for transferring service from one residential location to another, bill dispute and bill correction, processing of late payments, and so on.

Campaign Management

Following the deregulation of the utilities companies in many markets, utility companies now suddenly find themselves without monopolies in their markets and having to compete. Campaign management allows utility companies to market services using customer segmentation based on factors such as demographic profiles, sample marketing results, and customer response analysis modeling.

Contract Management

The SAP industry solution for utilities provides templates to support quotations and sales contracts using different sales methodologies. Quotations can be offered based on customer consumption behavior. Contracts can be created based on data from multiple IT systems such as SAP Utilities (IS-U), SAP CRM, or a non-SAP electronic document management (EDM) system. Regardless of where contacts are stored, SAP CRM provides utility companies with an integrated view of sales processes across all channels.

Meter Reading and Billing

Utility companies can leverage the SAP IS-U solution to handle a variety of flexible billing options, including metered billing, contract-based billing, real-time pricing, and time-of-use billing. The solution also supports unmetered billing and enables simulations and plausibility checks.

Meter readings and billing information can also be made available to customers online via a Web self-service application. Allowing customers to access their meter reading and billing information online reduces costs and increases customer satisfaction.

Invoice and Revenue Management

The SAP IS-U solution, which is integrated with SAP CRM, can be used to support credit risk and collections management scenarios via SAP ERP functionality. Utility companies can segment customers based on credit profiles and determine the required security deposit amount (if applicable) when offering products and services to consumers (see Figure 12.12).

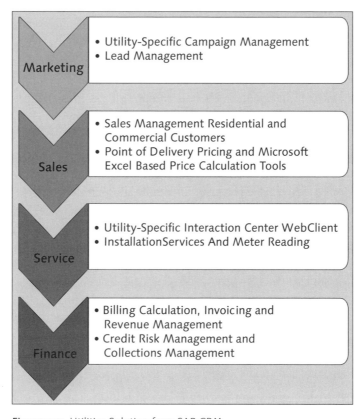

Marketing
- Utility-Specific Campaign Management
- Lead Management

Sales
- Sales Management Residential and Commercial Customers
- Point of Delivery Pricing and Microsoft Excel Based Price Calculation Tools

Service
- Utility-Specific Interaction Center WebClient
- InstallationServices And Meter Reading

Finance
- Billing Calculation, Invoicing and Revenue Management
- Credit Risk Management and Collections Management

Figure 12.12 Utilities Solution from SAP CRM

Case Study

A comfort bed company that manufactures bedding, pillows, mattress pads, sheets, comforters, and feather beds implemented ERP E-Commerce (formerly called ISA R/3) and strengthened relationships with B2B customers by providing Web-based order entry. The company has sales revenues of $300 million plus per year. The company is faced with the challenge of how to give the same attention to the small retail customers as is given to enterprise-size customers.

The business objectives the company wants to meet are the following:

> Provide a customer-focused, easy-to-use business solution

> Make it possible to send the midnight reporting to the plant maintenance system using an Internet connection

> Optimize the effectiveness of interactions with small retailers

The technological challenge that the company must meet is how to Web-enable the SAP R/3-based order management system to provide a Web-based interface to the B2B customers rapidly. With this requirement in mind, the company deployed the SAP CRM ISA R/3 solution with a backend SAP R/3 system. This solution created the following value for the company:

> Increased sales revenue and newly acquired B2B customers

> Decreased cost of order management

With this solution in place, the company is now in the process of implementing SAP CRM Web channel to provide cross-selling and up-selling functionality on the Web.

Conclusion

Business processes differ from industry to industry. Of course, some things are the same: every industry has customers, and every industry needs to support basic marketing, sales, and customer service processes. However, companies that operate in different industry verticals require SAP CRM systems that support their industry-specific business processes. For example, utilities companies need to support meter readings and move-in and move-out procedures, pharmaceutical companies need to adhere to various government safety legislation, and telecommunications companies need special financial customer care solutions for handling billing disputes and allowing customers to check their accounts and balances online.

Here are the most important things to remember about the SAP CRM industry solutions:

> SAP provides a number of industry solutions that leverage SAP CRM as well as other SAP products and tools such as SAP ERP, SAP Supply Chain Management (SCM), SAP Project Lifecycle Management (PLM), SAP NetWeaver Business Intelligence (BI), and SAP NetWeaver.

> SAP CRM supports more than 25 different industries, including automotive, chemicals, consumer products, high tech, life sciences, media, professional services, retail, telecommunications, oil and gas, professional services, public sector, media, and utilities.

> In most cases, the SAP CRM industry solutions provide industry-specific functionality and business process support, in addition to access to standard SAP CRM Marketing, Sales, and Service functionality.

> Certain SAP CRM application components, such as the interaction center, provide industry-specific functionality. For example, special industry "flavors" of the interaction center are available for the automotive, Telco, and utilities industries.

In the next chapter, we'll discuss SAP CRM analytics to see how historical data can be analyzed to find and correct problems, model and predict future customer behavior, and help enable more informed decision making.

SAP CRM Analytics

So far, you've learned a lot about how to use SAP CRM Marketing, Sales, and Service to automate and streamline your business processes. You discovered the different business channels that can be used to access SAP CRM functionality such as the Web channel, interaction center, mobile applications, and partner channel management. You also learned about the underlying technical platform and technology of SAP CRM and the importance of master data management in SAP CRM projects. In the previous chapter, you learned how companies in different industry verticals can leverage SAP CRM to meet their unique industry requirements.

All of this has taught you how to use SAP CRM technology to provide the people involved in your SAP CRM processes — including your employees, channel partners, and even customers themselves — with the tools to serve your customers successfully. This is a great start to any SAP CRM program and will certainly drive quick wins in terms of ROI. However, SAP CRM is about more than just tools, technology, and business process automation. SAP CRM is also about intelligently using all of the data that is generated and collected by your SAP CRM and IT systems to enable your people to make good business decisions. This is where SAP CRM Analytics comes into play.

Use your data to make optimal decisions and develop realistic models

For our purposes, we'll define *analytics* as the process of using data analysis to make optimal decisions and develop realistic models and predictions about the future outcome of business operations with some degree of certainty. Analytics is different from reporting in that reports summarize historical data, analytics uses statistical and mathematical models to discover important trends, relationships, and patterns in your data. A report can tell you what happened, while analytics can tell you why it happened and how to prevent or improve it next time.

SAP CRM provides both reporting and analytics. Historical and real-time reports are both available directly in SAP CRM using data stored in the SAP CRM system. SAP CRM enables so-called actionable intelligence, or the ability to drill in an SAP CRM report to access the actual underlying data objects that are being reported on, such as accessing an individual service ticket from a report about open service tickets. SAP CRM also provides out-of-the-box analytics via SAP NetWeaver Business Intelligence (SAP NetWeaver BI) using historical data stored in SAP's centralized data warehouse — the SAP Business Information Warehouse (BW). One way to access analytics is by logging into the SAP NetWeaver BI system. However, embedded analytics — analytics that are included inside a business application — are also available, in many cases, directly inside the SAP CRM system. For example, a configurable customer fact sheet is available that can be used to display information about a customer, including SAP NetWeaver BI analytics embedded directly in the customer fact sheet, along with SAP CRM-based data such as the customer's marketing preferences, open service ticket, and recent sales orders. In this chapter, we'll uncover many of the details and functions of SAP CRM Analytics.

SAP CRM Analytics

SAP NetWeaver BI allows you to consolidate all of the data captured from the various business applications in your SAP CRM system. SAP NetWeaver BI provides data mining and analysis of this data, which provides a 360-degree view of your customers that can be invaluable in product development decisions, marketing campaign planning, sales strategizing, and much more. SAP CRM analytical tools help you analyze the quality of your company's customer relationships. The outcome of the analysis can also help you plan a strategy for relationship building and enable more personalized customer service. SAP CRM Analytics uncovers hidden patterns and trends that affect your business. You can use the results of data analysis to help predict future shifts in customer behavior and to help optimize your business processes. SAP CRM Analytics also empowers your employees to make informed decisions.

Additionally, SAP CRM Analytics provides secure, role-based access that allows companies to create their own *dashboards* providing vital information that the business requires. In essence, SAP CRM Analytics provides easy-to-use, best-of-breed analytical capabilities.

Dashboards provide single-click access to analytical and collaborative tools.

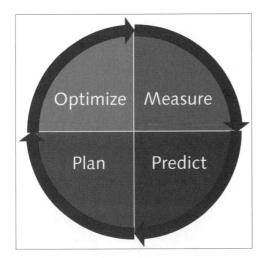

Figure 13.1 Closed Loop SAP CRM Analytics

One aspect that makes SAP CRM Analytics so powerful is the closed-loop approach. Closed-loop analytics enable you to measure, predict, plan, and optimize business operations (see Figure 13.1). SAP CRM Analytics answers a host of business and operational questions by providing detailed analyses. For example, you can find answers to all of these questions:

> Who are your most profitable customers?
> Who are the customers that contribute the most to your company's revenue?
> How can your employees optimize and strengthen the relationships with the most profitable customers?
> How can you win new customers and retain existing ones?
> What is the cost of winning a new customer or retaining an existing customer?
> What are your customer's priorities and preferences?
> What products do most customers buy?
> What products do your best customers buy?
> How do customers rate their level of satisfaction with your products?
> What is the customer satisfaction rate of post-sales service?
> What products and services do regional sales offices sells most?
> Which sales office sells the most products and services?
> Which sales office generates the most profit?
> What is the cost of warranty service?
> Are your current warranty plans profitable for the company?
> Is our organization making or losing money on warranty sales?

This list just gives you a brief idea of the types of things SAP CRM Analytics can help you answer about your business and your customers. To help you answer these types of questions about your customers, SAP CRM enables four different analytical methods: measurement, prediction, planning, and optimization. Table 13.1 provides examples of these four analytical methods and the type of information they can help reveal.

Measure	Predict	Plan	Optimize
What Is Happening	What Will Happen	What Should Happen	How to Leverage
Daily Sales Report	Sales and Service Forecast	Territory	Customer Segmentation Strategies
KPI Monitoring	Buying Propensities	Customer	Campaign Optimization
Call Reporting	Customer Lifetime Value (CLV)	Opportunity	Cross-Selling/ Up-Selling
Customer Profitability	Customer Loyalty	Campaign	Churn Management
Customer's 360° View	Growth Potential	Trade Promotion	

Table 13.1 Embedded Analytics

In addition to these analytical methods, SAP CRM also supports the following *analytical scenarios*: marketing, sales, service, interaction channel, customer, and product. For each scenario, SAP CRM delivers everything you need to use Analytics via SAP NetWeaver BI, including out-of-the-box data-mining models, as well as preconfigured SAP NetWeaver BI extractors, pre-InfoCubes, and queries. You don't have to be familiar with the technical details of SAP NetWeaver BI, which you can read about in other books. Rather, it's sufficient here to know that SAP CRM provides everything you need to get started. Of course, you can also create your own custom extractors, InfoCubes, and queries as well, but that is also outside the scope of this book. Let's take a look at the analytical scenarios for marketing, sales, service, interaction channel, customers, and products.

SAP CRM comes with more than 300 ready-to-use analytical queries. The broad spectrum of Analytics provides best practices to drive closed-loop SAP CRM scenarios. SAP CRM Analytics comes with tight integration to the SAP world and provides open connectors to inte-

SAP CRM provides 300 ready-to-use analytical queries

grate third-party applications. SAP CRM Analytics is built on the SAP NetWeaver platform, which provides proven SAP NetWeaver BI technology. SAP provides standard SAP NetWeaver BI analytical content with SAP CRM to deliver configurable and ready-to-use analytics. The standard SAP NetWeaver BI content includes a preconfigured, role-based, and task-related information model that is based on consistent metadata in SAP NetWeaver BI. SAP NetWeaver BI provides selected SAP CRM business roles (such as sales manager, service manager, and so on) with the information they need to carry out specific tasks. A partial list of standard, ready-to-use, out-of-the-box analytics for the SAP CRM marketing, sales, and service scenarios is presented in Table 13.2.

Marketing Analytics	Sales Analytics	Service Analytics
Market Exploration	Sales Planning	Strategic Service Planning
External List Analysis	Sales Pipeline Analysis	Service Quality Analysis
Marketing Budget Planning	Sales Funnel Analysis	Service Contract Analysis
Campaign Planning	Activity Analysis	Service Order Analysis
Marketing Optimization and Refinement	Opportunity Planning and Analysis	Service Warranty Analysis
Lead Analysis	Contract Analysis	Service Profitability Analysis
Marketing Plan Analysis	Sales Quotation and Order Analysis	Service Performance Analysis
Campaign Monitoring/ Success Analysis	Sales Analysis and Planning by Territory	
	Sales Performance Analysis	
	Billing Analysis	

Table 13.2 Partial List of Ready-to-Use Application Analytics

In addition to the standard analytics provided for marketing, sales, and service scenarios, analytics are also available for individual business channels, such as the interaction center, Web channel, partner channel management, and so on; collectively these analytics are known as interaction channel analytics. Additionally, there are a number of cross-application analytics available independent of business scenario or business channel, including customer analytics and product analytics. We'll discuss all of these applications in detail in the next sections, but for a quick preview of the features, see Table 13.3.

Customer Analytics	Product Analytics	Channel Analytics
Customer Satisfaction and Loyalty Analysis	Cross-Selling Analysis	Web Channel Analytics: Website Monitoring
Customer Segmentation with Clustering	Profitability Analysis	Web Channel Analytics: Web Analytics
Customer Migration Analysis (CMA)	Revenue Analysis	Interaction Center Analytics
Churn Management	Best-Selling Products	Channel and Partner Analytics
Customer Profitability Analysis	Complaints by Product	Field: Offline Reporting
Customer Lifetime Value (CLV) Analysis		

Table 13.3 Partial List of Ready-to-Use Cross Application Analytics

With this in the background, let's take a detailed look at the various analytics offered by SAP CRM.

Cross-application analytics

Marketing Analytics

With marketing analytics, you can learn how well your marketing programs and campaigns are performing. In addition, marketing pro-

Marketing analytics functionality

fessionals can find the information they need — such as customer preferences and demographic details — to conduct proper customer segmentation when creating customer target lists for new marketing campaigns. Marketing analytics encompass several processes as described in Figure 13.2. We'll discuss each of these in the following sections.

Figure 13.2 Components of Marketing Analytics

Market Budget Planning

Marketing analytics can help drive improvements in the marketing budget-planning process. For example, using data analysis provided by SAP NetWeaver BI, the campaign manager of a company's marketing department could see how closely the company's actual marketing expenses matched the budgeted amounts. This allows the campaign manager to make the necessary adjustments to optimize future results based on the historical data.

Campaign Planning

Campaign planning and optimization tools allow the campaign manager at a company to monitor the success of marketing campaigns that have already been carried out in order to improve future campaigns. For example, campaign managers can measure the success of previous campaigns based on factors such as customer response rate, conversion rates, contribution margin, and campaign ROI (see Figure 13.3).

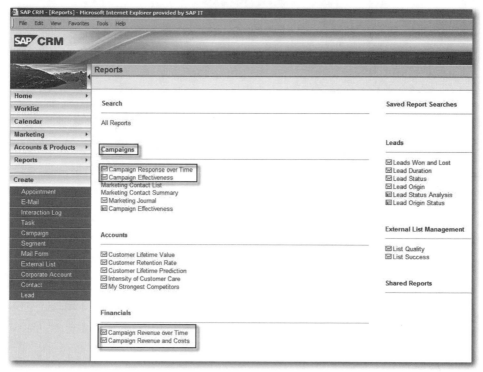

Figure 13.3 Marketing Analytics User Menu in SAP CRM 2007

Target Group Optimization

To create optimal target groups for new marketing campaigns, a marketing manager needs to be able to fine-tune the customer segmentation process. Analytical methods, such as RFM (recency, frequency, and monetary) value analysis, are used to maximize target group optimization for marketing campaigns. RFM analyzes which customer bought your company's products and services recently and provides details about the frequency of buying such products and services along with their monetary value of revenue (see Figure 13.4).

Recency, frequency, and monetary (RFM) value

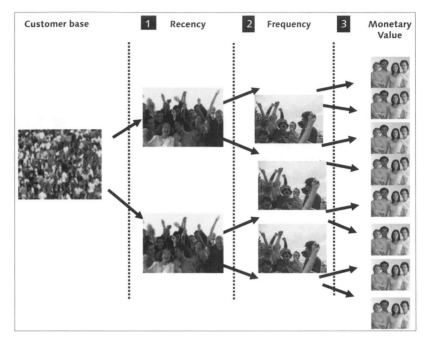

Figure 13.4 RFM Analysis for Target Group Optimization

Market Plan Analysis

Marketing managers need to be able to analyze the historical performance of marketing plans in terms of cost and revenue — and to compare planned values against actual results —to optimize future marketing plans.

Campaign Monitoring and Success

Track the effectiveness of your marketing campaigns

If a marketing campaign isn't performing as well as expected, the marketing manager should terminate the campaign and redistribute the funds and resources associated with the campaign to other marketing efforts. To do this, the marketing manager needs need to know when the actual data deviates from the expected, budgeted values. For example, the system could be configured to send an alert to the marketing manager — based on analytical data — when a campaign is performing poorly and appears unlikely to reach the planned targets. For well-performing campaigns that are allowed to run until completion, the campaign manager needs to be able to evaluate the success of the campaign afterwards. To do this, the marketing manager needs an overview of both the planned key figures and the actual data of the fully executed campaign. To have a more exact view, the marketing manager can even view the key figures according to different milestones and due dates.

Lead Analysis

The marketing manager at a company responsible for sales leads is empowered by information such as the duration of leads, changes in the lead qualification level, number of leads won, expected order quantity per lead, and number of activities per lead. SAP CRM Analytics provides standard queries for lead-channel analysis and lead-efficiency reporting, lead qualification-level analysis, lead historical-evaluation analysis, and lost leads analysis.

Ex   Example

XYZ is a midsize consumer products company that depends on external list providers for leads. The marketing manager at XYZ, Jack, is responsible for sales leads. Three lead qualifiers report to Jack: Mike, Dave, and Brian. XYZ recently conducted a massive campaign to promote a new product. Now the company wants to explore the quality of the leads received from external list providers to find out how each of the lead qualifiers is performing. Jack was delighted to find a standard lead-efficiency query in SAP NetWeaver BI as part of the standard SAP CRM business content. However, when he ran the lead-efficiency report, Jack was unpleasantly surprised to find that the win-rate of leads was only around 25 % (see Figure 13.5).

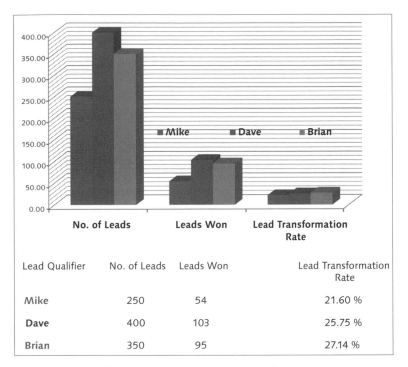

Lead Qualifier	No. of Leads	Leads Won	Lead Transformation Rate
Mike	250	54	21.60 %
Dave	400	103	25.75 %
Brian	350	95	27.14 %

Figure 13.5 Lead Efficiency Reporting in SAP CRM Analytics

Ex Continued...

> Jack called an emergency meeting with the three lead qualifiers to evaluate why the conversion rate was so poor. The lead qualifiers reported that the external lead providers were supplying XYZ with poor-quality leads, including outdated telephone numbers, incorrect email addresses, and so on.

External List Analysis

With list quality analysis, the campaign manager at a company can evaluate the quality of a lead list. The analysis determines the number of incorrect addresses, the number of duplicated addresses, and the revenues generated. This information can be used to aid decision makers when choosing between address list providers in the future. In addition, the analysis can be used to determine the number of addresses that reacted positively to the campaign and the number of addresses that were ultimately won as customers (see Figure 13.6).

The list success analysis evaluates the address list by applying key figures such as number of leads created in the SAP CRM system, number of contacts per lead, number of leads that are converted to customers, and average revenue per new customer.

Ⓔⓧ Continued...

The external list quality analysis confirmed that the quality of the leads generated by the external lists for XYZ was poor (see Figure 13.6). When Jack ran an external list success analysis, he found that approximately 70% of the leads supplied by the external list providers were inaccurate, which was hurting the campaign.

The lead qualifiers also mentioned to Jack that lead responses to email were higher than the lead qualification via telephone, and that Website traffic driven from trade shows was driving strong sales. Jack ran the lead channel analysis and confirmed the same (see Figure 13.7).

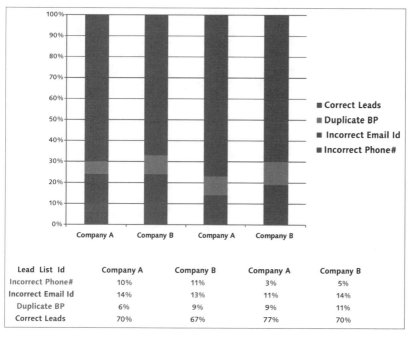

Lead List Id	Company A	Company B	Company A	Company B
Incorrect Phone#	10%	11%	3%	5%
Incorrect Email Id	14%	13%	11%	14%
Duplicate BP	6%	9%	9%	11%
Correct Leads	70%	67%	77%	70%

Figure 13.6 External List Quality Analysis

Ex **Continued...**

Jack was grateful that SAP CRM Analytics helped him find the root cause of the low conversion-rate for leads, and he called a meeting with his external list providers to resolve the issues. Jack decided to increase the focus on posting campaigns and trade shows aggressively on the Web because the success rate of the Web as a lead channel was so high — around 80%. Jack also decided to press external list providers to make email addresses mandatory in the lead lists because the email channel proved more successful when compared to the telephone

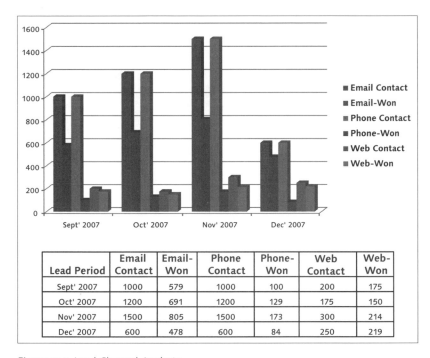

Lead Period	Email Contact	Email-Won	Phone Contact	Phone-Won	Web Contact	Web-Won
Sept' 2007	1000	579	1000	100	200	175
Oct' 2007	1200	691	1200	129	175	150
Nov' 2007	1500	805	1500	173	300	214
Dec' 2007	600	478	600	84	250	219

Figure 13.7 Lead Channel Analysis

External List Cost and Revenue Analysis

SAP CRM is tightly integrated with the backend SAP ERP Financials application and is coupled with the SAP NetWeaver BI system. The landscape makes it possible to ascertain the cost and revenue analysis of the external lead lists bought.

Ex Continued...

Using external list cost and revenue analysis, Jack found that Company A had supplied more accurate leads than Company B (see Figure 13.8). He also needed to know which external supplier leads were effective in increasing XYZ's revenue so that he could end the contract with the under-performing external suppliers. SAP CRM Analytics helped Jack by providing a list success analysis report. Jack was immensely impressed with the SAP CRM Analytics that assisted him at every stage of campaign analysis with accurate reports.

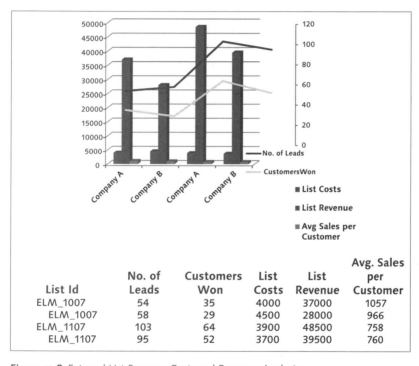

List Id	No. of Leads	Customers Won	List Costs	List Revenue	Avg. Sales per Customer
ELM_1007	54	35	4000	37000	1057
ELM_1007	58	29	4500	28000	966
ELM_1107	103	64	3900	48500	758
ELM_1107	95	52	3700	39500	760

Figure 13.8 External List Success, Cost, and Revenue Analysis

Ex Continued...

Jack decided to give Company A preferred vendor status and continue to give Company B a chance to improve the quality of the lead lists based on the list success analysis. Jack plans to use external list analysis reports as negotiation tools when renewing the vendor contracts.

This concludes the marketing analytics overview. Now that you have a good idea about the wide array of information marketing analytics can provide for your business needs, let's move onto sales analytics.

Sales Analytics

Sales analytics provide details on how the sales group is performing

Sales analytics provide business information that can be used to drive the entire sales cycle, from territory management to billing. Sales analytics enable complete reporting functionality for measuring your sales processes across your entire sales department — providing sales managers and sales people with the information they need for the areas they are responsible for. Sales analytics also deliver integrated business information, allowing sales managers to view sales figures from different perspectives to get an overall picture, and to drill-down into specific areas for a more detailed perspective. Sales people can also analyze specific sales figures by territory or by customer. And, sales analytics incorporate alerts to allow sales managers to monitor sales on a daily basis.

There are nine major sales analytical processes, so let's discuss these next (see Figure 13.9).

Figure 13.9 Sales Analytics in SAP CRM

Territory Management Analysis

SAP CRM provides standard analytical content — including SAP NetWeaver BI extractors, InfoCubes, and queries — to enable sales reporting by territory, territory hierarchy, territory level, territory attributes, and responsible territory. Several predefined queries are available to meet your business needs, including the number of activities per territory, the number of contracts signed per territory, and the open sales orders and quotations per territory. In addition, out-of-the-box reports are included, such as net revenues per territory level, as well as a comparison of planned versus actual key figures, which are provided in conjunction with SAP Strategic Enterprise Management (SEM).

> Territory management with predefined queries and out-of-the-box reports

Activity Management Analysis

SAP CRM provides standard analytical content to enable out-of-the-box reports for activity management, including sales calls via telephone and in-person sales visits. The reports display the value of sales generated because of each such customer-facing activity. The reports also provide information about activities of previous months, including success/failure analysis of activities as well as the level of pre-sales investment per customer, and so on.

Opportunity Management Analysis

SAP CRM Analytics delivers a specific set of analyses that covers opportunity-related reports such as sales volume forecast; opportunity win/loss analysis; and targeting based on competitors, competitors in current opportunities (see Figure 13.10), expected product value, top 10 opportunities by value, and competitor products by price.

> Generate a variety of reports for activity and opportunity management analysis

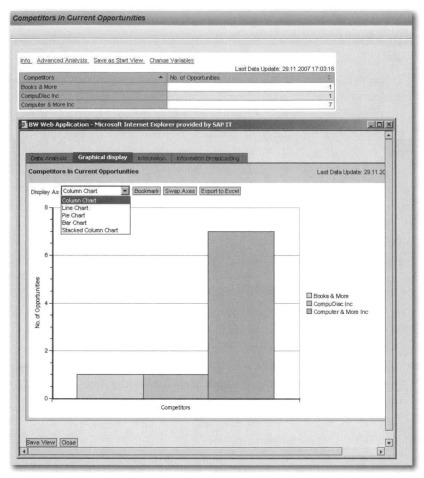

Figure 13.10 Competitors in Current Opportunities

Sales Quotation and Order Management Analysis

Manage sales
quotes, orders, and
contracts effectively

SAP CRM Analytics also provide a range of analyses for sales quotations and sales orders, which deliver detailed analytical information about the sales order process in your organization. Quotation tracking, quotation success rate, incoming sales orders, net value of sales quotations and sales order (see Figure 13.11), and top 10 products sold are a few examples of the out-of-the-box quotation and order analysis functionality.

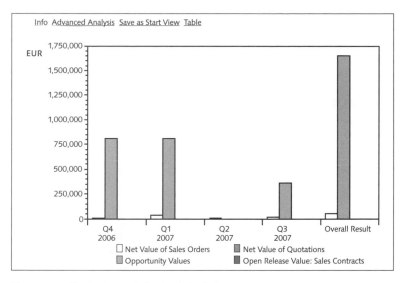

Figure 13.11 Quotation and Contract Analysis

Contract Management Analysis

Standard analytical content delivers ready-to-use queries, such as completed sales contracts, canceled sales contracts, top five contracts, and products in sales contracts (see Figure13.12). The complete analysis of how many contracts you have and what their value is will unlock the information that will help you manage contracts successfully.

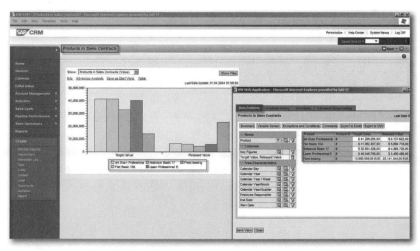

Figure 13.12 Products in Sales Contracts

Sales Pipeline Analysis

Evaluate current
business
developments
with sales pipeline
analysis

This analysis is an evaluation of your current business development, expected sales revenue, and volume. The pipeline analysis reports information on opportunities, quotations, open sales orders, and open sales contracts (see Figure 13.13).

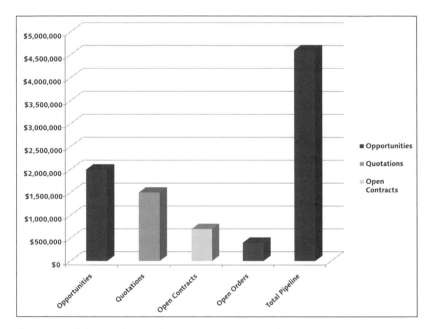

Figure 13.13 Sales Pipeline Analysis Using SAP CRM Analytics.

Sales Funnel Analysis

Sales funnel analysis provides an analysis of sales performance and generates reports about all sales documents, regardless of their status. This includes analysis of marketing campaigns, sales contracts, and sales order from a historic perspective. Funnel analysis evaluates the success of a sales manager's sales strategy. Sales funnel analysis includes lead funnel analysis, opportunity funnel analysis, and quotation funnel analysis (see Figure 13.14).

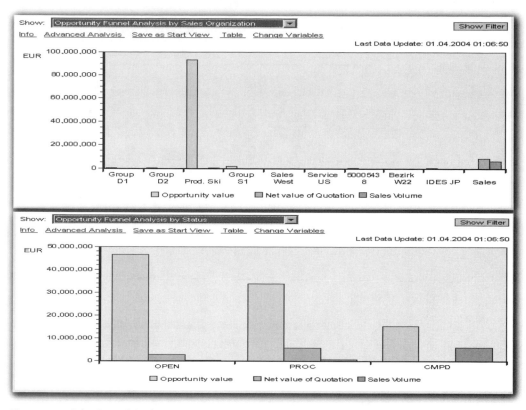

Figure 13.14 Sales Funnel Analysis

Sales Performance Analysis

Sales performance analysis helps you gain insight into your sales processes across the entire sales cycle — from leads, to opportunities, to sales orders. Out-of-the-box reports analyze sales performance based on predefined key figures. Sales performance analysis also includes ABC analysis of customers, customer profitability, and CLV. Sales performance analysis enables sales managers to access up-to-date information about customers, relationships and market information (see Figure 13.15).

Get complete sales funnel and performance analysis

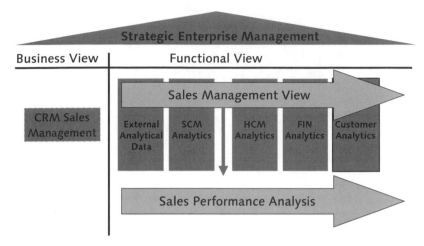

Figure 13.15 Sales Performance Analysis

 Tip

> ABC classification is a common analytical technique that can be used to
> group your customers into different classes based on some characteristic,
> such as size, revenue, or profitability. For example, you might group your
> largest customers into class A, your midsize customers into class B, and
> your small customers into class C.

Sales performance analysis relies on SAP Strategic Enterprise Management (SAP SEM), part of SAP ERP, which works together with SAP NetWeaver BI to generate analysis of real-time sales data and consolidated financial reporting.

Billing Analysis

Generate accurate
billing data for
legal and internal
purposes

The analysis of billing and invoicing data is generally required for legal and internal purposes. The internal analysis is particularly important for gaining a better overview of billing transactions and figures, supporting sales activities, identifying critical transactions, and realizing improvement potential. Unbilled revenue reporting is used to determine and evaluate quantities billed and extrapolated for the balance sheet of the closing accounting period.

This wraps up the discussion of sales analytics, so now we'll move onto service analytics.

Service Analytics

Service analytics provide companies with an overview of service-related metrics such as customer satisfaction, product quality, service revenue, and so on. You can use service analytics to compare service revenues with cost of service to improve service profitability. You can even drill down to view detailed service revenue and cost information by type of service item, such as service contract, warranty, service order, and so on. The service manager of a company can use service analytics to check the historic level of service that a particular customer or customer group has received. The service manager can also access key information about warranties and service contracts that are about to expire, including remaining term length and net value. Service analytics also support early identification of quality issues, enable real-time cost control, and help improve service quality, customer satisfaction, and service profit.

Access to service-related metrics

Service analytics support your organization by helping you plan service-revenue and profitability targets for your service area and helping you communicate those targets to management. This enables managers to closely align the operational activities of the service areas with the strategic goals of the service organization as a whole (see Figure 13.16).

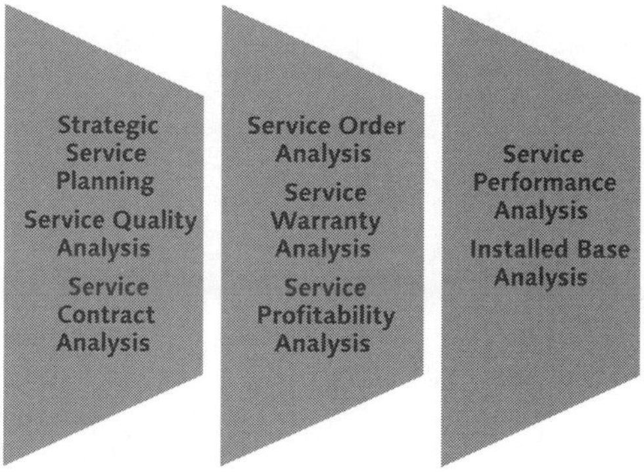

Figure 13.16 Service Analytics

327

Let's look at each of the areas within service analytics.

Service Quality Analysis

Service quality analysis provides you with the number of service-related complaints logged during a specified period, enabling you to resolve product quality issues and improve customer service. Service quality analysis also helps you monitor service timeliness to better meet Service Level Agreements (SLAs).

> **Ex** **Example**
>
> Paul is a service manager for Comp Tech, a high tech company. Bob is the sr. vice president of service, and he has entrusted Paul with the job of improving customer satisfaction, service efficiency, and service profitability. To begin this task, Paul runs the customer satisfaction (C-SAT) survey and finds that the C-SAT is dropping month-by-month (see Figure 13.17).
>
> Paul conducted further investigations into SLA compliance and found the company faltering on SLAs (see Figure 13.18).

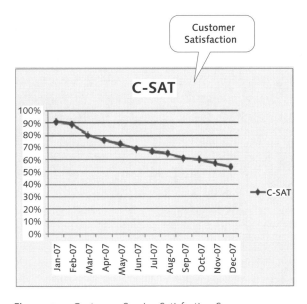

Figure 13.17 Customer Service Satisfaction Survey

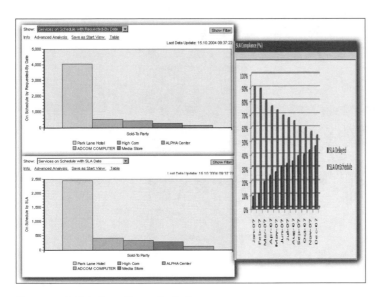

Figure 13.18 SLA Compliance Analysis

Ex **Continued...**

Paul then looked into the service business profitability and found that service profitability has been going south as well (see Figure 13.19).

And if that weren't enough, Paul discovered via service order analysis that service order volume has been increasing and has a backlog of unre-solved service orders (see Figure 13.20).

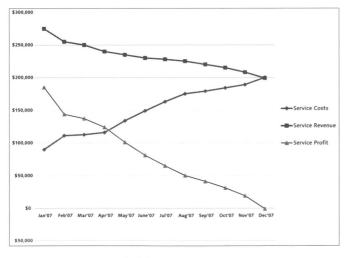

Figure 13.19 Service Profitability Analysis

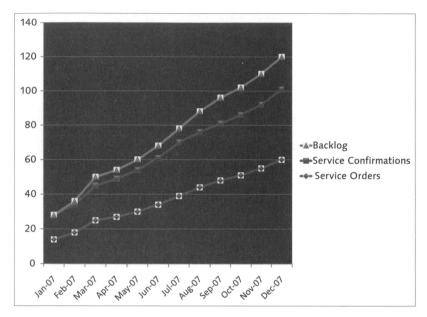

Figure 13.20 Service Order Analysis

Ex Continued...

Paul found the following by using service quality analysis:

Planned versus unplanned service orders analysis
Paul found that the number of unplanned service orders is significantly exceeding the planned service orders, which is a cause of concern.

Service labor analysis
Paul ran the service labor analysis and found that service technicians' overtime has risen, causing increased service costs. However, the overtime isn't helping with increased service confirmations. Paul needs to find a solution to this problem.

Service warranty analysis
Service warranty analysis shows that revenue is slipping because the costs of servicing the warranties are greatly exceeding the revenue generated by the sale of the warranties.

Continued...

Service contract analysis

Service contract analysis shows that service costs outweighed the contract revenues because SLAs are unduly in favor of customers. Paul also ran highest revenue products in service analysis (see Figure 13.21). Only a handful of products are generating top service contract revenues.

Service revenue analysis

Service revenue analysis by account showed that only two customers contributed the majority of the revenue (see Figure 13.22).

Highest-Revenue Products in Service Contracts

CRM Product	Gross Value of Contracts	Number of Items
SLA Support Platinum	575.718,00 MIX	64
Support 24 x 7	459.615,00 MIX	42
Harddisk, 20 GB	$ 427.160,00	176
Cable with grounded	$ 377.462,00	58
Immediate Response S	326.479,00 MIX	146

Selection   Details   Personalize

Top-Selling Products in Service Contracts

Product	Number of Items
Repair Service	1.756
Standard 5x10	225
Harddisk, 20 GB	176
160 GB Hard Drive	152
Immediate Response S	146

Selection   Details   Personalize

Figure 13.21 Highest Revenue and Top Selling Products in Service Contracts

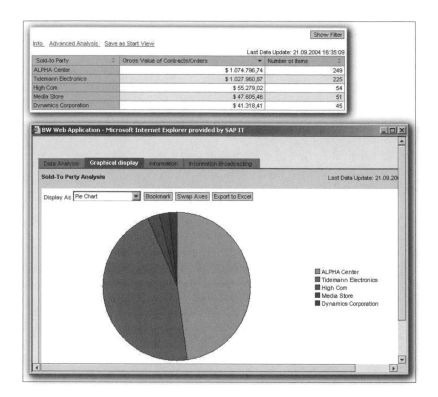

Figure 13.22 Service Revenue Analysis by Account

Ex Continued...

Installed base analysis

Installed base analysis shows that the service orders for notebooks are on the high side (see Figure 13.23).

This analysis shows that most of the notebooks have setup problems as found from the analysis of the service problem codes. Paul found that the unavailability of skilled technicians causes excessive overtime costs and a backlog of unresolved service orders.

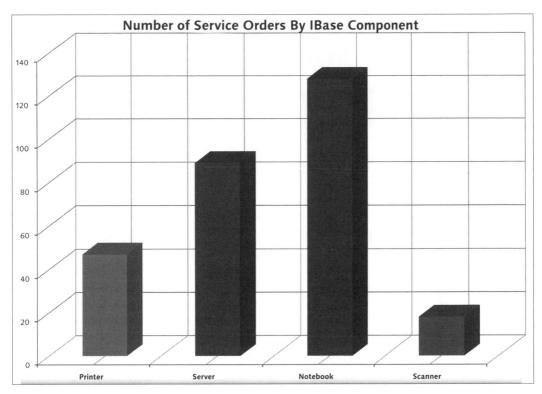

Figure 13.23 IBase Analysis

(Ex) Continued...

To solve these problems, Paul conducted a service campaign targeting platinum consultants and offered onsite resolution of setup issues at a special rate. Paul also conducted an email campaign with instructions in an email attachment about how to resolve the setup issues. These campaigns reduced the service orders to a normal level. Additionally, because the current warranties were unprofitable, Paul renegotiates the service contracts with customers as the old warranties expire. A C-SAT survey was conducted three months after the sweeping changes, and it showed an increased level of customer satisfaction. Service profit revenues started climbing again as well.

This brief case study gives you a good idea of what you can do with the service analytics tools in SAP CRM. Now that we have discussed the marketing, sales, and service analytical scenarios, let's move on to discuss the analytical scenarios for customers and products, as well as for the interaction channel.

Customer Analytics

Customer analytics provide valuable insight into the value of a customer to your organization, their buying behavior, satisfaction level, loyalty, and churn rate. Successful business relationships are fostered by knowing more about your customers, which also allows you to better focus your limited resources on your most important customers.

Evaluate the reliability of your customer segmentation process

The most important customer analytics include customer migration analysis, churn management, customer loyalty, and CLTV. We'll discuss them in detail in the following sections.

Customer Migration Analysis

Customer migration analysis evaluates the reliability of your customer segmentation process and tracks changes in segment memberships (who are the customers that joined or left a particular customer segment) over a period. This analysis uses data mining techniques such as ABC classification, clustering, and decision trees. *ABC classification* is a common analytical technique that can be used to group your customers into different classes based on some characteristic such as size, revenue, or profitability. *Clustering* involves grouping entries in a database into subsets that share common traits. A *decision tree* is a predictive modeling tool that uses a graph or model of decisions and their possible consequences.

Ex Example

Julie is a customer manager at Lucy's department store. One day, her boss tells her that sales are dropping and asks her to find out why. Lucy's had recently implemented SAP CRM Analytics, so Julie is able to generate an analysis of the customers over a specific period. The analysis shows that a considerable number of high-value class "A" customers migrated to class "B" during March, and then to low-value class "C" by June. This affected the sales revenue of the company over those two quarters. So Julie engages the marketing manager to run a special campaign to attract the attention of the customers who slipped from class A to class C. The campaign is conducted at the end of the second quarter and succeeds in helping move customers up from class C to class B. Julie then conducts a second campaign to push the customers from class B to class A, which is the category of the highest value to the company (see Figure 13.24).

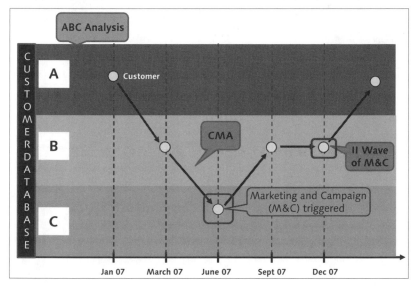

Figure 13.24 Customer Migration Analysis Using ABC Classification

Churn Management

Churn management helps organizations understand, predict, and manage customer behavior with an aim to reduce turnover of profitable customers and build healthy and profitable long-term relationships

Understand your customers better with churn management

with customers. Churn-rate reports evaluate the number of customers who have defected during a particular period, such as the past year. Reports are also available to predict the likelihood of future customer defections. Decision-tree techniques are used to help predict future churn rates (see Figure 13.25).

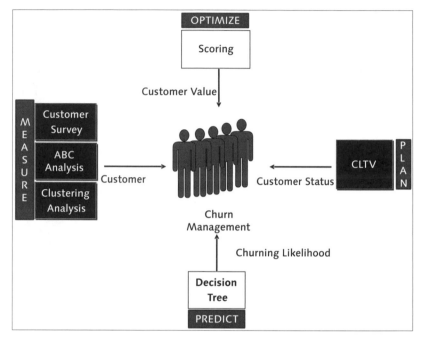

Figure 13.25 Churn Management in Customer Analytics

Customer Lifetime Value (CLTV)

Customer lifetime value (CLTV)

Knowing the likelihood that your customers will defect is only one side of the equation. Knowing the value of the customer to your company is also very critical in deciding how much effort and resource to invest in retaining a customer. CLTV analysis helps businesses make better decisions by determining how much a company should invest in a particular customer or group of customers. CLTV can be defined as net present value (NPV) of all future profits over the customer's lifetime resulting from buying your company's goods and services.

SAP CRM Analytics offers weighted score tables that can calculate a number of indexes, including a customer-value index based on the amount of profit generated by the relationship with the customer, as well as a value-churn index that combines the value and churn dimensions into a single measure. These indexes help you identify high-value customers who are likely to churn, allowing you to take preemptive action to save the account.

Customer Satisfaction and Loyalty Analysis

Customer satisfaction and loyalty analysis enables you to conduct surveys to determine the level of satisfaction and loyalty among your customers. You can use the results of the surveys to better understand the overall drivers of customer satisfaction and loyalty. You can also leverage customer feedback to improve the quality or your products and services in hopes of improving customer satisfaction and thus increasing customer loyalty.

Product Analytics

Product analytics help companies produce the right products and services by identifying the product attributes and features that are important to customers. Product analytics also help reveal which products are selling profitably and which products aren't. The goal of product analytics is to help you improve product quality and customer service (see Figure 13.26), increase product-related revenues, and reduce operating costs by eliminating inefficiencies. Product analytics include two important areas of analysis: cross-selling proposals and product profitability analysis.

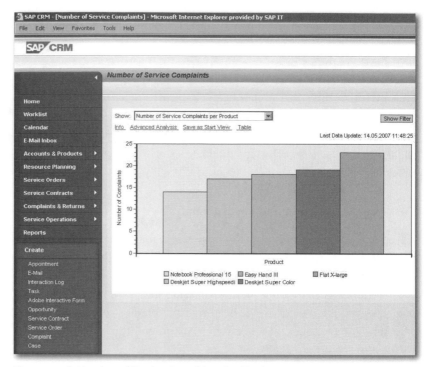

Figure 13.26 Number of Service Complaints Per Product

Cross-Selling Proposals

Discover sales
patterns for your
products

Cross-selling analysis looks at transaction-based product data (such as sales orders) and discovers sales patterns for different products. Product analytics can establish, for example, whether a given product is usually sold in combination with one or more other products. This analysis opens up new opportunities to offer profitable product combinations to customers. For example, the information can be used in the interaction center of the E-Commerce Web shop to make intelligent cross-sell recommendations. This analysis further helps position cross-selling products near each other on retail store shelves or together in a product catalog in the Web shop.

Product Profitability Analysis

Product profitability analysis enables margin contribution analysis, indicating which products are adding the most to your bottom line and which products aren't selling well or aren't producing significant profits. Product profitability analysis can also be used to determine which product features are most important to customers. Additionally, companies can use the results of product profitability analysis to determine products that sell well together.

Interaction Channel Analytics

Interaction channel analytics provide detailed business figures for measuring and optimizing the success of your interaction channels, including Web channel, interaction center, and partner channel management. Out of the box, analytics for each channel allow companies to drill down into the health of their marketing, sales, and service operations per channel. Channel analytics can be used to analyze the various channels that customers use to contact your company. For example, you could use channel analytics to determine the average customer usage level of particular channels, including the amount of sales revenue generated by each channel (see Figure 13.27).

Determine the usage and success of your channels

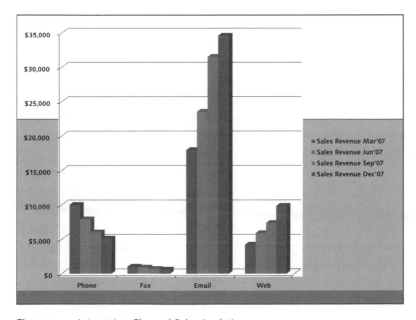

Figure 13.27 Interaction Channel Sales Analytics

As you can see in the example presented in Figure 13.27, a quarter-by-quarter analysis clearly indicates that in this example, email and the Web are the most commonly used channels by customers to order products and services, whereas phone and fax are less frequently used. This information could indicate, for example, that the company should invest more in the email and Web channels, and train employees to handle these requests in a timely manner to help increase company revenues and customer satisfaction.

Web Channel Analytics

Keep track of your Web shop performance

Web channel analytics provide information about the health and performance of your Web shop, including the number of visitors, server performance, and response time. Web channel analytics generate insights about how customers navigate through the Web shop by capturing the user interaction in the Web shop at predefined events such as user login; adding products to the shopping basket, checking out, and so on. Web channel analytics also provide dedicated reports outlining the sales revenue generated by your Web shop.

Interaction Center Analytics

Resolve issues quickly and improve customer satisfaction

Interaction center analytics enable call center managers to improve customer satisfaction and loyalty by detecting and resolving issues that affect the amount of time it takes to process and resolve customer issues. For example, telephony and multi-channel data can be imported from third-party communication management software to provide reports about the volume of incoming telephone calls, average speed of the answer, average-handling time, abandonment rate, and so on. Similarly, reports are also available showing the overall volume of email received, as well as the number of emails received and processed per agent or agent group. In addition to reports about the volume and handling time of specific communication channels, such as telephone and email, you can also view reports about service issues, including the amount of trouble tickets logged, the ratio of high and very high priority issues, the percentage of unresolved issues, and so on. In SAP CRM 2006s and SAP CRM 2007, you can even create your own on-the-fly OLTP (online transaction processing) service-related reports that provide real-time SAP CRM-based analytics without the need for an actual SAP NetWeaver BI system.

Conclusion

This chapter has given you a solid understanding of the reporting and analytical tools that SAP CRM provides. With more than 300 out-of-the-box reports, we obviously couldn't provide detailed coverage of everything. In fact, complete books have been written that talk only about SAP CRM Analytics. Here are the key things to remember:

> You can access a lot of ready-to-run analytical content that is provided by SAP CRM. Standard, out-of-the-box analytics address every business areas, answering the most commonly asked business questions.

> You can integrate SAP CRM Analytics with other SAP products such as Supply Chain Management (SCM) and SAP ERP Financials and Human Resources, providing a broader perspective on your business operations.

> You can leverage customer profitability metrics to measure not only contribution margins but also the costs of acquiring, serving, and retaining your customers.

> You can leverage customer churn analytics to predict the likelihood of a customer leaving your business. You can also classify customers based on their projected CLTV, allowing you to optimally use your resources to retain your most valuable customers.

> You can harness RFM value analysis to estimate response rates to your marketing campaigns. Based on this information, you can then optimize your campaign target.

> You can use the wide range of sales metrics to see, for example, how effective your organization is at converting leads and opportunities to sales orders.

> You can also take advantage of a comprehensive set of service-related KPIs to see how well your service organization is meeting customer expectations in terms of number of customer complaints,

service level compliance, and profitability of your service activities.

> Finally, you can even break down customer analytics by channel to see, for example, whether you generate more sales revenue from your Web channel E-Commerce Web shop, your interaction center, or your partner channel.

In the next chapter, we'll discuss how SAP enables "anywhere, anytime" customer relationship management by allowing users to access the SAP CRM system via a variety of devices and connectivity options, including laptops, tablet PCs, smartphones, PDAs, BlackBerrys, and so on.

14

SAP CRM User Access

To use any computer system effectively, the users need to understand how the system's user interface (UI) operates. The UI is the primary means by which users interact with the system, including how the user inputs data into the system and how the output from the system is presented back to the user. The planning and design of the UI affects how effectively the end user can work with the system, including how much time is required for a user to learn how to effectively enter data into the system and analyze output from the system. If you remember the early days of DOS, you know how unfriendly and difficult computers originally were to use. However, thankfully, in the early 1980s, Apple Computer developed a graphical user interface (GUI) that made personal computers accessible to everyone. Making computer systems easy to access and simple and straightforward to use is absolutely critical.

In this chapter, we'll discuss the various ways in which SAP users can interact with the SAP CRM system. In particular, we'll focus on the different devices (or access modes) that are supported by SAP CRM, such as laptops, tablet PCs, and handheld devices. We'll also discuss how the different user access modes affect the user experience.

This chapter is very timely because SAP recently delivered a new Web-based SAP CRM UI with release SAP CRM 2006s and SAP CRM 2007: the SAP CRM WebClient. SAP, analysts, and customers are praising the WebClient for its usability, simplicity, and power.

User Access Modes

User access modes affect the user's experience

Users can access and input data into SAP CRM using a variety of devices, including desktop PCs, laptops, notebooks, tablet PCs, PDAs, smartphones, and BlackBerrys. In this chapter, we'll discuss the various UI and user access modes supported by SAP CRM (see Figure 14.1).

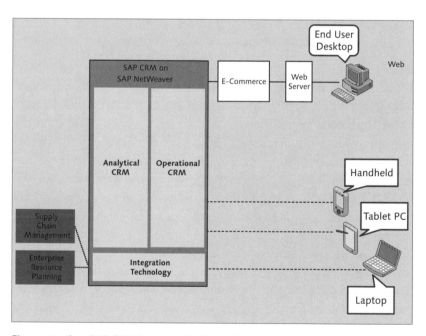

Figure 14.1 One SAP CRM System With Many User Access Modes

Desktop/Laptop

Minimum SAP CRM system requirements

Although many desktops are being replaced today by laptops with docking stations and flat panel monitors, the personal computer (PC) is still a very powerful office computer system.

344

The minimum recommended system requirements for a desktop or laptop to run SAP CRM applications are a 17-inch monitor with a screen resolution of 1024 x 768, 300Mhz processor, and 128MB memory. However, you may have to consider other application resource needs along with the SAP CRM applications when deciding on the final desktop configuration.

Notebook Computers

A notebook computer with a built-in high-speed (3Mbps or more) broadband wireless has become the number one tool for external sales forces. SAP CRM delivers Marketing, Sales, and Service applications to run in both a connected and disconnected mode. And, every day, PC and wireless companies are working hard to provide notebooks with even better mobility and connectivity for mobile workers. In addition to the standard SAP CRM applications, SAP also supports groupware integration and workgroup solutions for notebooks. When you use SAP CRM on a laptop, it runs on a standalone database with a local pricing engine. This way the sales person has access to the customer, product, and pricing data without connecting to the main SAP CRM server.

Give sales people access whether they're connected or not

PDA Companion

To run SAP CRM on a PDA, you need to use the PDA Companion, which is an extension of the Mobile Sales application that allows the Mobile Sales application to run on a PDA and synchronize with the Mobile Sales application running on a laptop. This solution works similarly to how enterprise email received by an Outlook application on a desktop or notebook is synchronized with a PDA device, such as a BlackBerry.

The PDA Companion solution became available to the pharmaceutical and consumer products industry verticals beginning with SAP CRM 4.0. The PDA Companion is used to manage the activities, appointments, accounts, and drug *detailing* efforts.

> **Note**
>
> Detailing in the pharmaceutical industry refers to the practice of pharmaceutical sales people providing physicians with free product samples.

PDA companion is great for the Pharmaceuticals industry

However, the PDA Companion can also now be used in other industries outside of pharmaceuticals. To work properly, the PDA must be running on Windows Mobile (WM) 2005 and Windows Mobile 2003 SE. Microsoft Active Sync must also be installed on the PDA device (see Figure 14.2).

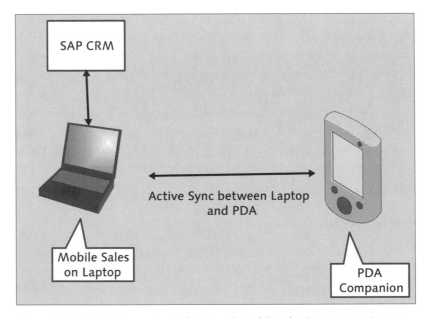

Figure 14.2 The PDA Companion Solution with Mobile Sales Running on a Laptop

Tablet PC

SAP CRM supports tablet PCs running Windows Tablet PC versions. Tablet PCs allows users to interact with the touch screen using a stylus device, and they support drawing, writing, handwriting recognition, erasing, and speech navigation and control. Figure 14.3 highlights the tablet PC features that are supported by SAP CRM applications.

Example

> Running SAP CRM sales on a tablet PC is handy for pharmaceutical sales people because it allows them to capture the digital signature of a physician during the sales call.

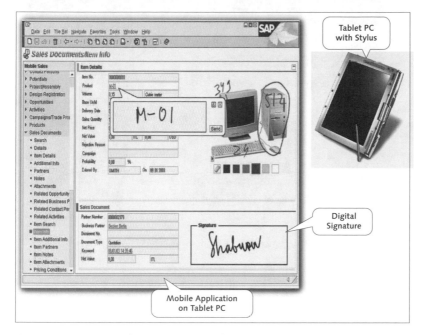

Figure 14.3 SAP CRM Sales Running on a Tablet PC

Handheld Devices

SAP CRM also supports handheld devices running the Pocket PC and PalmOS® operating systems. Handheld devices are supported with JSP-based sales and service applications using a Mobile Infrastructure (MI) engine connected to SAP CRM as shown in Figure 14.4. This allows field reps to manage their accounts with their handhelds and then sync the data back up with the main SAP CRM server.

Sync data from handhelds to the SAP CRM server with MI

347

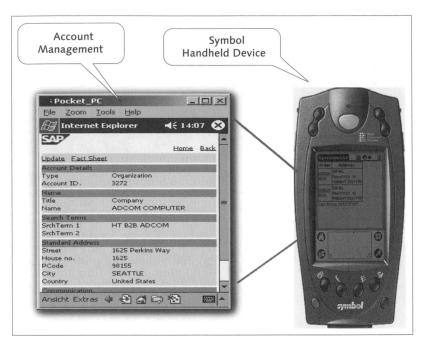

Figure 14.4 Account Management on a Symbol Handheld Device

Smartphone

Smartphones give
SAP CRM users
secure, real-time
access

Smartphones are the result of the converging communication devices into one. Smartphones allow the integration of handheld functionality with a voice-centric handset to combine voice communications, text messaging, Internet access, and wireless email messaging in one mobile device. Smartphones provide SAP CRM users with secure, real-time access to customer data and transactions using wireless access to the corporate network via the built-in Internet browser. Critical alerts can also be broadcast to field professionals using SMS (Short Message Service) and email messaging capabilities, while providing the simplicity and convenience of device consolidation.

Bidirectional synchronization with groupware solutions (Outlook and Lotus Notes) also ensures that contact, calendar, activity, and email interactions remain up to date.

SAP CRM Enhanced Usability

With the latest releases of SAP CRM 2006s and SAP CRM 2007, the usability of SAP CRM has improved greatly. SAP CRM now offers a single Web-based UI that replaces the People Centric User Interface (PCUI) and the SAP GUI for business users, based on the proven SAP CRM interaction center WebClient technology. It's no longer required to use the SAP Enterprise Portal (EP) to run SAP CRM in a Web browser; EP is still supported but is now optional rather than mandatory. The new UI was built based on feedback from customers, competitor analysis, pilot application experiences, and SAP CRM on-demand. Therefore, a lot of thought and work went into the design of the new SAP CRM WebClient (see Figure 14.5).

New SAP CRM Web UI built based on customer feedback

Figure 14.5 New SAP CRM WebClient UI in SAP CRM 2006s and Above Releases

The new L-Shape provides easy global navigation through the entire SAP CRM application, and generic shortcuts provide faster data entry and access. The L-Shape consists of a few header areas: A for the page header, and B for the navigation area. The specific content of the L-Shape can be configured based on business roles, such as sales

SAP CRM WebClient has a home page starting point for every user professional, service professional, interaction center agent, and so on. The L-Shape makes your life easier by allowing you to save common search criteria in the Saved Searches area and by allowing you to easily create new documents via the Quick Links (see Figure 14.5).

The new SAP CRM WebClient UI also has a home page as the starting point for every user, which contains the following:

> Personalized information
> Most frequently used tools
> An individual work center page for every first-level menu
> A complete view of information pushed to the user, such as alerts and workflow tasks in a worklist
> A current view of the user email inbox (Outlook, Lotus Notes), and the option to transfer the emails to SAP CRM with additional details
> A calendar page to provide a graphical view of appointments and tasks
> A report page to access all of the reports for a specific role or business area

SAP CRM also provides many other configuration options to improve usability and UI optimization. For instance, the configuration tools are used to set the properties of the fields/toolbar events/tabs to hide, display, and so on. It also comes with UI configuration tools and design-layer customization tools. The SAP CRM WebClient UI is easy to configure and use, so let's take a look at what you can do with the tools:

> Use the UI tools to add new fields to business objects, such as business partner, product, and so on.
> Position the fields in a view, and rename the field labels.
> Define captions, define navigation bar entries, and create business roles.

The tools available for UI configuration include the following:

Multiple tools are available for UI configuration

> BSP WD component workbench

> UI configuration tool

> Easy Enhancement Work Bench (EEWB)

> Role and navigation bar customizing

> Design layer customizing

One of the tools in the preceding list, the Easy Enhancement Work Bench (EEWB) tool, is used to add new fields to the database of business objects such as business partner or product, as well as transactional objects such as opportunities without modifying the table entries directly or making changes to the screens by programming (see Figure 14.6).

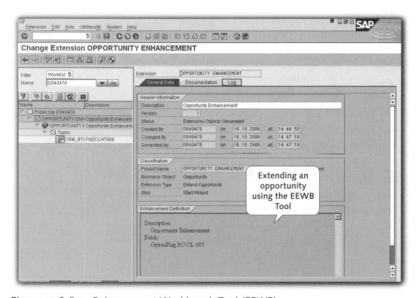

Figure 14.6 Easy Enhancement Workbench Tool (EEWB)

Design Layer Customizing

Design layer configuration can be used to hide fields so that the hidden field isn't visible to the end user in an application. Design layer configuration can also be used to exclude a field from a field set, causing the field not to be visible in the UI config tool.

The design layer configuration can also be used to rename field labels or set a field as mandatory. For example, some companies may prefer to change the default field label for "business partner" to something else such as "customer," "subscriber," "tax payer," or "resident," to better fit with their line of business and industry.

Conclusion

As you learned in this chapter, SAP CRM can be accessed via many modes, including desktop, laptop, notebook, tablet PC, smartphone, and BlackBerry. You also learned that SAP CRM can be run in disconnected mode via various mobile devices, with SAP CRM data stored directly on the mobile device and easily synched back to the main SAP CRM application when the device is connected to the central SAP CRM server.

In this chapter, we also discussed the new SAP CRM WebClient UI available in SAP CRM 2006s, SAP CRM 2007, and above, which provides increased usability and Web-based access to all SAP CRM applications. The SAP CRM WebClient UI also provides a single consolidated toolset that allows you to configure all SAP CRM screens and applications to meet your specific business needs. The single UI and consolidated toolset reduces the complexities involved with making UI changes and allows IT and business users to change screens without any knowledge of coding. The new SAP CRM UI has come a long way to meet your usability dreams.

Some important points to remember from this chapter:

> You can access SAP CRM with your desktop, laptop, notebook, tablet PC, PDA, smartphone, or BlackBerry.

> SAP GUI and PCUI are no longer supported for business users as of SAP CRM 2006s and SAP CRM 2007 and beyond. SAP GUI is still necessary for IT users. However, business users will exclusively use the SAP CRM WebClient.

> It's no longer required to use EP to run SAP CRM inside a Web browser. The new Web-based SAP CRM WebClient runs in a

browser without the need for EP. Existing EP customers can still continue to use EP, and it's possible to integrate the new SAP CRM WebClient UI into EP. However, EP is now optional rather than mandatory.

> The SAP CRM WebClient UI provide a single UI and one consolidated set of tools for configuring and customizing all of your SAP CRM applications, screens, and fields without any coding or modifications.

In Chapter 15, we'll look at the process of implementing SAP CRM, from discovery and requirements gathering, to planning and design, to blueprinting, to the actual realization and deployment.

Building an SAP CRM System

Now that you're familiar with the SAP CRM product and its capabilities, it's time to learn about the implementation methodologies that will allow you to design and implement a system to suit your business needs. SAP CRM is incredibly flexible and allows almost unlimited implementation possibilities. Because the success of your SAP CRM program hinges upon how the system is configured, implemented, and used, it's absolutely critical to carefully plan, design, and implement your SAP CRM system based on your business requirements — both stated and unstated. In this chapter, we'll discuss the tools and methodologies you can use to discover, analyze, design and develop, validate, and deploy SAP CRM successfully (see Figure 15.1).

Successful SAP CRM implementations require preplanning

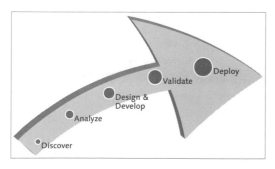

Figure 15.1 Stages of Building an SAP CRM System

Discover Your Business Needs

The first step in your SAP CRM implementation is to conduct an internal discovery session to determine your business needs and requirements. SAP CRM isn't just a technology but a strategy for doing business successfully by leveraging IT systems such as SAP CRM. So it's essential to unearth your real business needs, requirements, and pain points before designing a business system that will be handling your company's business needs for at least the next five years.

Set Up a Team and/or Hire an SAP CRM Business Application Consultant

Create a diverse discovery team

The first step in undertaking any SAP CRM project is to set up an internal team or hire an SAP CRM business consultant to help with your business discovery planning. If you choose to hire a consultant, it's important to hire someone who has experience in the industry and understands your company's business model. If you use an internal team only, be sure to involve people from all areas that will be affected by the implementation, from both IT and management. Be sure to provide the consultant with detailed information about your current business processes, challenges, pain points, and future vision to ensure that the consultant has the necessary information to properly plan your SAP CRM project. You should also be sure to involve the business process owners from your company in those early discussions with the consultant. Based on thorough discussions with your team, the consultant will come up with a discovery and analysis plan.

Conduct Discovery Sessions

Create a discovery team consisting of business process owners, subject matter experts, IT managers, and the external consultant. The business process owners provide the leadership during the discovery sessions. The discovery team will study the existing business processes and scenarios and record the best business practices, shortcomings, and pitfalls. This discovery study should be done for each of the business divisions that will use the SAP CRM system. Evolve a global business template based on the discovery study that should be used by all of the divisions with some changes to accommodate division-specific business needs.

Business Scenario Analysis

The team may use the existing tools and methodologies available in your company to conduct business scenario analysis based on the discovery sessions documents. The business process owner leads the analysis with the help of subject matter experts, the external consultant, and the IT personnel with the goal of understanding the capabilities of the existing IT landscape and then deciding how to make a smooth transition to SAP CRM.

Design your system based on customer experience and employee usability

SAP CRM projects often struggle because the project team doesn't design the system with customer experience and employee usability in mind. The project team gets tunnel vision focusing on how to migrate the business processes from the legacy systems to the SAP CRM system and how to enable additional business processes that the SAP CRM system supports; as a result, little thought or planning is given to usability. When designing your new SAP CRM system, it's critical to measure customer and user experience with the legacy systems and consider improvements suggested by the customers and users (both internal and external) in the past.

Several methods are available for conducting business analysis and capturing high-level requirements. The proven method is to hold a series of meetings with business process owners or business process leads and subject matter experts. The business process owner leads the meetings with assistance from the SAP CRM functional and technical consultants. High-level business requirements are collected as an outcome of these meetings.

Design and Development

Your high-level business requirements are typically gathered in a spreadsheet during the discovery and analysis phases and then are handed over to the SAP CRM lead business systems analyst (BSA). The BSA should have experience in implementing the SAP CRM systems, with at least two full-cycle project designs and implementations. It's wise to hire an external consultant, if your organization does not have an internal analyst with the requisite experience.

The BSA analyzes the high-level requirements and may call for a series of discussions with your design team, including the business process owners, subject matter experts, and IT leads. It's a good idea to engage the lead BSA early in the initial discovery sessions because this resource needs to thoroughly understand all of the business process details to quickly produce the system design requirements. The SAP CRM consultant could be the potential candidate for the lead BSA position, and you are better off engaging a SAP CRM consultant in the discovery phase who will serve as your BSA in the later phases.

The BSA conducts a series of meetings with the design team to analyze the high-level business requirements, drivers, and goals as well as the business objects behind the requirements. The BSA will come up with multiple, detailed system-level business requirements for each of the high-level business requirements. The detailed business requirements are discussed, adjusted, agreed on, and then signed off on by both business and IT.

Functional Design

Functional design document

The IT lead will take the approved, detailed system-level business requirements and develop a functional design document on how the requirements should be implemented in the SAP CRM system using screen mockups and other tools. In small teams, the BSA may also take on the role of SAP CRM functional consultant and create a functional design document. The functional design document will be accompanied by business process procedures or SAP CRM configuration documents.

Technical Design

A technical design document will be created for system modifications and enhancements needed to implement the business requirements. In general, the SAP CRM standard out-of-the-box solution satisfies around 75% of the requirements of large companies that run complex business processes, and up to 90% of the requirements of small and midsize businesses (SMBs) with just a little tweaking of the business processes. Small or large, you'll have one or more technical design documents. The technical design document will have pseudo-code, coding-quality requirements, and program performance metrics. The technical design document is then handed over to the developers. It's a good idea to involve the lead developer early in the design phase. Everyone must sign off on the functional and design documents, including the IT lead, the SAP CRM functional consultants, and the BSA.

The technical design document details the required system modification and enhancements

Implementation/Configuration/Development

The IT team — consisting of both the functional and the technical team — will configure the SAP CRM system according to the functional and technical documents. The BSA can also take the role of functional consultant in small teams. The IT team completes the unit testing and integration testing of the applications that are developed and or configured.

End-to-End Deployment

All of the development and configuration will be migrated from the development system to the quality analysis (QA) system for business validation. The lead BSA will come up with the business validation scenarios and create the scripts for testing. The business team — consisting of business process owners, subject matter experts, and super-users — will complete the business validation and record any issues in a tracking database. The system is then presented for user acceptance testing (UAT) after successful sign-off at the end of the business validation phase.

System configuration based on the functional and technical design docs

User acceptance
testing (UAT)

The QA team will write the test scripts and users will participate in the UAT. The system is ready to roll upon successfully completing the UAT. The business team should come up with the deployment plan well ahead of the business validation. All necessary resources for application deployment will be identified, informed, and brought on board the deployment team. The deployment team secures the infrastructure and local resources necessary for training and coordinates all training activities. End-user training can actually begin in parallel to the business validation testing. Usually, companies run a separate training system. A well-laid-out training plan is very important for the successful deployment of your SAP CRM application because your SAP CRM system will ultimately only be considered a success if it's appreciated and adopted by your end users.

So now that you understand the various phases and process steps necessary for implementing an SAP CRM system, let's shift our discussion to the different project methodologies available for implementing SAP CRM.

Project Methodologies

Several project methodologies are available for implementing an SAP CRM project. The most commonly used methodologies are the ASAP, Conference Room Pilot, and Cycle methodologies. Let's take a look at each of these methodologies in detail.

ASAP Methodology

All of the solutions
you need for
a successful
implementation

SAP's own ASAP methodology is a proven, reliable, and successful approach to implementing SAP solutions across industry and business environments. An outline of the phases, as well as the tasks associated with each phase will be discussed next. An initial draft project work plan should be created that represents the major tasks that need to be accomplished for your project. SAP-provided tools such as solution maps, SAP Solution Composer, and SAP Solution Manager help manage a complex SAP CRM project. Solution maps provide templates to be used during the different phases of project implementation. The

SAP Solution Composer is useful in the discovery phase to map your requirements and business processes against the capabilities of the SAP offering. The SAP Solution Manager is a central repository of tools and methodologies needed to actually implement an SAP project (see Figure 15.2).

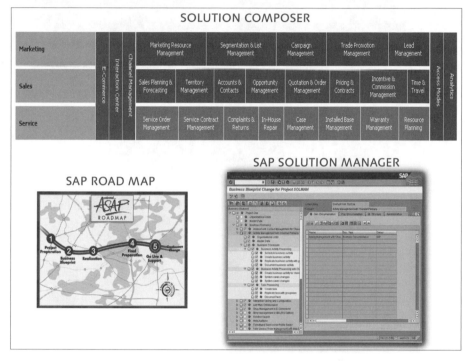

Figure 15.2 ASAP Tools

Discovery and Evaluation

The discovery and evaluation model of ASAP involves performing the initial business process evaluation, identifying improvements, and delivering a business case and program charter. During this phase, you perform an "as-is" business-process analysis to identify areas of improvement based on industry-specific SAP Best Practices. This helps you determine which metrics are necessary to develop a business case for your SAP CRM implementation and to arrive at a project charter (see Figure 15.3).

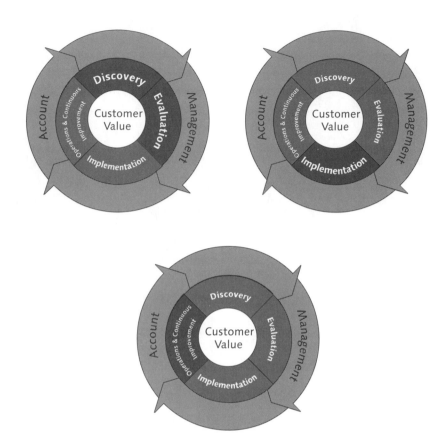

Figure 15.3 Discovery and Evaluation

The ASAP Phases

Five phases in ASAP
methodology

The ASAP methodology has the following five phases:

1. Project preparation

2. Business blueprinting

3. Realization

4. Final preparation

5. Go live

Next, let's discuss these phases and key activities (see Figure 15.4).

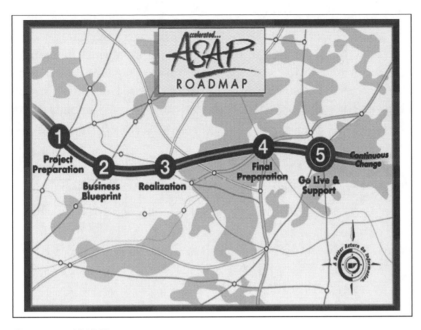

Figure 15.4 ASAP Phases

Project Planning

The purpose of the project planning phase is to provide initial planning and preparation for your SAP CRM project. Although each SAP CRM project has its own unique objectives, scope, and priorities, the steps in this phase help identify and plan the primary focus areas to be considered (see Table 15.1).

Initial Project Planning	Project Procedures
Establish system landscape strategy	Plan the training project
Kick off project	Plan the technical requirements
Conduct SAP CRM functional review	Schedule sample deliverables
Create the project plan	Organize the project
Develop an implementation strategy	Define management standards
Set implementation standards	Create a training plan
Establish development system	Define system administration

Table 15.1 Key Activities

363

Business Blueprint

The purpose of this phase is to create the *business blueprint*, which is a detailed documentation of the results gathered during the requirements workshops. The business blueprint also documents the business process requirements of the company. Based on this, you can achieve a common understanding of how the company intends to run its business within the SAP CRM System (see Table 15.2).

Key Activities	Sample Deliverables
Define the business process	Hold SAP CRM business workshops
Create the training blueprint	Conduct an SAP CRM functional review
Conduct a SAP CRM review at the end of this phase	Finalize the baseline scope of project
Hold workshops to review the results of the requirements	Refine the overall project schedule and implementation sequence
Set a training schedule and plan	Develop a prototype (if needed)
Define the SAP CRM design (authorization design, organization hierarchy technical design, interface design)	

Table 15.2 Key Activities and Sample Deliverables

Realization Phase

During the realization phase, the project team configures the development environment and implements authorization concepts to control which users have access to various data and transactions. A key task of this phase is prototyping solutions and testing in the SAP CRM environment. Additionally, during the realization phase, the team defines test plans for system tests, data tests, data access tests, and authorizations tests (see Table 15.3).

Key Activities	Sample Deliverables
Begin with the project management realization	Create test plans
Configure the development environment	Develop in-scope interfaces and/ or conversions
Schedule development configuration workshops	Establish production environment
Training realization phase	Define the production configuration
Define test plans	Create end user documentation
Define system procedures	Establish the SAP CRM administration procedures
Establish QA environment	
Configure QA	
Hold QA configuration workshops	
Execute test plans in QA environment	

Table 15.3 Key Activities and Sample Deliverables During the Realization Phase

Final Preparation

The overall purpose of the final preparation phase is to *finalize* activities to roll out the SAP CRM system to the end user community. Tight integration and coordination across the required technology areas and skill disciplines are necessary for timely and high-quality implementations. This coordination is also the key to successful knowledge transfer to your business personnel (see Table 15.4).

Key Activities	Sample Deliverables
Tuning	Database and SAP CRM tuning
End user training	Approval for going live
System management	Go live checklist
Go Live Checks (provided by SAP)	Production support plan
Cut-over	

Table 15.4 Key Activities and Deliverables of the Final Preparation Phase

Go Live

The overall purpose of the go-live phase is to roll out the SAP CRM system to the end user community. This phase also provides up to two weeks of post go-live support (see Table 15.5).

Provide production support	Validate live business process results
Perform strategic SAP CRM planning (as/if required)	Provide post-implementation support

Table 15.5 Key Activities of the Go-Live Phase

Go live when everything is tested and finalized

Usually, companies have maintenance support contracts with SAP, who provides support on a global basis, up to 24/7 — based on your Service Level Agreement (SLA).

This concludes our discussion of ASAP. Now we'll turn our discussion to the Cycle methodology and Conference Room Pilot (CRP) methodologies, both of which are essentially ASAP methodologies with variations in the realization and final preparation phases.

Cycle Methodology

Keep timelines while involving key users

Using the Cycle methodology, the project team divides the project into several cycles from the realization to final preparation phases, including baseline configuration. The Cycle methodology permits key users to participate from the early stages of the project implementation. This methodology keeps the project timelines hard while building a robust SAP CRM system for complex business scenarios. However, proper resource availability is the key to the success of a project implemented using this functionality (see Figure 15.5).

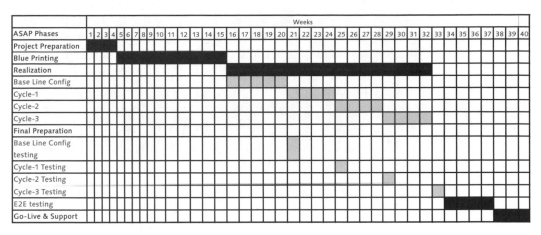

Figure 15.5 A Sample Project Plan Using the Cycle Methodology

In this method, the project preparation and blue printing phases are completed per ASAP methodology. The realization and final preparation phases are done in cycles. The realization phase starts with a baseline configuration, which is built based on the standard out-of-the-box functionality of SAP CRM that meets the business requirements. The baseline configuration is delivered for testing by business leads and super users. The configuration team moves on to Cycle 1 configuration, which may consist of standard configuration and enhancements, without waiting for the results of the baseline configuration testing.

The results of testing will be available during the second week of Cycle 1 configuration. The project teams take the testing feedback and make suitable changes during the Cycle 1 configuration. When delivered, Cycle 1 contains the newest functionality of Cycle 1 and the baseline functionality. The project team delivers Cycle 1 for testing and moves to configure Cycle 2. The cycles of realization and testing go on until the last cycle is completed. The end-to-end testing, go-live, and support phases are completed per standard ASAP methodology.

Conference Room Pilot (CRP) Methodology

The Conference Room Pilot (CRP) methodology helps project team members better understand the capabilities of SAP CRM software and

Use CRP for out-of-the-box SAP CRM implementations

develop business processes accordingly. This methodology is suitable for companies that want to implement SAP CRM out of the box, using internal resources without any assistance (or with only minimal assistance) from external consultants. The IT team provides knowledge transfer of the SAP CRM system configuration to the business leads. The business, armed with the system knowledge, conducts a complete testing of the functionality as delivered in each round of CRP. The delivered functionality is adjusted according to the suggestions and issues reported in each CRP delivery phase.

The next round of CRP does not start until the business signs off, acknowledging that the delivered system functionality meets the business requirements. This methodology usually involves conducting several rounds of CRP that adjust the business processes and configuration of SAP CRM from one CRP to another CRP until the desired business processes are totally configured in the system. CRP follows the waterfall method of development, where in essence, one CRP does not start until the previous CRP is fully completed and tested. It's hard to estimate the timelines associated with realization and final preparation phases of the project when using the CRP methodology because each round of CRP is highly dynamic. This method is most applicable when time isn't a constraint.

Conclusion

The success of your SAP CRM project will highly depend on your ability to accurately assess the technical capabilities of your IT team, as well as the availability of required business resources. SAP CRM projects require detailed workshops with key stakeholders, business leads, and IT leads before you embark on the long mission. The complexity of your business requirements determines the degree of detail that you go through when choosing a methodology, building a project plan, and implementing the SAP CRM system successfully.

The following are key points to keep in mind from this chapter:

> Even companies with strong internal IT departments should consider hiring an experienced SAP CRM business consultant who can provide invaluable advice and assist with the discovery, blueprinting, realization, and validation phases of the SAP CRM project.

> In addition to the various software implementation methodologies available from different consulting companies, SAP offers the ASAP methodology, which can reduce standard implementations timelines by up to 50% by using templates and tools based on industry best practices.

> To help manage complex projects, SAP software provides standard tools, such as business solution maps that contain various templates for each stage of the project; the SAP Solution Composer, which helps map business requirements to SAP's CRM functionality; and the SAP Solution Manager, which assists with configuration and implementation activities.

In the next chapter, we'll look at a case study of an industry-leading company that successfully implemented a highly advanced SAP CRM project.

Varian Medical Systems Case Study

Varian Medical Systems (VMS) is a world leader in radiation therapy for cancer treatment. VMS has 4,500 employees with a global presence, including manufacturing facilities in the United States, the United Kingdom, Switzerland, Germany, and China. The 800-plus field service engineers provide around-the-clock service and support to the customers. VMS revenues for the financial year 2007 were $1.77 billion. VMS is being traded on the NYSE under the symbol VAR. VMS was formerly part of Varian Associates, Inc., which was incorporated in 1948.

Business Challenge

The company, which designs and manufactures equipment and software for treating cancer with radiation, struggled with a suboptimal customer service process that leveraged a homegrown solution built on top of SAP R/3. The need for an efficient CRM-based solution became increasingly pressing as Varian's business began to shift from purely hardware-based products toward increasingly software-enabled product lines. Varian's executives hoped that the addition of SAP CRM was just what the company needed to improve service to its hardware and software customers.

The company's legacy helpdesk and customer service applications were product-centric. The business challenge was to provide a customer-centric helpdesk and dispatch service solutions and structure the solution knowledge and experience gained over several years in a way to be used in solving the product issues and resolving customer service requests quickly. Varian also needed to be able to categorize customer issues using multiple category levels to pinpoint the exact issue. The need of the day was "Total Customer Solutions." The challenge was to make a seamless transition to the new system while enhancing customer service without any loss of currently supported features.

Business Objectives

"It's important to think big to have a good vision and a holistic view of the end solution. But it's practical to start small."

Satish Subramanian, EAS Manager and CRM project manager (IT), Varian Medical Systems

The following business objectives drove the initial helpdesk and customer service implementation using the SAP CRM interaction center WebClient:

> Improve organizational efficiency

> Simplify the customer's ability to get a rapid response

> Provide a single 1-800 telephone number for customers to contact helpdesk and services

> Improve the management of service resources

> Reduce the response time of agents and field service engineers to customer service requests

> Track issues/cases/complaints

> Retain knowledge for easy retrieval

> Integrate customer data

> Maintain growth and market leadership in a solutions-based (versus product-based) market

> Ready the business for future challenges related to the increasing complexity of product/service offerings

The following additional business objectives drove the upgrade from SAP CRM 4.0 to SAP CRM 2005 (SAP CRM 5.0) and implementation of additional functionality:

> Link all customer service agents

> Track customer issues from end to end

> Solve customer problems remotely

> Leverage internal resources and knowledge

> Reduce response time of agents and field service technicians

> Dispatch field service technicians effectively

> Match the best resource with the customer issue

> Enable decision-support tools for management

The business objectives that drove the helpdesk and dispatch efforts are shown in Figure 16.1.

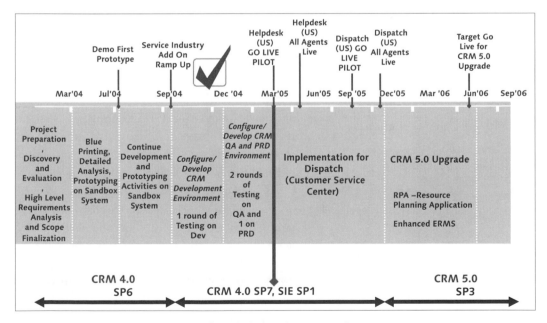

Figure 16.1 Customer Interaction Center for Helpdesk and Service Implementation Timeline Based on the Business Objectives

Technology Challenge

VMS has developed a homegrown helpdesk and dispatch solution on top of the SAP R/3 customer service application. It was a great solution for its day. However, the solution was product-centric and not customer-centric. The solution experienced several limitations, including limited abilities to do the following:

> View available agents because there was no out-of-the-box resource planning in R/3

> Transfer telephone calls because R/3 customer service supported fewer contact center features

> View installed base (IBase) information

> Transfer service notifications

> Assign field service resources because no dispatch solution was available in R/3

> View service entitlements

> Track solutions to known problems

The IT department at VMS had solid experience with SAP products and services, so SAP CRM became an obvious choice as the company's future CRM solution. VMS started testing the SAP CRM applications since the SAP CRM 3.1 release. However, SAP CRM 3.1 did not yet offer the Web-based interaction center WebClient user interface or service dispatch functionality — both of which were important to support VMS's service business scenarios. In addition, users didn't like the SAP GUI-based CRM application and wanted a Web-based solution. SAP CRM 4.0 offered both the interaction center WebClient and the Resource Planning Tool (RPT) for service dispatch. Users loved the Web-based interaction center WebClient, and VMS kicked off helpdesk and service projects using SAP CRM 4.0 in March 2004. During this time, VMS realized that some of the additional functionality that the company required — multi-level problem categorization and Email Response Management System (ERMS) functionality — were only available with an add-on package for SAP CRM 4.0 known as the Add-on for Service Industries (also sometimes referred to as the

Service Industry Extension or SIE). VMS joined the SAP CRM 4.0 SIE ramp-up program in September 2004. VMS became the first SAP customer to go live with the SAP CRM 4.0 Add-on for Services Industries in April 2005 with the following solutions:

> Service Ticket
> ERMS
> Call categorization
> SAP NetWeaver BI analytics
> People-Centric User Interface (PCUI) using SAP Enterprise Portal (EP)
> Integration with backend SAP ERP

The new system, based on the SAP CRM 4.0 Add-on for Service Industries, is fully integrated with all other required systems. For example, service notifications are created in R/3 with reference to a SAP CRM service ticket requiring field service. The service notifications are replicated to the field service technician's notebook from a home-grown Lotus Notes field-service application. The project is considered a success and was made possible by the leadership of VMS's Business and IT team (see Figure 16.2).

Figure 16.2 The Leadership of VMS Business and IT Team That Made the SAP CRM Project a Grand Success

From left, seated in the first row are Satish Subramanian, EAS Manager, and IT Project Manager, Jim Duffy, Business Project Manager, Customer Service, and Support.

In the second row are Biju Appu, Sr. Business Systems Analyst; Taru Gupta, CRM Technical and BI Analyst; Gert Beukema, Sr. Technical Analyst; Julie Hayashi, Sr. Business Systems Analyst and EAS Lead; Jitendra Pongurlekar, Sr. Technical Analyst; and Vickie Farnsworth, Helpdesk Lead.

Solution Deployment

The solution was deployed as a pilot program to a limited number of contact center helpdesk agents during April 2005.

All U.S. helpdesk agents were brought onto the SAP CRM system during June 2005.

A pilot group of dispatch agents went live with SAP CRM system in September 2005.

All remaining dispatch agents went live during December 2005.

The SAP CRM system was upgraded to SAP CRM 2005 (SAP CRM 5.0) during June 2006.

The upgrade enabled additional functionality, including ERMS as well as the Web-based resource planning application (RPA), which replaced the SAP GUI-based RPT.

The system landscape after going live with SAP CRM 2005 (SAP CRM 5.0) is shown in Figure 16.3.

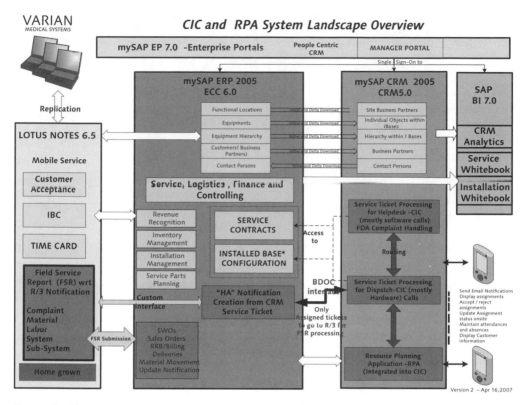

Figure 16.3 The Customer Interaction Center and Resource Planning Landscape After Upgrading to SAP CRM 5.0

Value Achieved

The new system provides the following benefits:

> The ability to respond to an increasing volume of helpdesk and dispatch calls

> Cost per customer call reduction

> The ability to provide the same level of support to customers for all products and services

> The ability to identify customer-specific history, requirements, and needs

> Agents have key information for increasingly complex product offerings

"We now have a system that gives us a complete look at all of the information relevant to a customer who is calling."

Penny Howie, Director, Technical Training, and Support

> Service dispatchers can schedule field engineers with greater efficiency

> Accurate and rapid data is available to district managers to improve planning and responsiveness

> VMS can now meet or exceed customers' expectations

"We now have a system that gives us a complete look at all of the information relevant to a customer who is calling," says Penny Howie, Director, Technical Training, and Support. "We can see how many times they've called before, who they talked to, the types of problems they're having. And we can move that information to other people at Varian who need to see it."

"This project was important because it enhanced our ability to help customers quickly and effectively."

Bette Snyder
Manager, North American Helpdesk

For example, if a customer service and support (CSS) representative wants to "escalate" a customer call to someone in management, it can be done quickly and easily using the new tool. "We used to have to research the issue and manually compile a report on the problem, so that the manager would know what had happened to that point. This new tool holds the information in one place, and the manager can see what's going on and quickly determine what should happen next," Howie explains.

According to Bette Snyder, Manager, North American Help Desk, this project was important because it enhanced the company's ability to help customers quickly, particularly when a problem is compromising their ability to care of patients. "We need to be able to respond as quickly and effectively as possible when customers come to us looking for assistance. The faster we can respond, the better," she said.

Lessons Learned

Have a Focused Approach and Implement SAP CRM in Small Pieces

SAP CRM is a complex system serving many facets of customer-facing organizations, from service to sales and marketing. Determining and prioritizing business requirements ahead of time will make the project run smoothly.

Get Key Users Involved Very Early, Preferably During Sandbox Testing

The Varian team struggled in the initial stages of its project, especially as they moved into the prototyping stage. They realized that it would have been valuable to have key users engage the system to see what SAP has to offer ahead of time.

Establish Direct Communication with SAP Product Developers — Especially in a Ramp-Up Scenario

Working with the interaction center WebClient, which was a new technology at the time of the initial implementation, Varian needed additional support, Satish Subramanian said. "When you are at the cutting edge, you realize that the folks who can really help in bottleneck situations are the product developers at SAP. Nobody knows the technology better than them," he said.

In the initial stage, Varian senior developers made their own enhancements to the system, but they were stuck with some bugs in the redesign screen. They recruited an SAP product developer from SAP Labs in nearby Palo Alto, who visited their office and helped them out of the bottleneck.

Pilot with a Smaller Group If Possible to Mitigate Risks

"Employing a small group of users at the time of go-live means the implementation team has fewer users to support and there is less of a chance of any business disruption," Subramanian said.

If anything goes wrong with the new application, the majority of the users are still on the legacy system. Subramanian also pointed out that pilot users at Varian provided valuable feedback on issues and bugs that could be fixed before bringing all of the users onto the new system.

Varian used 4 users in the pilot deployment, and the group was able to resolve all system bugs within a month. Then they rolled out the system to 2 to 3 agents at a time until all 23 helpdesk agents in North

America were live. They used a similar method with the dispatch agents.

"We also need to consider that most of our helpdesk agents are home-based in North America and dispatch agents work out of four offices in North America," Subramanian said. "The Pilot deployment made it easier to plan training schedules for all the users with the new application."

Subramanian added that no system will be perfect when it goes live. "No matter how much testing we do, we will never be able to catch all of the bugs [on the system]!" he said.

Get the Right People on the Bus

Varian chose key internal employees from the IT department to work full time on the project, including three business employees and two consultants. Subramanian was the project manager between Laptop, and the group chose consultants to augment the knowledge of the internal team.

"We looked at [a number of] consultants, but we decided on Srini Katta [independent consultant] and Casper Kan [SAP consultant] because both were experienced and had been involved in several previous implementations. We used these two for expertise and knowledge that we did not have at the beginning of the project. Their role was to help us come up to speed with the applications," Subramanian said (see Figure 16.4).

By the end of the implementation, the internal Varian IS team was autonomous. Srini Katta worked with the team until just three days after the initial go-live and Casper Kan until a few weeks after the go-live, according to Subramanian.

"We have been live successfully for eight months now and have been completely self-sufficient," he said.

Figure 16.4 All Cheerful IS Team on the SAP CRM Go-Live Day

Sitting in the front row are Srini Katta, SAP CRM Subject Matter Expert; Jitendra Pongurlekar, Sr. Technical Analyst; Satish Subramanian, CRM Project Manager (IT); and Casper Kan, SAP Platinum Netweaver Consultant.

Standing from left are Julie Hayashi, the Lead CRM Customer Service; Sree Bheemasenachar, the SAP CRM Middleware Analyst; Gert Beukema, Sr. Technical Analyst; and Taru Gupta, CRM technical and BI Analyst.

Relieve the Core Team of Users from Their Daily Jobs So They Can Dedicate Their Time to the Project

"We realized pretty early on that in order for us to make progress in this initiative, it was important for us to have the business team committed to the project," Subramanian said. "But it's also important for the core user team to play with the sandbox system to come up with detailed requirements and identify the gaps in the system ahead of time. This is clearly a full-time job."

In addition to the IT team, Varian's business team appointed a project manager and one former helpdesk agent and dispatch agent who were dedicated full time to the project. This group evaluated out-of-the-box functionality, identified gaps, came up with detailed specifications, and completed testing. They also communicated with the rest of the users and were responsible for creating training materials and executing the training sessions for all end users.

Have Dedicated Project Managers from the Business and IT Teams

"The project clearly needs to be business driven and should not be IT driven," Subramanian said. "We had a project manager appointed by the business side as well as an IT project manager, and both had a lot to accomplish. It's important to have a successful partnership and they need to complement each other well."

Use SAP Best Practices for SAP CRM

This SAP-authorized guide on best practice scenarios can be accessed online at *http://help.sap.com.*

"We follow [this guide] step-by-step to accomplish good connectivity and downloads from R/3," Subramanian said. "The best practice guide to middleware connectivity to R/3 [has been] especially helpful for our team."

Looking Ahead

"Today, Varian is in the process of creating a Global Contact Center, which will be built on top of the SAP CRM 5.0 platform," said Doug Cook, Sr. Director of Customer Support Services.

"One of the key Contact Center project objectives is to provide a globally consistent customer experience. The first step in reaching this objective is to establish a common call logging process for all agents, worldwide. This involves replacing legacy applications and providing each agent with access to the interaction center. The interaction center will become the only system that Varian's customer service agents will use to log calls and document support activities. The common platform will enable Varian to migrate all of the dispatch agents on to the resource planning application, and this will fulfill another project objective, which is to centralize scheduling activities for field service personnel. The Mobile Service Online (or MSOn) is the third component of the GCC Strategy. The MSOn enables mobile communication between Varian's agents and field service representatives. The field reps have the ability to update their assignments and availability via the intranet or a BlackBerry device. The SAP Business Information Warehouse is the final project component of Varian's GCC vision. Varian has already developed a set of queries, which allow them to track contact center activity and analyze trends across the entire customer install base."

The integration that an SAP-based CRM solution provides was a key driver for Varian's Contact Center project. In addition, Varian believes that some of the payback will be realized through process improvement and global standardization. For example, SAP CRM has provided Varian's Contact Center managers to determine the level of centralization that best supports their local customer activity, and the RPA allows dispatch agents to assign the closest qualified engineers who are available to support the customer. In the end, Varian realizes that the application will continue to evolve (as it has over the past two years), so the company will continue to build upon the features in the existing solution while extending the contact center globally.

"Today, Varian is in the process of creating a Global Contact Center, which will be built on top of the SAP CRM 5.0 platform."

Doug Cook, Sr. Director of Customer Support Services.

The common platform will enable Varian to migrate all of the dispatch agents on to the RPA, and this will fulfill another project objective, which is to centralize scheduling activities for field service personnel. MSOn is the third component of the GCC Strategy.

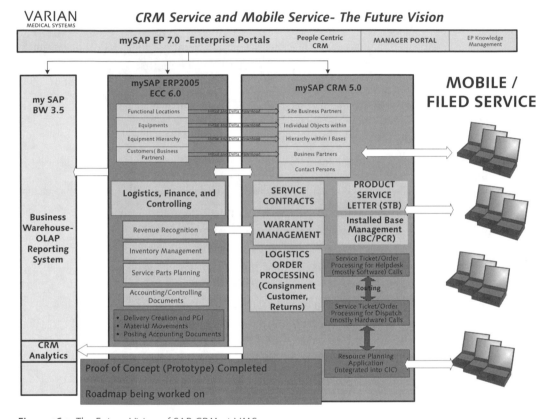

Figure 16.5 The Future Vision of SAP CRM at VMS

A   Glossary

ABAP (Advanced Business Application Programming)   A high-level programming language created by SAP. ABAP is currently positioned alongside the more recently introduced Java as the language for programming SAP's Application Server (AS), part of the SAP NetWeaver platform for building business applications. Its syntax is somewhat similar to COBOL.

abstraction   A method of presenting technology so that users see only what they need without exposing the underlying complexity.

access management   A feature that allows IT people to set up specific accesses for various users on a network.

Adobe Interactive PDF Forms (SAP Interactive Forms by Adobe)   A digital forms technology used in SAP software for collaborative electronic forms documentation.

analytics   Data analyses typically generated in the form of reports, charts, and so on.

ASAP   A systematic project methodology for speeding up an SAP system implementation.

authentication   The process of verifying the identity of a computer user to provide access to a system or data.

Best Practice   A management concept that involves devising a method or process that most effectively produces a desired outcome. SAP applications use business Best Practices to automate common business processes. (See also SAP Best Practices.)

Bill of Material (BOM)   A list of all of the items that make up a product or assembly. The list has a formal structure and states the name, quantity, and unit of measure for each component. A comprehensive product Lifecycle Management solution should offer support for the following categories of BOM: feature and requirements structures, material BOM, document structures, equipment BOM, functional location BOM, sales order BOM, and work breakdown structure BOM.

business analysis   Helps an organization to improve how it conducts its functions and activities to reduce overall costs, provide more efficient use of resources, and better support customers. It introduces the notion of process orientation, of concentrating on and rethinking end-to-end activities that create value for customers while removing unnecessary, nonvalue added work.

business analyst   A person who practices the discipline of business analysis.

Business Application Programming Interface (BAPI) An application programming interface (source code that systems use to request services from computer applications) with certain business rules attached.

business content Predefined sets of business data, called business content, provided based on a user's role in the company.

business needs A set of requirements that organizations must follow such as keeping the employee records, maintaining the material stock levels, handling transactions, and so on.

business object Items in an object-oriented computer application that match an abstract business concept such as an order, invoice, or product. Business objects are used as part of a domain model to encapsulate their associated behavior in programming.

business package Solutions that create an optimal user experience through preconfigured collections of portal content designed to serve specific roles within the enterprise. Business packages deliver ready-to-use solutions that minimize time to deployment, streamline common processes, and improve productivity.

business process A set of related steps performed to create a defined result in a business setting. SAP applications support typical business processes such as invoicing.

business requirements A specification of what the business wants usually expressed in terms of broad outcomes the business requires rather than specific functions the system may perform. Specific design elements are usually outside the scope of this document, although design standards may be referenced. Business requirements are system agnostic.

business scenario End-to-end collaborative business processes that can also leverage the Internet and include the content and expertise necessary to execute the business scenario.

Business Server Pages (BSPs) A page-based programming model (provided in the SAP NetWeaver Application Server) with server-side scripting as well as server page technology for developing, designing, and implementing Web applications. Server-side scripting enables direct access to all elements in the SAP NetWeaver AS (such as function modules, database tables, ABAP objects, and so on).

Business Server Pages (BSP) application A complete, functional application, such as a classic SAP transaction that is executed in a Web browser rather than in the SAP GUI. HTTP or HTTPS is the protocol used to access the application across the network, thus allowing the use of standard products such as firewalls and proxy servers.

Business Server Pages (BSP) programming model Similar to the server page technology, this model focuses on points that ensure optimum structure in interfaces and business logic.

business-to-business (B2B) Services or products delivered not to end users but to another business, such as transportation services.

business-to-consumer (B2C) E-commerce business process where consumers can buy goods and services via Internet.

business workflow SAP concept that is designed to enhance business processes through integrated, multifunctional business processes.

change management A structured approach to the process of strategizing and managing change for individuals, teams, and departments in an organization.

channel On the Web, a channel is a preselected Web site that can automatically push updated information for immediate display or viewing on request.

collaboration room Online portals where members of a team can collaborate by sharing documents, applications, schedules, and tasks, and where the members can communicate via chats or discussions.

compliance The process businesses use to comply with regulations such as Sarbanes-Oxley or health and safety regulations.

composite application An application that rests on other applications or components to use their service-enabled functions and data to build business scenarios.

Composite Application Framework (CAF) A part of SAP NetWeaver that is a development environment for services used to create composite applications.

composition platform This is used to build model-based business processes using services; for example, SAP NetWeaver is a composition platform.

customizing Modification of the software to meet special customer requirements.

dashboard A user interface, typically provided through a portal, that offers tools and data in a centralized location.

database An electronic collection of information organized for easy access by computer programs.

data warehouse A centralized repository for an enterprise's data.

e-commerce Doing business — primarily buying and selling of goods and services — on the Web. Also known as electronic commerce or EC.

electronic data interchange (EDI) The electronic communication of business transactions, such as orders, confirmations, and invoices, between organizations. Third parties provide EDI services that enable organizations with different equipment to connect. Traditional EDI data formats include X12, EDIFACT, and TRADACOMS.

electronic form   See Adobe Interactive PDF Forms.

embedded analytics   Incorporating SAP NetWeaver Business Intelligence within operational applications and business processes.

employee self-service   One of two self-service features provided by SAP NetWeaver that enables employees to access data and complete processes related to their roles in a company, such as submitting vacation leave requests or signing up for employee training. See also manager self-service.

encryption   The process used to obscure information so that it cannot be read without special tools or knowledge to unscramble it.

enterprise   Any business or organization.

enterprise computing   Computer systems and processes used within an enterprise.

Enterprise Resource Planning (ERP)   A type of application that is used to integrate all of the data and processes of a business or organization with the goal of maximizing the efficiency of operations. See also SAP ERP.

enterprise service   A Web Service used to execute one-step of a business process. Enterprise services can be used and combined to build business processes. See also Web Service.

enterprise service oriented architecture (enterprise SOA)   SAP's blueprint for implementing a service-oriented architecture to use services as building blocks for business processes, based on open standards. See also enterprise service.

enterprise service oriented architecture (SOA) adoption   A support program offered by SAP to help enterprises move toward an enterprise SOA environment.

Enterprise Services Repository (ESR)   The centralized storage place in SAP NetWeaver for services, business objects, and business processes, along with metadata (data that provides information about the characteristics of other data).

Extensible Markup Language (XML)   Used to share data across a variety of information systems.

FDA (Food and Drug Administration)   The federal agency responsible for ensuring that foods are safe, wholesome, and sanitary; human and veterinary drugs, biological products, and medical devices are safe and effective; cosmetics are safe; and electronic products that emit radiation are safe. FDA also ensures that these products are honestly, accurately, and informatively represented to the public.

Financials SAP ERP Financials is a comprehensive solution for finance and accounting, and for enterprise management. It delivers tools enabling finance and payment processes to be performed, administered, and analyzed efficiently in a network of many different companies using e-business. It also provides users with up-to-date, consistent financial data and information about the performance and strategy of an enterprise.

functional design document This document constitutes "how" the business requirements are going to be configured in the chosen system.

functional requirements Describe what the system, process, or product/service must do to fulfill the business requirement(s). Note that the business requirement often can be broken up into detailed business requirements and many functional requirements. These are often referred to as system requirements.

governance Strategic directives for an enterprise to follow; including corporate policies and procedures.

granularity An approach to defining services that breaks them down in relation to the steps of a business process. See also business process.

guided procedure A wizard-like workflow tool in SAP NetWeaver that guides users through collaborative business processes using templates.

HTML (Hypertext Markup Language) A markup language used to create Web pages; HTML describes the characteristics of text in a document involving a request from a client to a server and a response.

HTTP (Hypertext Transfer Protocol) A method of accessing information stored on the Web.

HTTPS (Hypertext Transfer Protocol via SSL) A secure form of HTTP using encryption. See also HTTP, encryption.

Human Capital Management (HCM) SAP ERP HCM enables you to plan short-term staff deployment, long-term staff development, recruitment, and continuous staff training. Assessments or reimbursement strategies can be generated automatically by defining goals.

inbox Area in the interaction center WebClient that agents can use to review, select, access, and edit elements from a central worklist.

industry solution map Industry-specific maps from SAP that guide users and help them focus on core processes and functions relevant to their types of business.

industry value network Any of eight industry-focused organizations that involve customers, partners, and SAP employees who work together to innovate solutions within particular industries.

integration   The ability for data generated by one software application or device to be used by another software application or device.

interaction center WebClient   A thin-client, highly optimized desktop application for interaction center agents. It provides a framework for processing interaction center WebClient functions.

interaction history   Contains a search area and an overview of business transactions that exist for a customer. Agents can search for business transactions using various search criteria. The results are displayed in the form of a list.

interactive forms   See Adobe Interactive PDF Forms.

iView   Small applications that typically run in a portal and connect to the underlying data and applications in your system.

Java 2 platform, Enterprise Edition (J2EE)   Defines the standard for developing multitier enterprise applications based on Java. This standard has been defined by an open community, including SAP, and is driven by Sun Microsystems Inc.

key performance indicator (KPI)   Both financial and nonfinancial measurements that help to quantify and analyze strategic performance objectives of an organization.

knowledge management   Various efforts by an enterprise to create, classify, and represent information and distribute it throughout the organization.

Lifecycle Data Management   Part of SAP Product Lifecycle Management related to using enterprise SOA to manage product-related data.

Lifecycle Process Support   Part of SAP Product Lifecycle Management for integrating SAP PLM with other SAP Business Suite applications.

Logistics Execution System (LES)   Part of SAP Supply Chain Management (SAP SCM) that links production, procurement, warehouse and inventory management, distribution, transportation, and sales.

manager self-service   One of two self-service features provided by SAP NetWeaver that enables managers to access data and complete processes related to their management roles in a company, such as hiring or creating budgets. See also employee self-service.

Master Data Management (MDM)   See SAP Master Data Management (MDM).

middleware   Communication software that resides on a server and replicates, synchronizes, monitors, and distributes data between headquarters (networked offices) and field users (disconnected or untethered users) or other solutions. For example, field users dial in to the central database or hub on a daily basis to download changes. They work offline throughout the course of the day. In the evening, field users upload their changes to the central database.

Mobile Application Studio (MAS)   This object-oriented, visual development tool is tailored to the architecture of SAP mobile client applications. It allows you to customize mobile client applications, delivered by SAP, according to your specific business requirements, or develop your own applications.

Mobile Business — SAP Mobile Procurement   Enterprises use this application to extend online procurement to sales employees and provide them with online access to workflows and online catalogs. Employees work with the SAP procurement solution that runs on their mobile devices, such as palmtops, personal digital assistants (PDAs), and laptops, completely without a connection to the backend system.

Mobile Infrastructure (MI)   See SAP Mobile Infrastructure (MI).

Mobile Sales   The SAP CRM Mobile Sales application supports field sales people during the sales activities at the customer site as well as in their office work. It helps synchronize the activities of sales people, managers, and sales teams.

Mobile Service   The SAP CRM Mobile Service application is designed to meet the needs of the field service force. This application runs on mobile clients in the offline mode and allows service representatives to manage the service lifecycle (creating service orders, creating complaints, and reporting confirmations) efficiently. Service employees also have offline access to essential data, such as business partners (BPs) and products, on their mobile clients.

model-driven development   See modeling.

modeling   A system of programming that describes what a software application's function is by defining relationships between components.

NetWeaver   See SAP NetWeaver.

open architecture   Software product's components can conform to nonproprietary standards of other software suppliers, which permits multi-tiered functioning on database servers, application servers, PCs, workstations, or Web-browsers.

Personal Digital Assistant (PDA)   A handheld computer, also known as palmtop computer or small computer.

personalization   Application on an employee's desktop that works together with a Web browser to provide a personalized, role-specific view of the entire business world. This business world includes marketplaces, applications, and services provided by the employer over the intranet or other companies over the Internet.

portal   Typically, a main site on the Web or on an intranet that provides capabilities users can personalize for their needs.

procurement   Acquiring goods or services at the optimum price and quality.

protocol   In object-oriented software applications, protocols are used to help objects communicate with each other.

risk management   Identifying and planning for potential risk in business, including performing risk analysis, monitoring, and developing responses for possible risk scenarios. SAP GRC Risk Management is a portion of an SAP solution for Governance, Risk, and Compliance.

role-based   The concept of providing information and services to end users based on their role in an enterprise.

SAP Advanced Planner & Optimizer (APO)   A software solution that enables dynamic Supply Chain Management (SCM). It includes applications for detailed planning, optimization, and scheduling, allowing the supply chain to be accurately and globally monitored even beyond enterprise boundaries. SAP APO is a component of Supply Chain Management (SCM).

SAP Best Practices   A set of preconfigured business templates based on industry Best Practices to accelerate implementations and upgrades. Used

substantially in SAP Business All-in-One.

SAP Business All-in-One   An integrated software system built on business SAP Best Practices for the small to midsize company.

SAP Business ByDesign   A new addition to the SAP solutions for small businesses and midsize enterprises (SMEs) that is targeted to the unmet needs of these companies, which have traditionally not purchased an integrated business application. SAP Business ByDesign is a complete and adaptable on-demand business solution designed to unify and streamline core business operations for midsize companies.

SAP Business One   SAP's offering for the smaller end of the mid-market.

SAP Business Suite   A comprehensive business solution from SAP that includes SAP ERP, SAP Customer Resource Management (CRM), SAP Product Lifecycle Management (PLM), SAP Supply Chain Management (SCM), and SAP Supplier Relationship Management (SRM).

SAP Customer Resource Management (SAP CRM)   Part of the SAP Business Suite that deals with managing the business interactions and relationships with customers.

SAP Developer Network (SDN)   A centralized resource for those developing applications on the SAP NetWeaver platform. SDN involves software developers, systems integrators, and consultants, and can be viewed at http://sdn.sap.com.

SAP Enterprise Portal (EP)   Enables heterogeneous system landscapes to be integrated into one standardized platform based on open standards.

SAP ERP   A suite of software applications that focuses on the core business requirements of midsize to large companies, including areas of Human Capital Management (HCM), financials, operations, and corporate services.

SAP ERP Financials   The area of SAP ERP that helps you to predict performance and manage compliance, and helps you to automate financial accounting and Supply Chain Management (SCM).

SAP ERP Human Capital Management (HCM)   The area of SAP ERP that helps you manage human resources processes, including talent management, workforce deployment, and core HR processes such as hiring and training.

SAP ERP Operations   The area of SAP ERP that involves managing procurement and the flow of materials, the manufacturing lifecycle, and sales and service.

SAP Manufacturing   An SAP software package that enables you to integrate manufacturing with other areas of your business operations and detect exceptions in your operation.

SAP Mobile Asset Management   Empowers mobile workers to perform their daily activities related to plant maintenance and customer service in the field — at customer sites and within plants — while disconnected from the backend SAP system. The application delivers an extension of asset Lifecycle Management features and functions that are provided in Product Lifecycle Management (PLM). Engineers and technicians in the field can handle order management, inventory management, notification management, measurements and counter readings, business partner (BP) management, technical object management, and customizing management. SAP Mobile Asset Management is available in either a standard version or an industry version tailored for ISU utilities. The application is designed for a handheld device but runs on both handheld and laptop computers.

SAP Mobile Business   SAP software that enables you to access SAP Business Suite solutions via mobile devices. See also SAP Mobile Infrastructure (MI).

SAP Mobile Direct Store Delivery   Supports workers in the business scenario used in the consumer-products industry for distribution of consumer products directly to the retail outlet, bypassing the retailer's warehouses. SAP Mobile Direct Store Delivery provides enterprise functionality for delivery personnel to service customers and manage relationships while working away from their main office. Delivery personnel can issue invoices, collect cash, take orders for future deliveries, manage truck inventory, and perform other related activities.

SAP Mobile Infrastructure (MI) A part of SAP NetWeaver that provides an open standards platform used to give access to data and processes via a variety of channels. SAP MI is the technology that works with SAP Mobile Business to provide access to mobile devices. See also SAP Mobile Business.

SAP Mobile Time and Travel SAP Mobile Time and Travel allows workers to track business trips, related expenses, and work completed while they are away from the office, without a connection to the backend system. The application includes components for both time sheet and travel expense management, which can be deployed separately or together. SAP Mobile Time and Travel's time sheet management functionality enables workers to record their working times on laptop computers anytime, anywhere.

SAP NetWeaver SAP's technology platform for most of its solutions. SAP NetWeaver allows for the integration of various application components and for composing services using a model-based approach. SAP NetWeaver is also the location of a centralized services repository whereby technologies enable activities such as mobile computing.

SAP NetWeaver Business Intelligence (SAP NetWeaver BI) A component of the SAP NetWeaver platform that offers data warehousing functional-

ity via repositories of data and offers tools for information integration.

SAP NetWeaver Developer Studio This application builds on the open-source Eclipse framework. As a starting point for all Java development tools and the integration basis for all infrastructure components, SAP NetWeaver Developer Studio supports efficient development of Web Dynpro, Web Services, and Java/J2EE business applications as well as Java projects on a large-scale basis for both SAP technologies and standard technologies.

SAP NetWeaver Exchange Infrastructure (SAP NetWeaver XI) A building block of SAP NetWeaver that runs on SAP NetWeaver Application Server (SAP NetWeaver AS). Through the strength of its integration, SAP NetWeaver XI enables a new breed of adaptive business solutions.

SAP NetWeaver Master Data Management (MDM) Enables you to store, augment, and consolidate master data while ensuring consistent distribution to all systems and applications in an IT infrastructure. Working across heterogeneous systems at multiple locations, SAP NetWeaver MDM leverages existing IT investments in business-critical data, delivering vastly reduced data maintenance costs. In addition, by ensuring cross-system data consistency, SAP NetWeaver MDM accelerates the execution of business processes, greatly improves decision making, and helps you maintain a competitive advantage.

SAP NetWeaver Master Data Management (SAP NetWeaver MDM) A system for managing data that receives and sends out data to the various databases in your enterprise. With SAP NetWeaver MDM, you can create a universal database and even store information about relationships between databases.

SAP Product Lifecycle Management (SAP PLM) An SAP software solution that helps a company manage product development, projects, product structures, and quality.

SAP R/3 The SAP client/server architecture-based software introduced in 1992, which was a predecessor of SAP ERP.

SAP Service and Asset Management An SAP software solution for managing service delivery and management and optimization of assets.

SAP Service Marketplace Internet platform that offers all of the functionality needed for collaboration among SAP, customers, and partners. Provides central access and guided navigation to the complete portfolio of SAP's service offerings.

SAP Solution Manager A solution support set that includes tools, content, and access to SAP to help companies deploy SAP products.

SAP Supplier Relationship Management (SAP SRM) An application that is part of the SAP Business Suite, which helps organizations manage the procurement process.

SAP Supply Chain Management (SAP SCM) An application that is part of the SAP Business Suite used to coordinate supply and demand; monitor the supply chain to manage distribution, transportation, and other logistics; and provide collaborative and analytical tools.

SAP Strategic Enterprise Management (SEM) A suite of tools and processes that managers and executives can use to introduce enterprise-wide, value-chain-orientated management practices. SAP SEM provides an integrated, real-time overview of the performance of a company over and beyond its organizational structures. This enables managers to gauge — and even increase — the value of their company.

SAP Tech Ed An annual SAP conference spotlighting technical knowledge and skills related to eSOA and SAP NetWeaver, including hands-on workshops and technical lectures.

SAP Total Cost of Ownership (TCO) Model A framework for modeling TCO for SAP ERP software, which provides an analysis of specific customer data to support SAP implementations.

SAP xApps Composite applications that customers of SAP can buy to enable additional business processes. See also composite application. The use of xApps is being discontinued.

Sarbanes-Oxley Act A U.S. regulation initiated in 2002 to regulate financial reporting and accountability in response to corporate scandals such as Enron and WorldCom.

scalability The ability of a system to be grown or built on easily.

scenario A set of business processes that can be performed in sequence to reach a desired outcome. An example of a scenario in SAP is Procure2Pay, managing an entire procurement process.

scratchpad A temporary workspace in the interaction center WebClient that you use as an electronic notepad to store miscellaneous information during an interaction.

SEM See SAP Strategic Enterprise Management (SEM).

service See Web Service and enterprise service.

service oriented architecture (SOA) A software architecture that allows for the use of services with an exchange relationship to build business processes.

shared services center A method of sharing pieces of business process scenarios via a centralized location, often used in outsourcing business processes to third parties.

Simple Object Access Protocol (SOAP) A protocol for accessing services on the Web. It employs XML syntax to send text commands across the Internet using HTTP.

Single Sign-On Mechanism that enables the user to log on to several systems without having to enter a password for each individual system. The user enters the name and password once only and can then log on to all systems that belong to the Single Sign-On environment.

small and midsize businesses (SMBs) Companies with less than 100 employees are small enterprises or small businesses. Companies with 100 to 999 employees are called mid-sized enterprises or businesses. They require a cost-effective solution that can be up and running quickly — and that will continue to meet their needs as the business grows. SAP Smart Business Solutions are specifically designed for companies in the SMB marketplace. They are divided into three Solutions: SAP Business One, SAP Business ByDesign, and SAP Business All –in- One

small and midsized enterprises (SMEs) See small and midsize businesses (SMBs).

SMB See small and midsize businesses (SMBs).

Solution Composer An SAP tool used to manipulate SAP Solution Maps and Business Solution Maps to visualize, plan, and implement various IT solutions in an enterprise.

Solution Manager   See SAP Solution Manager.

solution map   A table of SAP software applications organized within a single solution category that define a set of requirements either within or across industries.

standardization   Setting up a single technical standard that various entities can agree to.

Supply Chain Management (SCM)   See SAP Supply Chain Management (SCM).

Technical Design document   Provides detailed information and pseudo-code about the development objects and enhancements that are required to bridge the gap between the out-of-the-box system functionality and business requirements.

Total Cost of Ownership (TCO)   See SAP Total Cost of Ownership (TCO) Model.

user interface   The visual definition of a communication between a software program and a user.

value-based services for SAP solutions   A method of evaluating the potential value of the implementation of SAP products or product enhancements.

vertical solution   An industry-specific solution. See also industry solution map.

Visual Composer   A modeling tool included in SAP NetWeaver used to create customized user interfaces.

xApp   See SAP xApps.

XML (Extensible Markup Language)   Used to share data across a variety of information systems.

Web Service   Web application programming interfaces (APIs) that can be accessed via a network. Web Services encapsulate a function of an application in a way that it can be accessed by another application.

Web Service Description Language (WSDL)   A way of describing Web Services using XML to hide complexity and focus on functionality.

work center   A kind of user portal that focuses on a certain set of tools or data that supports one kind of work or functionality.

workflow   Automatic routing of business documents to the responsible persons to work on them based on certain business rules and conditions.

work trigger   A role-based initiation of data or other functionality being pushed to a user based on a need to know.

Index

A

ABAP, 248
  Advanced Business Application Programming, 248
Access sequence, 275
Account and contact management, 80, 81, 293
Account management, 185
Account planning, 185
Actionable intelligence, 306
Activity management, 80, 185
Activity Menu, 188
Adobe Forms, 236
Adobe Interactive Form, 237
Advanced Planner and Optimizer
  APO, 91
Advertising sales management, 293
Agent desktop productivity tools, 139
Allgemeiner Berichts Aufbereitungs Prozessor, 248
Analytical method, 308
  Measurement, 308
  Optimization, 308
  Planning, 308
  Prediction, 308
Analytical scenario
  Customer, 309
  Interaction channel, 309
  Marketing, 309
  Product, 309
  Sales, 309
  Service, 309
ASAP methodology, 360
ASAP phase, 362
Attribute set type, 264
Available-to-Promise
  ATP, 91

B

Backend ERP integration, 75
Batch management, 282

Billing and contract management, 80
Blended business scenario, 144
Brand marketing, 284
Business blueprint, 364
Business Addins (BAdIs), 142
Business Communications Management (BCM), 129
Business Object Layer (BOL), 248
Business package, 241
Business partner (BP) master data, 255
Business partner category, 256
  Groups, 256
  Natural persons, 256
  Organizations, 256
Business partner classification, 258
  Account group, 258
  Competitor, 259
  Consumer, 259
  Customer, 259
  prospect, 259
Business partner relationship, 260
Business partner role, 257
  Account, 257
  Bill-to party, 257
  Business Partner (Gen), 257
  Consumer, 257
  Contact Person, 257
  Employee, 257
  Payer, 257
  Prospect, 257
  Ship-to party, 257
  Sold-to party, 257
Business to Business (B2B), 29
Business to Consumer (B2C), 29

C

Calendar and task management, 185
Call center, 123, 287
Call Me Back, 133
Campaign and trade promotion management, 185

Campaign management, 48, 70, 293
  Campaign automation, 209
  Marketing calendar, 209
  Marketing planner, 209
Case management, 110
Catalog management, 157
Categorization, 284
Category performance analysis (CPA), 285
Channel commerce, 202
  Partner order management, 202
Channel intermediary, 201
Channel marketing, 202
  Campaign management, 209
  Catalog management, 209
  Lead management, 210
  Marketing funds, 210
  Partner communication, 209
  Partner locator, 211
Channel partner management, 49
Channel sales, 202
  Account and contact management, 213
  Activity management, 213
  Channel sales analytics, 214
  Opportunity management, 214
Channel service, 202
  Complaints and returns management, 223
  Knowledge management, 221
  Live support, 222
  Service order management, 222
Collaborative Project (cProject), 296
Commodity chemical, 282
Communication Management Software (CMS), 140
Complaint management, 185
Complaints and returns, 114
  Quality notification (QM), 114
  Return material authorization (RMA), 114
Condition record, 273
Condition table, 275
Condition technique, 273, 274
Condition type, 275
Consignment process, 283

Consumer decision tree (CDT), 285
Consumer products
  Brand management, 284
  Category management, 285
Consumer products (CP), 283
Contact center, 123
Contact center software, 129
Contract management, 185
Credit card management, 299
CRM Marketing
  Marketing plan, 62
  Marketing strategy, 62
CRM middleware, 242
CRM Mobile applications, 177
  Offline mode, 177
CRM sales force automation system
  SFA, 93
CRM Service, 99
  Contract and entitlement management, 105
CRM Service order management, 112
CRM WebClient, 95, 159, 247, 344
CRM WebClient user interface, 247
Cross-application analytics, 311
CRP methodology, 367
Customer analytics, 334
  Churn management, 334
  Customer lifetime value (CLTV), 334
  Customer loyalty, 334
  Customer migration, 334
  Customer satisfaction and loyalty, 337
Customer fact sheet, 306
Customer-first approach, 37, 38
Customer Lifetime Value (CLTV), 39
Customer service, 293
Cycle methodology, 366

D

Dashboard, 148, 307
Delivery-related billing, 92
Demand-driven distributed order management, 282
Distributed order management, 282
Document Management, 283

E

E-Commerce, 49, 154
EDI transaction document
  EDI 940, 166
  *EDI 945 shipment confirmation
  form, 166*
Embedded analytics, 306
Employee interaction center
  EIC, 147
End-to-end deployment, 359
Enterprise Java Beans (EJB), 240
Enterprise Portal (EP), 240
Enterprise services, 47
Enterprise SOA
  Support from NetWeaver, 231
Entitlement management, 106
E-Service
  Customer self-service, 171
Exchange Infrastructure (XI), 238
External List Management (ELM),
68

F

Field sales, 49
  Handheld sales, 51
  Mobile sales, 51
Full-cycle solution, 45
Functional design, 358

G

Grantor Management, 297
Groupware integration, 243

H

Handheld device, 177
  BlackBerry, 178
  PDA, 177
  Smartphone, 177
Home and home office business
(HHO), 30

I

Implementation method, 355
Incentives and commissions manage-
ment, 81, 93
Industry vertical, 28
Industry vertical solution, 279
  Automotive, 280
  Banking, 280
  Chemical, 280
  Consumer products, 280
  Engineering and construction, 280
  Financial services, 280
  High-tech, 280
  Insurance, 280
  Leasing, 280
  Life sciences, 280
  Media, 280
  Oil and gas, 280
  Pharmaceuticals, 280
  Professional services, 280
  Public sector (government), 280
  Retail, 280
  Telecommunications, 280
  Utilities, 280
In-house repair, 115
Inquiries, 90
Installed base management, 101
  IBase, 101
  Individual object, 101
  IObject, 101
Installed base object
  Object, 101
Intellectual Property Management
(IPM), 294
Interaction center, 49, 287, 305
Interaction channel analytics, 311,
339
  Interaction center, 340
  Web channel, 340
Interaction Layer (genIL), 248
Interactive selling, 159
Interactive voice response, 133
Internet Customer Self-Service
  ICSS, 136

Internet customer self-service portal, 136
Internet Pricing and Configurator
  IPC, 88
Internet Pricing and Configurator
(IPC), 160, 162
Internet Pricing Configurator (IPC),
240
Internet Sales, 154
IP-PBXs, 129

J

Java 2 Platform Enterprise Edition
(J2EE), 240
Java Database Connectivity (JDC), 240
Java Message Service (JMS), 240
Java Server Pages (JSP), 159
Java Virtual Machine (JVM), 240

K

Key performance indicator (KPI), 235
Knowledge management, 108, 171
  *Text Retrieval and EXtraction
  (TREX) engine, 108*

L

Large enterprise business, 30
Lead business systems analyst (BSA),
358
Lead management, 48, 73
List management, 68

M

Marketing analytics, 48, 75, 311
  *Campaign monitoring and success,
  314*
  Campaign planning, 312
  Lead analysis, 315
  Market budget planning, 312
  Market plan analysis, 314
  Target group optimization, 313
Marketing automation , 66
Marketing plan
  Campaign, 62
  Trade promotion, 62
Marketing Resource Management
(MRM), 48, 64
Master data, 253
  Business partner, 259
  Customer, 259
Material Safety Data Sheets (MSDS),
283
Microsoft Active Sync, 346
Microsoft Windows, 231
Mobile application, 305
Mobile Application Studio (MAS), 180
Mobile client, 180
Mobile Infrastructure (MI), 347
Mobile Sales Laptop solution, 185
Mobile Service, 191
  Service order management, 192
Mobile system landscape, 181
Multi-channel integration, 140

N

NetWeaver Application Server, 159
NetWeaver Mobile, 230

O

Object
  component, 101
Operational planning, 85
Opportunity management, 80, 86,
185
Order to cash, 163
Organizational master data, 267
  *Organizational attributes and busi-
  ness attributes, 269*
  Organizational object, 268
  Organizational structure, 267
  Organizational unit, 270

P

PalmOS Æ operating system, 347
Partner and channel analytics, 223
Partner channel management, 305
Partner management, 202
   Partner compensation, 208
   Partner networking, 207
   Partner planning and forecasting,
   208
   Partner profiling and segmenta-
   tion, 205
   Partner recruitment, 203
   Partner training and certification,
   205
Partner order management
   Collaborative showrooms, 216
   Distributed order management,
   218
   Interactive selling and configura-
   tion, 216
   POS and channel inventory, 216
   Quotation and order management,
   215
Pay-for-promotion, 72
PBXs, 129
People-Centric User Interface
   PCUI, 95
Personalization, 158
Planning and forecasting, 84
Point of Sale (POS) data, 285
Portfolio Management (xRPM), 296
Price and Margin Management, 286
Price optimization, 286
Pricing, 162
Pricing master data, 272
Pricing procedure, 275
Product analysis
   Product profitability, 338
Product analytics, 337
   Cross-selling proposals, 338
Product attribute, 264
Product category and hierarchy, 265
Product configuration and pricing,
80, 87

Product master data, 262
Product Modeling Environment
   PME, 88
Product relationship, 266
Product search and display, 185
Product type, 263
   Financial Services, 264
   Financing, 264
   Intellectual Property, 264
   Material, 264
   Service, 264
   Warranty, 264
Project planning, 363
Push to talk, 133

Q

Quotation and order management,
80, 89

R

Realization phase, 364
Real-Time Offer Management (RTOM),
141
Recency, frequency, and monitor
value (RFM), 313
Remote Function Cases (RFCs), 142
Resource planning, 107
   Route optimization, 108
   Van stock, 108

S

SaaS, 58
   Software as a Service, 58
Sales analytics, 81, 185, 320
   Activity management, 321
   Billing, 326
   Contract management, 323
   Opportunity management, 321
   Sales Funnel, 324
   Sales performance, 325
   Sales pipeline, 324

Sales quotation and order management, 322
Territory management, 321
Sales Configuration Engine
    SCE, 88, 273
Sales order management, 185
Sales planning and forecasting, 80
Sales Pricing Engine
    SPE, 88, 273
Sample management, 283
SAP Business Information Warehouse (BI), 230
SAP Business Information Warehouse (BW), 306
SAPconnect, 140
SAP CRM, 43
SAP CRM Analytics, 53, 305
    Interaction center analytics, 54
    Marketing analytics, 53
    Sales analytics, 54
    Service analytics, 54
SAP CRM interaction center, 123
SAP CRM Marketing, 48
SAP CRM Mobile application
    Mobile Sales Laptop (MSA LPT), 178
    Mobile Sales Online (MSOn), 178
SAP CRM Mobile Application
    Mobile Service Handheld (MSE HH), 178
    Mobile Service Laptop (MSE LPT), 178
SAP CRM Mobile Device
    Mobile Sales Handheld (MSA HH), 178
SAP CRM on-demand, 44
SAP CRM on-premise, 44
SAP CRM partner channel management, 199
SAP CRM partner channel management solution map, 201
SAP CRM Rental, 286
SAP CRM Rule Modeler, 87
SAP CRM Sales, 49
    Activity management, 183
    Contact management, 183
SAP CRM Service , 100

SAP CRM Service Parts Management, 286
SAP CRM solution map, 47
SAP Direct Store Delivery (ERP), 180
SAP Enterprise Portal (EP), 230
SAP ERP, 44
SAP ERP Sales and Distribution (SD), 258
SAP Incentive and Commission Management (ICM), 290
SAP Internet Pricing and Configurator (IPC), 272
SAP Leasing, 291
SAP Mobile BI (NetWeaver), 180
SAP Mobile Procurement (SRM), 180
SAP Mobile Sales (CRM), 180
SAP Mobile Sales (ERP), 180
SAP Mobile Service (CRM), 180
SAP Mobile Time and Travel (ERP), 180
SAP Mobile Warehouse Management (SCM), 180
SAP NetWeaver, 229, 231
    Adoptions in 2006, 231
    Composition platform, 235
SAP NetWeaver Application Server, 84, 233
SAP NetWeaver Business Intelligence (BI), 306
SAP NetWeaver Business Process Management, 235
SAP NetWeaver. E-Commerce, 159
SAP NetWeaver Enterprise Portal, 236
SAP NetWeaver Exchange Infrastructure (SAP NetWeaver XI), 230
SAP NetWeaver Master Data Management (MDM), 254
SAP NetWeaver Process Integration (SAP NetWeaver PI), 238
SAP NetWeaver TREX, 236
SAP Price and Margin Management, 274
SAP Real-Time Offer Management, 63
SAP SME portfolio
    Definition, 56

SAP xApps Mobile Time and Travel, 94
SAP XI, 238
Segment and list management, 48
Segmentation, 67
    Customer segment, 67
Segment Builder, 67
SEM-BPS, 94
Service analytics, 117, 327
    Service quality, 328
Service contract management, 106
Service Level Agreement, 105
    SLA, 105
Service management, 172
Service order, 112, 287
Service order and service ticket, 111
Service order management, 185
Service ticket, 112, 287
Shared-Service Center, 147
    SSC, 147
Shelf management, 185
Small and medium business (SMB), 30
Smartphone
    Short Message Service (SMS), 348
Specialty chemicals, 282
Strategic planning, 84
Subscription sales, 293
Supplier Relationship Management (SRM), 166
Supply Chain Management (SCM), 282

T

Technical design, 359
Telco, 299
Telephone system hardware, 128
Territory management, 80, 85, 185
Three Pillars of SAP CRM, 45
Time and travel management, 81, 185
Total cost of ownership (TCO), 33
Trade Promotion Management (TPM), 48, 71
Transaction-related billing, 92
Transaction Tax Engine
    TTE, 88

U

Usability, 349
User acceptance testing (UAT), 359
User access, 343
    PDA Companion, 345
User access mode
    Desktop/PC, 344
    Handheld, 347
    Laptop, 344
    Notebook Computers, 345
    Smartphone, 348
    Tablet PC, 346
User access modes, 344

V

Varian Medical Systems , 371
Variant configuration, 273
Virtual interaction center, 124
Visit planning and route optimization, 185

W

Warranty management, 103
Web auctions, 170
Web channel, 305
Web Channel Analytics, 173
Web Channel Enablement
    E-Analytics, 154
    E-Commerce, 154
    E-Marketing, 154
    E-Service, 154
    Web Channel Anlaytics, 154
Web Channel Enablement solution, 153
Web chat, 137
Web form, 134, 136
Web Service Description Language (WSDL), 237
Web Services, 236
Windows Mobile 2003 SE, 346
Windows Mobile (WM) 2005, 346